The Samurai Series:

The Book of Five Rings

by Miyamoto Musashi

Hagakure
The Way of the Samurai

by Yamamoto Tsunetomo

Bushido
The Soul of Japan

by Inazo Nitobe

The Samurai Series:The Book of Five Rings, Hagakure -The Way of the Samurai & Bushido - The Soul of Japan
by Miyamoto Musashi, Yamamoto Tsunetomo & Inazo Nitobe

First Printing - December 2006

Published by
EL Paso Norte Press
404 Christopher Ave
El Paso, Texas 79912

ISBN: 1-934255-01-7
ISBN13: 978-1-934255-01-8

Printed in the United States of America

The Samurai Series

Contents

The Samurai Series

The Book
of
Five Rings

by

Miyamoto Musashi

CONTENTS

The Samurai Series

Introduction

I have been many years training in the Way of strategy, called Ni Ten Ichi Ryu, and now I think I will explain it in writing for the first time. It is now during the first ten days of the tenth month in the twentieth year of Kanei (1645). I have climbed mountain Iwato of Higo in Kyushu to pay homage to heaven, pray to Kwannon, [God(dess) of mercy in Buddhism. - Slaegr] and kneel before Buddha. I am a warrior of Harima province, Shinmen Musashi No Kami Fujiwara No Genshin, age sixty years.

From youth my heart has been inclined toward the Way of strategy. My first duel was when I was thirteen, I struck down a strategist of the Shinto school, one Arima Kihei. When I was sixteen I struck down an able strategist Tadashima Akiyama. When I was twenty-one I went up to the capital and met all manner of strategists, never once failing to win in many contests.

After that I went from province to province dueling with strategist of various schools, and not once failed to win even though I had as many as sixty encounters. This was between the ages of thirteen and twenty-eight or twenty-nine.

When I reached thirty I looked back on my past. The previous victories were not due to my having mastered strategy. Perhaps it was natural ability, or the order of heaven, or that other schools' strategy was inferior. After that I studied morning and evening searching for the principle, and came to realize the Way of strategy when I was fifty.

Since then I have lived without following any particular Way. Thus with the virtue of strategy I practice many arts and abilities - all things with no teacher. To write this book I did not use the law of Buddha or the teachings of Confucius, neither old war chronicles nor books on martial tactics. I take up my brush to explain the true spirit of this Ichi school as it is mirrored in the Way of heaven and Kwannon.

The time is the night of the tenth day of the tenth month, at the hour of the tiger.

The Earth Book

Strategy is the craft of the warrior. Commanders must enact the craft, and troopers should know this Way. There is no warrior in the world today who really understands the Way of strategy.

There are various Ways. There is the Way of salvation by the law of Buddha, the Way of Confucius governing the Way of learning, the Way of healing as a doctor, as a poet teaching the Way of Waka, [a type of poem. - Slaegr] tea, archery, and many arts and skills. Each man practices as he feels inclined.

It is said the warrior's is the twofold Way of pen and sword, and he should have a taste for both Ways. Even if a man has no natural ability he can be a warrior by sticking assiduously to both divisions of the Way. Generally speaking, the Way of the warrior is resolute acceptance of death. Although not only warriors but priests, women, peasants and lowlier folk have been known to die readily in the cause of duty or out of shame, this is a different thing. The warrior is different in that studying the Way of strategy is based on overcoming men. By victory gained in crossing swords with individuals, or enjoining battle with large numbers, we can attain power and fame for ourselves or our lord. This is the virtue of strategy.

The Way of Strategy

In China and Japan practitioners of the Way have been known as "masters of strategy". Warriors must learn this Way.

Recently there have been people getting on in the world as strategists, but they are usually just sword-fencers. The attendants of the Kashima Kantori shrines of the province Hitachi received instruction from the gods, and made schools based on this teaching, travelling from country to country instructing men. This is the recent meaning of strategy.

In olden times strategy was listed among the Ten Abilities and Seven Arts as a beneficial practice. It was certainly an art but as a beneficial practice it was not limited to sword-fencing. The true value of sword-fencing cannot be seen within the confines of sword-fencing technique.

If we look at the world we see arts for sale. Men use equipment to sell their own selves. As if with the nut and the flower, the nut has become less than the flower. In this kind of Way of strategy, both those teaching and those learning the way are concerned with coloring and showing off their technique, trying to hasten the bloom of the flower. They speak of "This Dojo" and "That Dojo". They are looking for profit. Someone once said "Immature strategy is the cause of grief". That was a true saying.

There are four Ways in which men pass through life: as gentlemen, farmers, artisans and merchants.

The Way of the farmer. Using agricultural instruments, he sees springs through to autumns with an eye on the changes of season.

Second is the Way of the merchant. The wine maker obtains his ingredients and puts them to use to make his living. The Way of the merchant is always to live by taking profit. This is the Way of the merchant.

Thirdly the gentleman warrior, carrying the weaponry of his Way. The Way of the warrior is to master the virtue of his weapons. If a gentleman dislikes strategy he will not appreciate the benefit of weaponry, so must he not have a little taste for this?

Fourthly the Way of the artisan. The Way of the carpenter [architect and builder, all buildings were of wood. - Slaegr] is to become proficient in the use of his tools, first to lay his plans with a true measure and then perform his work according to plan. Thus he passes through life. These are the four Ways of the gentleman, the farmer, the artisan and the merchant.

Comparing the Way of the carpenter to strategy

The comparison with carpentry is through the connection with houses. Houses of the nobility, houses of warriors, the Four houses, [there are also four different schools of tea. - Slaegr] ruin of houses, thriving of houses, the style of the house, the tradition of the house, and the name of the house. The carpenter uses a master plan of the building, and the Way of strategy is similar in that there is a plan of campaign. If you want to learn the craft of war, ponder over this book. The teacher is as a needle, the disciple is as thread. You must practice constantly.

Like the foreman carpenter, the commander must know natural rules, and the rules of the country, and the rules of houses. This is the Way of the foreman.

The foreman carpenter must know the architectural theory of towers and temples, and the plans of palaces, and must employ men to raise up houses. The Way of the foreman carpenter is the same as the Way of the commander of a warrior house.

In the construction of houses, choice of woods is made. Straight un-knotted timber of good appearance is used for the revealed pillars, straight timber with small defects is used for the inner pillars. Timbers of the finest appearance, even if a little weak, is used for the thresholds, lintels, doors, and sliding doors, and so on. Good strong timber, though it be gnarled and knotted, can always be used discreetly in construction. Timber which is weak or knotted throughout should be used as scaffolding, and later for firewood.

The foreman carpenter allots his men work according to their ability. Floor layers, makers of sliding doors, thresholds and lintels, ceilings and so on. Those of poor ability lay the floor joists, and those of lesser ability carve wedges and do such miscellaneous work. If the foreman knows and deploys his men well the finished work will be good.

The foreman should take into account the abilities and limitations of his men, circulating among them and asking nothing unreasonable. He should know their morale and spirit, and encourage them when necessary. This is the same as the principle of strategy.

The Way of Strategy

Like a trooper, the carpenter sharpens his own tools. He carries his equipment in his tool box, and works under the direction of his foreman. He makes columns and girders with an axe, shapes floorboards and shelves with a plane, cuts fine openwork and carvings accurately, giving as excellent a finish as his skill will allow. This is the craft of the carpenters. When the carpenter becomes skilled and understands measures he can become a foreman.

The carpenter's attainment is, having tools which will cut well, to make small shrines, writing shelves, tables, paper lanterns, chopping boards and pot-lids. These are the specialties of the carpenter. Things are similar for the trooper. You ought to think deeply about this.

The attainment of the carpenter is that his work is not warped, that the joints are not misaligned, and that the work is truly planed so that it meets well and is not merely finished in sections. This is essential.

If you want to learn this Way, deeply consider the things written in this book one at a time. You must do sufficient research.

Outline of the Five Books of this Book of Strategy

The Way is shown as five books concerning different aspects. These are Ground, Water, Fire, Tradition (Wind), and Void.

The body of the Way of strategy from the viewpoint of my Ichi school is explained in the Ground book. It is difficult to realize the true Way just through sword-fencing. Know the smallest things and the biggest things, the shallowest things and the deepest things. As if it were a straight road mapped out on the ground, the first book is called the Ground book.

Second is the Water book. With water as the basis, the spirit becomes like water. Water adopts the shape of its receptacle, it is sometimes a trickle and sometimes a wild sea. Water has a clear blue color. By the clarity, things of Ichi school are shown in this book.

If you master the principles of sword-fencing, when you freely beat one man, you beat any man in the world. The spirit of defeating a man is the same for ten million men. The strategist makes small things into big things, like building a great Buddha from a one foot model. I cannot write in detail how this is done. The principle of strategy is having one thing, to know ten thousand things. Things of Ichi school are written in this the Water book.

Third is the Fire book. This book is about fighting. The spirit of fire is fierce, whether the fire be small or big; and so it is with battles. The Way of battles is the same for man to man fights and for ten thousand a side battles. You must appreciate that spirit can become big or small. What is big is easy to perceive: what is small is difficult to perceive. In short, it is difficult for large numbers of men to change position, so their movements can be easily predicted. An individual can easily change his mind, so his movements are difficult to predict. You must appreciate this. The essence of this book is that you must train day and night in order to make quick decisions. In strategy it is necessary to treat training as part of normal life with your spirit unchanging. Thus combat in battle is described in the Fire book.

Fourthly the Wind book. This book is not concerned with my Ichi school but with other schools of strategy. By Wind I mean old traditions, present-day traditions, and family traditions of strategy. Thus I clearly explain the strategies of the world. This is tradition. It is difficult to know yourself if you do not know others. To all Ways there are side-tracks. If you study a Way daily, and your spirit diverges, you may think you are obeying a good Way but objectively it is not the true Way. If you are following the true way and diverge a little, this will later become a large divergence. You must realize this. Other strategies have come to be thought of as mere sword-fencing, and it is not unreasonable that this should be so. The benefit of my strategy, although it includes sword-fencing, lies in a separate principle. I have explained what is commonly meant by strategy in other schools in the Tradition (Wind) book.

Fifthly, the book of the Void. By void I mean that which has no beginning and no end. Attaining this principle means not attaining the principle. The Way of strategy is the Way of nature. When you appreciate the power of nature, knowing rhythm of any situation, you will be able to hit the enemy naturally and strike naturally. All this is the Way of the Void. I intend to show how to follow the true Way according to nature in the book of the Void.

The Name Ichi Ryu Ni To (One school - two swords)

Warriors, both commanders and troopers, carry two swords at their belt. In olden times these were called the long sword and the sword; nowadays they are known as the sword and the companion sword. Let it suffice to say that in our land, whatever the reason, a warrior carries two swords at his belt. It is the Way of the warrior.

"Nito Ichi Ryu" shows the advantages of using both swords.

The spear and the halberd are weapons which are carried out of doors.

Students of the Ichi school Way of strategy should train from the start with the sword and the long sword in either hand. This is a truth: when you sacrifice your life, you must make fullest use of your weaponry. It is false not to do so, and to die with a weapon yet undrawn.

If you hold a sword with both hands, it is difficult to wield it freely to left and right, so my method is to carry the sword in one hand. This does not apply to large weapons such as the spear or halberd, but swords and companion swords can be carried in one hand. It is encumbering to hold a sword in both hands when you are on horseback, when running on uneven roads, on swampy ground, muddy rice fields, stony ground, or in a crowd of people. To hold the long sword in both hands is not the true Way, for if you carry a bow or spear or other arms in your left hand you have only one hand free for the long sword. However, when it is difficult to cut an enemy down with one hand, you must use both hands. It is not difficult to wield a sword in one hand; the Way to learn this is to train with two long swords, one in each hand. It will seem difficult at first, but everything is difficult at first. Bows are difficult to draw, halberds are difficult to wield; as you become accustomed to the bow so your pull will become stronger. When you become used to wielding the long sword, you will gain the power of the Way and wield the sword well.

As I will explain in the second book, the Water Book, there is no fast way of wielding the long sword. The long sword should be wielded broadly and the companion sword closely. This is the first thing to realize.

According to this Ichi school, you can win with a long weapon, and yet you can also win with a short weapon. In short, the Way of the Ichi school is the spirit of winning, whatever the weapon and whatever its size.

It is better to use two swords rather than one when you are fighting a crowd, and especially if you want to take a prisoner.

These things cannot be explained in detail. From one thing, know ten thousand things. When you attain the Way of strategy there will not be one thing you cannot see. You must study hard.

The Benefit of the Two Characters reading "Strategy"

Masters of the long sword are called strategists. As for the other military arts, those who master the bow are called archers, those who master the spear are called spearmen, those who master the gun are called marksmen, those who master the halberd are called halberdiers. But we do not call masters of the Way of the long sword "longswordsmen", nor do we speak of "companionswordsmen". Because bows, guns, spears and halberds are all warriors' equipment they are certainly part of strategy. To master the virtue of the long sword is to govern the world and oneself, thus the long sword is the basis of strategy. The principle is "strategy by means of the long sword". If he attains the virtue of the long sword, one man can beat ten men. Just as one man can beat ten, so a hundred men can beat a thousand, and a thousand can beat ten thousand. In my strategy, one man is the same as ten thousand, so this strategy is the complete warrior's craft.

The Way of the warrior does not include other Ways, such as Confucianism, Buddhism, certain traditions, artistic accomplishments and dancing. But even though these are not part of the Way, if you know the Way broadly you will see it in everything. Men must polish their particular Way.

The Benefit of Weapons in Strategy

There is a time and place for use of weapons.

The best use of the companion sword is in a confined space, or when you are engaged closely with an opponent. The long sword can be used effectively in all situations.

The halberd is inferior to the spear on the battlefield. With the spear you can take the initiative; the halberd is defensive. In the hands of one of two men of equal ability, the spear gives a little extra strength. Spear and halberd both have their uses, but neither is very beneficial in confined spaces. They cannot be used for taking a prisoner. They are essentially weapons for the field.

Anyway, if you learn "indoor" techniques, you will think narrowly and forget the true Way. Thus you will have difficulty in actual encounters.

The bow is tactically strong at the commencement of battle, especially battles on a moor, as it is possible to shoot quickly from among the spearmen. However, it is unsatisfactory in sieges, or when the enemy is more than forty yards away. For this reason there are nowadays few traditional schools of archery. There is little use nowadays for this kind of skill.

From inside fortifications, the gun has no equal among weapons. It is the supreme weapon on the field before the ranks clash, but once swords are crossed the gun becomes useless.

One of the virtues of the bow is that you can see the arrows in flight and correct your aim accordingly, whereas gunshot cannot be seen. You must appreciate the importance of this.

Just as a horse must have endurance and no defects, so it is with weapons. Horses should walk strongly, and swords and companion swords should cut strongly. Spears and halberds must stand up to heavy use: bows and guns must be sturdy. Weapons should be hardy rather than decorative.

You should not have a favorite weapon. To become over-familiar with one weapon is as much a fault as not knowing it sufficiently well. You should not copy others, but use weapons which you can handle properly. It is bad for commanders and troopers to have likes and dislikes. These are things you must learn thoroughly.

Timing in strategy

There is timing in everything. Timing in strategy cannot be mastered without a great deal of practice.

Timing is important in dancing and pipe or string music, for they are in rhythm only if timing is good. Timing and rhythm are also involved in the military arts, shooting bows and guns, and riding horses. In all skills and abilities there is timing.

There is also timing in the Void.

There is timing in the whole life of the warrior, in his thriving and declining, in his harmony and discord. Similarly, there is timing in the

Way of the merchant, in the rise and fall of capital. All things entail rising and falling timing. You must be able to discern this. In strategy there are various timing considerations. From the outset you must know the applicable timing and the inapplicable timing, and from among the large and small things and the fast and slow timings find the relevant timing, first seeing the distance timing and the background timing. This is the main thing in strategy. It is especially important to know the background timing, otherwise your strategy will become uncertain.

You win battles with the timing in the Void born of the timing of cunning by knowing the enemies' timing, and thus using a timing which the enemy does not expect.

All the five books are chiefly concerned with timing. You must train sufficiently to appreciate this.

If you practice day and night in the above Ichi school strategy, your spirit will naturally broaden. Thus is large scale strategy and the strategy of hand to hand combat propagated in the world. This is recorded for the first time in the five books of Ground, Water, Fire, Tradition (Wind), and Void. This is the way for men who want to learn my strategy:

Do not think dishonestly. The Way is in training. Become acquainted with every art. Know the Ways of all professions. Distinguish between gain and loss in worldly matters. Develop intuitive judgement and understanding for everything. Perceive those things which cannot be seen. Pay attention even to trifles. Do nothing which is of no use.

It is important to start by setting these broad principles in your heart, and train in the Way of strategy. If you do not look at things on a large scale it will be difficult for you to master strategy. If you learn and attain this strategy you will never lose even to twenty or thirty enemies. More than anything to start with you must set your heart on strategy and earnestly stick to the Way. You will come to be able to actually beat men in fights, and to be able to win with your eye. Also by training you will be able to freely control your own body, conquer men with your body, and with sufficient training you will be able to beat ten men with your spirit. When you have reached this point, will it not mean that you are invincible?

Moreover, in large scale strategy the superior man will manage many subordinates dexterously, bear himself correctly, govern the country and foster the people, thus preserving the ruler's discipline. If there is a Way involving the spirit of not being defeated, to help oneself and gain honor, it is the Way of strategy.

The Samurai Series

The Book of Five Rings

The Water Book

The spirit of the Ni Ten Ichi school of strategy is based on water, and this Water Book explains methods of victory as the long-sword form of the Ichi school. Language does not extend to explaining the Way in detail, but it can be grasped intuitively. Study this book; read a word then ponder on it. If you interpret the meaning loosely you will mistake the Way.

The principles of strategy are written down here in terms of single combat, but you must think broadly so that you attain an understanding for ten-thousand-a-side battles.

Strategy is different from other things in that if you mistake the Way even a little you will become bewildered and fall into bad ways.

If you merely read this book you will not reach the Way of strategy. Absorb the things written in this book. Do not just read, memorize or imitate, but so that you realize the principle from within your own heart study hard to absorb these things into your body.

Spiritual Bearing in Strategy

In strategy your spiritual bearing must not be any different from normal. Both in fighting and in everyday life you should be determined though calm. Meet the situation without tenseness yet not recklessly, your spirit settled yet unbiased. Even when your spirit is calm do not let your body relax, and when your body is relaxed do not let your spirit slacken. Do not let your spirit be influenced by your body, or your body be influenced by your spirit. Be neither insufficiently spirited nor over spirited. An elevated spirit is weak and a low spirit is weak. Do not let the enemy see your spirit.

Small people must be completely familiar with the spirit of large people, and large people must be familiar with the spirit of small people. Whatever your size, do not be misled by the reactions of your own body. With your spirit open and unconstricted, look at things

The Samurai Series 17

from a high point of view. You must cultivate your wisdom and spirit. Polish your wisdom: learn public justice, distinguish between good and evil, study the Ways of different arts one by one. When you cannot be deceived by men you will have realized the wisdom of strategy.

The wisdom of strategy is different from other things. On the battlefield, even when you are hard-pressed, you should ceaselessly research the principles of strategy so that you can develop a steady spirit.

Stance in Strategy

Adopt a stance with the head erect, neither hanging down, nor looking up, nor twisted. Your forehead and the space between your eyes should not be wrinkled. Do not roll your eyes nor allow them to blink, but slightly narrow them. With your features composed, keep the line of your nose straight with a feeling of slightly flaring your nostrils. Hold the line of the rear of the neck straight: instill vigor into your hairline, and in the same way from the shoulders down through your entire body. Lower both shoulders and, without the buttocks jutting out, put strength into your legs from the knees to the tips of your toes. Brace your abdomen so that you do not bend at the hips. Wedge your companion sword in your belt against your abdomen, so that your belt is not slack - this is called "wedging in".

In all forms of strategy, it is necessary to maintain the combat stance in everyday life and to make your everyday stance your combat stance. You must research this well.

The Gaze in Strategy

The gaze should be large and broad. This is the twofold gaze "Perception and Sight". Perception is strong and sight week.

In strategy it is important to see distant things as if they were close and to take a distanced view of close things. It is important in strategy to know the enemy's sword and not to be distracted by insignificant movements of his sword. You must study this. The gaze is the same for single combat and for large-scale strategy.

It is necessary in strategy to be able to look to both sides without moving the eyeballs. You cannot master this ability quickly. Learn what is written here; use this gaze in everyday life and do not vary it whatever happens.

Holding the Long Sword

Grip the long sword with a rather floating feeling in your thumb and forefinger, with the middle finger neither tight nor slack, and with the last two fingers tight. It is bad to have play in your hands.

When you take up a sword, you must feel intent on cutting the enemy. As you cut an enemy you must not change your grip, and your hands must not "cower". When you dash the enemy's sword aside, or ward it off, or force it down, you must slightly change the feeling in your thumb and forefinger. Above all, you must be intent on cutting the enemy in the way you grip the sword.

The grip for combat and for sword-testing is the same. There is no such thing as a "man-cutting grip".

Generally, I dislike fixedness in both long swords and hands. Fixedness means a dead hand. Pliability is a living hand. You must bear this in mind.

Footwork

With the tips of your toes somewhat floating, tread firmly with your heels. Whether you move fast or slow, with large or small steps, your feet must always move as in normal walking. I dislike the three walking methods know as "jumping-foot", "floating-foot" and "fixed-steps".

So-called "Yin-Yang foot" is important in the Way. Yin-Yang foot means not moving only one foot. It means moving your feet left-right and right-left when cutting, withdrawing, or warding off a cut. You should not move on one foot preferentially.

The Five Attitudes

The five attitudes are: Upper, Middle, Lower, Right Side, and Left Side. These are the give. Although attitude has these five divisions, the one purpose of all of them is to cut the enemy. There are none but these five attitudes.

Whatever attitude you are in, do not be conscious of making the attitude; think only of cutting.

Your attitude should be large or small according to the situation. Upper, Lower and Middle attitudes are decisive. Left Side and Right Side attitudes are fluid. Left and Right attitudes should be used if there is an obstruction overhead or to one side. The decision to use Left or Right depends on the place.

The essence of the Way is this. To understand attitude you must thoroughly understand the middle attitude. The middle attitude is the heart of attitudes. If we look at strategy on a broad scale, the Middle attitude is the seat of the commander, with the other four attitudes following the commander. You must appreciate this.

Th Way of the Long Sword

Knowing the Way of the long sword means we can wield with two fingers the sword we usually carry. If we know the path of the sword well, we can wield it easily.

If you try to wield the long sword quickly you will mistake the Way. To wield the long sword well you must wield it calmly. If you try to wield it quickly, like a folding fan or a short sword, you will err by using "short sword chopping". You cannot cut down a man with a long sword using this method.

When you have cut downwards with the longsword, lift it straight upwards; when you cut sideways, return the sword along a sideways path. Return the sword in a reasonable way, always stretching the elbows broadly. Wield the sword strongly. This is the Way of the longsword.

If you learn to use the five approaches of my strategy, you will be able to wield a sword well. You must train constantly.

The Five Approaches

The first approach is the Middle attitude. Confront the enemy with the point of your sword against his face. When he attacks, dash his sword to the right and "ride" it. Or, when the enemy attacks, deflect the point of his sword by hitting downwards, keep your long sword where it is, and as the enemy renews his attack cut his arms from below. This is the first method.

The five approaches are this kind of thing. You must train repeatedly using a long sword in order to learn them. When you master my Way of the long sword, you will be able to control any attack the enemy makes. I assure you, there are no attitudes other than the five attitudes of the long sword of Ni To.

In the second approach with the long sword, from the Upper attitude cut the enemy just as he attacks. If the enemy evades the cut, keep your sword where it is and, scooping up from below, cut him as he renews the attack. It is possible to repeat the cut from here.

In this method there are various changes in timing and spirit. You will be able to understand this by training in the Ichi school. You will always win with the five long sword methods. You must train repetitively.

In the third approach, adopt the Lower attitude, anticipating scooping up. When the enemy attacks, hit his hands from below. As you do so he may try to hit your sword down. If this is the case, cut his upper arm(s) horizontally with a feeling of "crossing". This means that from the lower attitudes you hit the enemy at the instant that he attacks.

You will encounter this method often, both as a beginner and in later strategy. You must train holding a long sword.

In this fourth approach, adopt the Left Side attitude. As the enemy attacks hit his hands from below. If as you hit his hands he attempts to dash down your sword, with the feeling of hitting his hands, parry the path of his long sword and cut across from above your shoulder.

This is the Way of the long sword. Through this method you win by parrying the line of the enemy's attack. You must research this.

In the fifth approach, the sword is in the Right Side attitude. In accordance with the enemy's attack, cross your long sword from below at the side to the Upper attitude. Then cut straight from above.

This method is essential for knowing the Way of the long sword well. If you can use this method, you can freely wield a heavy long sword.

I cannot describe in detail how to use these five approaches. You must become well acquainted with my "in harmony with the long sword" Way, learn large-scale timing, understand the enemy's long sword, and become used to the five approaches from the outset. You will always win by using these five methods, with various timing considerations discerning the enemy's spirit. You must consider all this carefully.

The "Attitude No-Attitude" Teaching

"Attitude No-Attitude" means that there is no need for what are know as long sword attitudes. Even so, attitudes exist as the five ways of holding the long sword. However you hold the sword it must be in such a way that it is easy to cut the enemy well, in accordance with the situation, the place, and your relation to the enemy. From the Upper attitude as your spirit lessens you can adopt the Middle attitude, and from the Middle attitude you can raise the sword a little in your technique and adopt the Upper attitude. From the lower attitude you can raise the sword and adopt the Middle attitudes as the occasion demands. According to the situation, if you turn your sword from either the Left Side or Right Side attitude towards the center, the Middle or the Lower attitude results.

The principle of this is called "Existing Attitude - Nonexisting Attitude".

The primary thing when you take a sword in your hands is your intention to cut the enemy, whatever the means. Whenever you parry, hit, spring, strike or touch the enemy's cutting sword, you must cut the enemy in the same movement. It is essential to attain this. If you think only of hitting, springing, striking or touching the enemy, you will not be able actually to cut him. More than anything, you must be thinking of carrying your movement through to cutting him. You must thoroughly research this.

Attitude in strategy on a larger scale is called "Battle Array". Such attitudes are all for winning battles. Fixed formation is bad. Study this well.

To Hit the Enemy "In One Timing"

"In One Timing" means, when you have closed with the enemy, to hit him as quickly and directly as possible, without moving your body or settling your spirit, while you see that he is still undecided. The timing of hitting before the enemy decides to withdraw, break or hit, is this "In One Timing".

You must train to achieve this timing, to be able to hit in the timing of an instant.

The "Abdomen Timing of Two"

When you attack and the enemy quickly retreats, as you see him tense you must feint a cut. Then, as he relaxes, follow up and hit him. This is the "Abdomen Timing of Two".

It is very difficult to attain this by merely reading this book, but you will soon understand with a little instruction.

No Design, No Conception

when word and actions are spontaneously the same.

In this method, when the enemy attacks and you also decide to attack, hit with your body, and hit with your spirit, and hit from the Void with your hands, accelerating strongly. This is the "No Design, No Conception" cut.

This is the most important method of hitting. It is often used. You must train hard to understand it.

The Flowing Water Cut

The "Flowing Water Cut" is used when you are struggling blade to blade with the enemy. When he breaks and quickly withdraws trying to spring with his long sword, expand your body and spirit and cut him as slowly as possible with your long sword, following your body like stagnant water. You can cut with certainty if you learn this. You must discern the enemy's grade.

Continuous Cut

When you attack and the enemy also attacks, and your swords spring together, in one action cut his head, hands and legs. When you cut several places with one sweep of the long sword, it is the "Continuous Cut". You must practice this cut; it is often used. With detailed practice you should be able to understand it.

The Fire and Stones Cut

The Fires and Stones Cut means that when the enemy's long sword and your long sword clash together you cut as strongly as possible without raising the sword even a little. This means cutting quickly with the hands, body and legs - all three cutting strongly. If you train well enough you will be able to strike strongly.

The Red Leaves Cut

The Red Leaves Cut [allusion to falling, dying leaves. - Slaegr] means knocking down the enemy's long sword. The spirit should be getting control of his sword. When the enemy is in a long sword attitude in front of you and intent on cutting, hitting and parrying, you strongly hit the enemy's long sword with the Fire and Stones Cut, perhaps in the spirit of the "No Design, No Conception" Cut. If you then beat down the point of his sword with a sticky feeling, he will necessarily drop the sword. If you practice this cut it becomes easy to make the enemy drop his sword. You must train repetitively.

The Body in Place of the Long Sword

Also "the long sword in place of the body". Usually we move the body and the sword at the same time to cut the enemy. However, according to the enemy's cutting method, you can dash against him with your body first, and afterwards cut with the sword. If his body is immovable, you can cut first with the long sword, but generally you hit first with the body and then cut with the long sword. You must research this well and practice hitting.

Cut and Slash

To cut and to slash are two different things. Cutting, whatever form of cutting it is, is decisive, with a resolute spirit. Slashing is nothing more than touching the enemy. Even if you slash strongly, and even if the enemy dies instantly, it is slashing. When you cut, your spirit is resolved. You must appreciate this. If you first slash the enemy's hands or legs, you must then cut strongly. Slashing is in spirit the same as touching. When you realize this, they become indistinguishable. Learn this well.

Chinese Monkey's Body

The Chinese Monkey's Body [short-armed monkey. - Slaegr] is the spirit of not stretching out your arms. The spirit is to get in quickly, without in the least extending your arms, before the enemy cuts. If you are intent upon not stretching out your arms you are effectively far away, the spirit is to go in with your whole body. When you come to within arm's reach it becomes easy to move your body in. You must research this well.

Glue and Lacquer Emulsion Body

The spirit of "Glue and Lacquer Emulsion Body" is to stick to the enemy and not separate from him. When you approach the enemy, stick firmly with your head, body and legs. People tend to advance their head and legs quickly, but their body lags behind. You should stick firmly so that there is not the slightest gap between the enemy's body and your body. You must consider this carefully.

To Strive for Height

By "to strive for height" is meant, when you close with the enemy, to strive with him for superior height without cringing. Stretch your legs, stretch your hips, and stretch your neck face to face with him. When you think you have won, and you are the higher, thrust in strongly. You must learn this.

To Apply Stickiness

When the enemy attacks and you also attack with the long sword, you should go in with a sticky feeling and fix your long sword against the enemy's as you receive his cut. The spirit of stickiness is not hitting very strongly, but hitting so that the long swords do not separate easily. It is best to approach as calmly as possible when hitting the enemy's long sword with stickiness. The difference between "Stickiness" and "Entanglement" is that stickiness is firm and entanglement is weak. You must appreciate this.

The Body Strike

The Body Strike means to approach the enemy through a gap in his guard. The spirit is to strike him with your body. Turn your face a little aside and strike the enemy's breast with your left shoulder thrust out. Approach with the spirit of bouncing the enemy away, striking as strongly as possible in time with your breathing. If you achieve this method of closing with the enemy, you will be able to knock him ten or twenty feet away. It is possible to strike the enemy until he is dead. Train well.

Three Ways to Parry His Attack

There are three methods to parry a cut:

First, by dashing the enemy's long sword to your right, as if thrusting at his eyes, when he makes an attack.

Or, to parry by thrusting the enemy's long sword towards his right eye with the feeling of snipping his neck.

Or, when you have a short "long sword", without worrying about parrying the enemy's long sword, to close with him quickly, thrusting at his face with your left hand.

These are the three methods of parrying. You must bear in mind that you can always clench your left hand and thrust at the enemy's face with your fist. For this it is necessary to train well.

To Stab at the Face

To stab at the face means, when you are in confrontation with the enemy, that your spirit is intent of stabbing at his face, following the line of the blades with the point of your long sword. If you are intent on stabbing at his face, his face and body will become rideale. When the enemy becomes as if readable, there are various opportunities for winning. You must concentrate on this. When fighting and the enemy's body becomes as if rideable, you can win quickly, so you ought not to forget to stab at the face. You must pursue the value of this technique through training.

To Stab at the Heart

To stab at the heart means, when fighting and there are obstructions above, or to the sides, and whenever it is difficult to cut, to thrust at the enemy. You must stab the enemy's breast without letting the point of your long sword waver, showing the enemy the ridge of the blade square-on, and with the spirit of deflecting his long sword. The spirit of this principle is often useful when we become tired or for some reason our long sword will not cut. You must understand the application of this method.

To Scold "Tut-TUT!"

"Scold" means that, when the enemy tries to counter-cut as you attack, you counter-cut again from below as if thrusting at him, trying to hold him down. With very quick timing you cut, scolding the enemy. Thrust up, "Tut!", and cut "TUT!" This timing is encountered time and time again in exchange of blows. The way to scold Tut-TUT is to time the cut simultaneously with raising your long sword as if to thrust the enemy. You must learn this through repetitive practice.

The Smacking Parry

By "smacking parry" is meant that when you clash swords with the enemy, you meet his attacking cut on your long sword with a tee-dum, tee-dum rhythm, smacking his sword and cutting him. The spirit of the smacking parry is not parrying, or smacking strongly, but smacking the enemy's long sword in accordance with his attacking cut, primarily intent on quickly cutting him. If you understand the timing of smacking, however hard your long swords clash together, your swordpoint will not be knocked back even a little. You must research sufficiently to realize this.

There are Many Enemies

"There are many enemies" applies when you are fighting one against many. Draw both sword and companion sword and assume a wide-stretched left and right attitude. The spirit is to chase the enemies around from side to side, even though they come from all four directions. Observe their attacking order, and go to meet first those who attack first. Sweep your eyes around broadly, carefully examining the attacking order, and cut left and right alternately with your swords. Waiting is bad. Always quickly re-assume your attitudes to both sides, cut the enemies down as they advance, crushing them in the direction from which they attack. Whatever you do, you must drive the enemy together, as if tying a line of fishes, and when they are seen to be piled up, cut them down strongly without giving them room to move.

The Advantage when coming to Blows

You can know how to win through strategy with the long sword, but it cannot be clearly explained in writing. You must practice diligently in order to understand how to win.

Oral tradition: "The true Way of strategy is revealed in the long sword."

One Cut

You can win with certainty with the spirit of "one cut". It is difficult to attain this if you do not learn strategy well. If you train well in this Way, strategy will come from your heart and you will be able to win at will. You must train diligently.

Direct Communication

The spirit of "Direct Communication" is how the true Way of the Ni To Ichi school is received and handed down.

Oral tradition: "Teach your body strategy."

Recorded in the above book is an outline of Ichi school sword-fighting.

To learn how to win with the long sword in strategy, first learn the five approaches and the five attitudes, and absorb the Way of the long sword naturally in your body. You must understand spirit and timing, handle the long sword naturally, and move body and legs in harmony with your spirit. Whether beating one man or two, you will then know values in strategy.

Study the contents of this book, taking one item at a time, and through fighting with enemies you will gradually come to know the principle of the Way.

Deliberately, with a patient spirit, absorb the virtue of all this, from time to time raising your hand in combat. Maintain this spirit whenever you cross swords with and enemy.

Step by step walk the thousand-mile road.

Study strategy over the years and achieve the spirit of the warrior. Today is victory over yourself of yesterday; tomorrow is your victory over lesser men. Next, in order to beat more skillful men, train according to this book, not allowing your heart to be swayed along a side-track. Even if you kill an enemy, if it is not based on what you have learned it is not the true Way.

If you attain this Way of victory, then you will be able to beat several tens of men. What remains is sword-fighting ability, which you can attain in battles and duels.

The Fire Book

In this the Fire Book of the Ni To Ichi school of strategy I describe fighting as fire.

In the first place, people think narrowly about the benefit of strategy. By using only their fingertips, they only know the benefit of three of the five inches of the wrist. They let a contest be decided, as with the folding fan, merely by the span of their forearms. They specialize in the small matter of dexterity, learning such trifles as hand and leg movements with the bamboo practice sword.

In my strategy, the training for killing enemies is by way of many contests, fighting for survival, discovering the meaning of life and death, learning the Way of the sword, judging the strength of attacks and understanding the Way of the "edge and ridge" of the sword.

You cannot profit from small techniques particularly when full armor is worn. ["Roku Gu" (six pieces): body armor, helmet, mask, thigh pieces, gauntlets and leg pieces. - Slaegr] My Way of strategy is the sure method to win when fighting for your life one man against five or ten. There is nothing wrong with the principle "one man can beat ten, so a thousand men can beat ten thousand". You must research this. Of course you cannot assemble a thousand or ten thousand men for everyday training. But you can become a master of strategy by training alone with a sword, so that you can understand the enemy's stratagems, his strength and resources, and come to appreciate how to apply strategy to beat ten thousand enemies.

Any man who wants to master the essence of my strategy must research diligently, training morning and evening. Thus can he polish his skill, become free from self, and realize extraordinary ability. He will come to possess miraculous power.

This is the practical result of strategy.

Depending on the Place

Examine your environment.

Stand in the sun; that is, take up an attitude with the sun behind you. If the situation dows not allow this, you must try to keep the sun on your right side. In buildings, you must stand with the entrance behind you or to your right. Make sure that your rear is unobstructed, and that there is free space on your left, your right side being occupied with your side attitude. At night, if the enemy can be seen, keep the fire behind you and the entrance to your right, and otherwise take up your attitude as above. You must look down on the enemy, and take up your attitude on slightly higher places. For example, the Kamiza [residence of the ancestral spirit of a house; often a slightly raised recess in a wall (with ornaments). - Slaegr] in a house is thought of as a high place.

When the fight comes, always endeavor to chase the enemy around to your left side. Chase him towards awkward places, and try to keep him with his back to awkward places. When the enemy gets into an inconvenient position, do not let him look around, but conscientiously chase him around and pin him down. In houses, chase the enemy into the thresholds, lintels, doors, verandas, pillars, and so on, again not letting him see his situation.

Always chase the enemy into bad footholds, obstacles at the side, and so on, using the virtues of the place to establish predominant positions from which to fight. You must research and train diligently in this.

The Three Methods to Forestall the Enemy

The first is to forestall him by attacking. This is called Ken No Sen (to set him up).

Another method is to forestall him as he attacks. This is called Tai No Sen (to wait for the initiative).

The other method is when you and the enemy attack together. This is called Tai Tai No Sen (to accompany him and forestall him).

There are no methods of taking the lead other than these three. Because you can win quickly by taking the lead, it is one of the most important things in strategy. There are several things involved in taking the lead. You must make the best of the situation, see through the enemy's spirit so that you grasp his strategy and defeat him. It is impossible to write about this in detail.

The First - Ken No Sen

When you decide to attack, keep calm and dash in quickly, forestalling the enemy. Or you can advance seemingly strongly but with a reserved spirit, forestalling him with the reserve.

Alternatively, advance with as strong a spirit as possible, and when you reach the enemy move with your feet a little quicker than normal, unsettling him and overwhelming him sharply.

Or, with your spirit calm, attack with a feeling of constantly crushing the enemy, from first to last. The spirit is to win in the depths of the enemy.

These are all Ken No Sen.

The Second - Tai No Sen

When the enemy attacks, remain undisturbed but feign weakness. As the enemy reaches you, suddenly move away indicating that you intend to jump aside, then dash in attacking strongly as soon as you see the enemy relax. This is one way.

Or, as the enemy attacks, attack still more strongly, taking advantage of the resulting disorder in his timing to win.

This is the Tai No Sen principle.

The Third - Tai Tai No Sen

When the enemy makes a quick attack, you must attack strongly and calmly, aim for his weak point as he draws near, and strongly defeat him.

Or, if the enemy attacks calmly, you must observe his movements and, with your body rather floating, join in with his movements as he draws near. Move quickly and cut him strongly.

This is Tai Tai No Sen.

These things cannot be clearly explained in words. You must research what is written here. In these three ways of forestalling, you must judge the situation. This does not mean that you always attack first; but if the enemy attacks first you can lead him around. In strategy, you have effectively won when you forestall the enemy, so you must train well to attain this.

To Hold Down a Pillow

"To Hold Down a Pillow" means not allowing the enemy's head to rise.

In contests of strategy it is bad to be led about by the enemy. You must always be able to lead the enemy about. Obviously the enemy will also be thinking of doing this, but he cannot forestall you if you do not allow him to come out. In strategy, you must stop the enemy as he attempts to cut; you must push down his thrust, and throw off his hold when he tries to grapple. This is the meaning of "to hold down a pillow". When you have grasped this principle, whatever the enemy tries to bring about in the fight you will see in advance and suppress it. The spirit is too check his attack at the syllable "at...", when he jumps check his jump at the syllable "ju...", and check his cut at "cu...".

The important thing in strategy is to suppress the enemy's useful actions but allow his useless actions. However, doing this alone is defensive. First, you must act according to the Way, suppressing the enemy's techniques, foiling his plans and thence command him directly. When you can do this you will be a master of strategy. You must train well and research "holding down a pillow".

Crossing at a Ford

"Crossing at a ford" means, for example, crossing the sea at a strait, or crossing over a hundred miles of broad sea at a crossing place. I believe this "crossing at a ford" occurs often in man's lifetime. It means setting sail even though your friends stay in harbor, knowing the route, knowing the soundness of your ship and the favor of the day. When all the conditions are meet, and there is perhaps a favorable wind, or a tailwind, then set sail. If the wind changes within a few miles of your destination, you must row across the remaining distance without sail.

If you attain this spirit, it applies to everyday life. You must always think of crossing at a ford.

In strategy also it is important to "cross at a ford". Discern the enemy's capability and, knowing your own strong points, "cross the ford" at the advantageous place, as a good captain crosses a sea route. If you succeed in crossing at the best place, you may take your ease. To cross at a ford means to attack the enemy's weak point, and to put yourself in an advantageous position. This is how to win large-scale strategy. The spirit of crossing at a ford is necessary in both large- and small-scale strategy.

You must research this well.

To Know the Times

"To know the times" means to know the enemy's disposition in battle. Is it flourishing or waning? By observing the spirit of the enemy's men and getting the best position, you can work out the enemy's disposition and move your men accordingly. You can win through this principle of strategy, fighting from a position of advantage.

When in a duel, you must forestall the enemy and attack when you have first recognized his school of strategy, perceived his quality and his strong and weak points. Attack in an unsuspecting manner, knowing his metre and modulation and the appropriate timing.

Knowing the times means, if your ability is high, seeing right into things. If you are thoroughly conversant with strategy, you will recognize the enemy's intentions and thus have many opportunities to win. You must sufficiently study this.

To Tread Down the Sword

"To tread down the sword" is a principle often used in strategy. First, in large scale strategy, when the enemy first discharges bows and guns and then attacks it is difficult for us to attack if we are busy loading powder into our guns or notching our arrows. The spirit is to attack quickly while the enemy is still shooting with bows or guns. The spirit is to win by "treading down" as we receive the enemy's attack.

In single combat, we cannot get a decisive victory by cutting, with a "tee-dum tee-dum" feeling, in the wake of the enemy's attacking long sword. We must defeat him at the start of his attack, in the spirit of treading him down with the feet, so that he cannot rise again to the attack.

"Treading" does not simply mean treading with the feet. Tread with the body, tread with the spirit, and, of course, tread and cut with the long sword. You must achieve the spirit of not allowing the enemy to attack a second time. This is the spirit of forestalling in every sense. Once at the enemy, you should not aspire just to strike him, but to cling after the attack. You must study this deeply.

To Know "Collapse"

Everything can collapse. Houses, bodies, and enemies collapse when their rhythm becomes deranged.

In large-scale strategy, when the enemy starts to collapse, you must pursue him without letting the chance go. If you fail to take advantage of your enemies' collapse, they may recover.

In single combat, the enemy sometimes loses timing and collapses. If you let this opportunity pass, he may recover and not be so negligent thereafter. Fix your eye on the enemy's collapse, and chase him, attacking so that you do not let him recover. You must do this. The chasing attack is with a strong spirit. You must utterly cut the enemy down so that he does not recover his position. You must understand how to utterly cut down the enemy.

To Become the Enemy

"To become the enemy" means to think yourself in the enemy's position. In the world people tend to think of a robber trapped in a house as a fortified enemy. However, if we think of "becoming the enemy", we feel that the whole world is against us and that there is no escape. He who is shut inside is a pheasant. He who enters to arrest is a hawk. You must appreciate this.

In large-scale strategy, people are always under the impression that the enemy is strong, and so tend to become cautious. But if you have good soldiers, and if you understand the principles of strategy, and if you know how to beat the enemy, there is nothing to worry about.

In single combat also you must put yourself in the enemy's position. If you think, "Here is a a master of the Way, who knows the principles of strategy", then you will surely lose. You must consider this deeply.

To Release Four Hands

"To release four hands" is used when you and the enemy are contending with the same spirit, and the issue cannot be decided. Abandon this spirit and win through an alternative resource.

In large-scale strategy, when there is a "four hands" spirit, do not give up - it is man's existence. Immediately throw away this spirit and win with a technique the enemy does not expect.

In single combat also, when we think we have fallen into the "four hands" situation, we must defeat the enemy by changing our mind and applying a suitable technique according to his condition. You must be able to judge this.

To Move the Shade

"To move the shade" is used when you cannot see the enemy's spirit.

In large-scale strategy, when you cannot see the enemy's position, indicate that you are about to attack strongly, to discover his resources. It is easy then to defeat him with a different method once you see his resources.

In single combat, if the enemy takes up a rear or side attitude of the long sword so that you cannot see his intention, make a feint attack, and the enemy will show his long sword, thinking he sees your spirit. Benefiting from what you are shown, you can win with certainty. If you are negligent you will miss the timing. Research this well.

To Hold Down a Shadow

"Holding down a shadow" is use when you can see the enemy's attacking spirit.

In large-scale strategy, when the enemy embarks on an attack, if you make a show of strongly suppressing his technique, he will change his mind. Then, altering your spirit, defeat him by forestalling him with a Void spirit.

Or, in single combat, hold down the enemy's strong intention with a suitable timing, and defeat him by forestalling him with this timing. You must study this well.

To Pass On

Many things are said to be passed on. Sleepiness can be passed on, and yawning can be passed on. Time can be passed on also.

In large-scale strategy, when the enemy is agitated and shows an inclination to rush, do not mind in the least. Make a show of complete calmness, and the enemy will be taken by this and will become relaxed. When you see that this spirit has been passed on, you can bring about the enemy's defeat by attacking strongly with a Void spirit.

In single combat, you can win by relaxing your body and spirit and then, catching on to the moment the enemy relaxes, attack strongly and quickly, forestalling him.

What is know as "getting someone drunk" is similar to this. You can also infect the enemy with a bored, careless, or weak spirit. You must study this well.

To Cause Loss of Balance

Many things can cause a loss of balance. One cause is danger, another is hardship, and another is surprise. You must research this.

In large-scale strategy it is important to cause loss of balance. Attack without warning where the enemy is not expecting it, and while his spirit is undecided follow up your advantage and, having the lead, defeat him.

Or, in single combat, start by making a show of being slow, then suddenly attack strongly. Without allowing him space for breath to recover form the fluctuation of spirit, you must grasp the opportunity to win. Get the feel of this.

To Frighten

Fright often occurs, caused by the unexpected.

In large-scale strategy you can frighten the enemy not just by what you present to their eyes, but by shouting, making a small force seem large, or by threatening them from the flank without warning. These things all frighten. You can win by making best use of the enemy's frightened rhythm.

In single combat, also, you must use the advantage of taking the enemy unawares by frightening him with your body, long sword, or voice, to defeat him. You should research this well.

To Soak In

When you have come to grips and are striving together with the enemy, and you realize that you cannot advance, you "soak in" and become one with the enemy. You can win by applying a suitable technique while you are mutually entangled.

In battles involving large numbers as well as in fights with small numbers, you can often win decisively with the advantage of knowing how to "soak" into the enemy, whereas, were you to draw apart, you would lose the chance to win. Research this well.

To Injure the Corners

It is difficult to move strong things by pushing directly, so you should "injure the corners".

In large-scale strategy, it is beneficial to strike at the corners of the enemy's force. If the corners are overthrown, the spirit of the whole body will be overthrown. To defeat the enemy you must follow up the attack when the corners have fallen.

In single combat, it is easy to win once the enemy collapses. This happens when you injure the "corners" of his body, and thus weaken him. It is important to know how to do this, so you must research deeply.

To Throw into Confusion

This means making the enemy lose resolve.

In large-scale strategy we can use our troops to confuse the enemy on the field. Observing the enemy's spirit, we can make him think, "Here? There? Like that? Like this? Slow? Fast?". Victory is certain when the enemy is caught up in a rhythm which confuses his spirit.

In single combat, we can confuse the enemy by attacking with varied techniques when the chance arises. Feint a thrust or cut, or make the enemy think you are going to close with him, and when he is confused you can easily win.

This is the essence of fighting, and you must research it deeply.

The Three Shouts

The three shouts are divided thus: before, during and after. Shout according to the situation. The voice is a thing of life. We shout against fires and so on, against the wind and the waves. The voice shows energy.

In large-scale strategy, at the start of battle we shout as loudly as possible. During the fight, the voice is low-pitched, shouting out as we attack. After the contest, we shout in the wake of our victory. These are the three shouts.

In single combat, we make as if to cut and shout "Ei!" at the same time to disturb the enemy, then in the wake of our shout we cut with the long sword. We shout after we have cut down the enemy - this is to announce victory. This is called "sen go no koe" (before and after voice). We do not shout simultaneously with flourishing the long sword. We shout during the fight to get into rhythm. Research this deeply.

To Mingle

In battles, when the armies are in confrontation, attack the enemy's strong points and, when you see that they are beaten back, quickly separate and attack yet another strong point on the periphery of his force. The spirit of this is like a winding mountain path.

This is an important fighting method for one man against many. Strike down the enemies in one quarter, or drive them back, then grasp the timing and attack further strong points to right and left, as if on a winding mountain path, weighing up the enemies' disposition. When you know the enemies' level attack strongly with no trace of retreating spirit.

What is meant by "mingling" is the spirit of advancing and becoming engaged with the enemy, and not withdrawing even one step. You must understand this.

To Crush

This means to crush the enemy regarding him as being weak.

In large-scale strategy, when we see that the enemy has few men, or if he has many men but his spirit is weak and disordered, we knock the hat over his eyes, crushing him utterly. If we crush lightly, he may recover. You must learn the spirit of crushing as if with a hand-grip.

In single combat, if the enemy is less skilful than yourself, if his rhythm is disorganized, or if he has fallen into evasive or retreating attitudes, we must crush him straightaway, with no concern for his presence and without allowing him space for breath. It is essential to crush him all at once. The primary thing is not to let him recover his position even a little. You must research this deeply.

The Mountain-Sea Change

The "mountain-sea" spirit means that it is bad to repeat the same thing several times when fighting the enemy. There may be no help but to do something twice, but do not try it a third time. If you once make an attack and fail, there is little chance of success if you use the same approach again. If you attempt a technique which you have previously tried unsuccessfully and fail yet again, then you must change your attacking method.

If the enemy thinks of the mountains, attack like the sea; and if he thinks of the sea, attack like the mountains. You must research this deeply.

To Penetrate the Depths

When we are fighting with the enemy, even when it can be seen that we can win on the surface with the benefit of the Way, if his spirit is not extinguished, he may be beaten superficially yet undefeated in spirit deep inside. With this principle of "penetrating the depths" we can destroy the enemy's spirit in its depths, demoralizing him by quickly changing our spirit. This often occurs.

Penetrating the depths means penetrating with the long sword, penetrating with the body, and penetrating with the spirit. This cannot be understood in a generalization.

Once we have crushed the enemy in the depths, there is no need to remain spirited. But otherwise we must remain spirited. If the enemy remains spirited it is difficult to crush him. You must train in penetrating the depths for large-scale strategy and also single combat.

To Renew

"To renew" applies when we are fighting with the enemy, and an entangled spirit arises where there is no possible resolution. We must abandon our efforts, think of the situation in a fresh spirit then win in the new rhythm. To renew, when we are deadlocked with the enemy, means that without changing our circumstance we change our spirit and win through a different technique.

It is necessary to consider how "to renew" also applies in large-scale strategy. Research this diligently.

Rat's Head, Ox's Neck

"Rat's head and ox's neck" means that, when we are fighting with the enemy and both he and we have become occupied with small points in an entangled spirit, we must always think of the Way of strategy as being both a rat's head and an ox's neck. Whenever we have become preoccupied with small detail, we must suddenly change into a large spirit, interchanging large with small.

This is one of the essences of strategy. It is necessary that the warrior think in this spirit in everyday life. You must not depart from this spirit in large-scale strategy nor in single combat.

The Commander Knows the Troops

"The commander knows the troops" applies everywhere in fights in my Way of strategy.

Using the wisdom of strategy, think of the enemy as your own troops. When you think in this way you can move him at will and be able to chase him around. You become the general and the enemy becomes your troops. You must master this.

To Let Go the Hilt

There are various kinds of spirit involved in letting go the hilt.

There is the spirit of winning without a sword. There is also the spirit of holding the long sword but not winning. The various methods cannot be expressed in writing. You must train well.

The Body of a Rock

When you have mastered the Way of strategy you can suddenly make your body like a rock, and ten thousand things cannot touch you. This is the body of a rock.

You will not be moved. Oral tradition.

What is recorded above is what has been constantly on my mind about Ichi school sword fencing, written down as it came to me. This is the first time I have written about my technique, and the order of things is a bit confused. It is difficult to express it clearly.

This book is a spiritual guide for the man who wishes to learn the Way.

My heart has been inclined to the Way of strategy from my youth onwards. I have devoted myself to training my hand, tempering my body, and attaining the many spiritual attitudes of sword fencing. If we watch men of other schools discussing theory, and concentrating on techniques with the hands, even though they seem skilful to watch, they have not the slightest true spirit.

Of course, men who study in this way think they are training the body and spirit, but it is an obstacle to the true Way, and its bad influence remains for ever. Thus the true Way of strategy is becoming decadent and dying out.

The true Way of sword fencing is the craft of defeating the enemy in a fight, and nothing other than this. If you attain and adhere to the wisdom of my strategy, you need never doubt that you will win.

The Wind Book

In strategy you must know the Ways of other schools, so I have written about various other traditions of strategies in this the Wind Book.

Without knowledge of the Ways of other schools, it is difficult to understand the essence of my Ichi school. Looking at other schools we find some that specialize in techniques of strength using extra-long swords. Some schools study the Way of the short sword, known as kodachi. Some schools teach dexterity in large numbers of sword techniques, teaching attitudes of the sword as the "surface" and the Way as the "interior".

That none of these are the true Way I show clearly in the interior of this book - all the vices and virtues and rights and wrongs. My Ichi school is different. Other schools make accomplishments their means of livelihood, growing flowers and decoratively coloring articles in order to sell them. This is definitely not the Way of strategy.

Some of the world's strategists are concerned only with sword-fencing, and limit their training to flourishing the long sword and carriage of the body. But is dexterity alone sufficient to win? This is not the essence of the Way.

I have recorded the unsatisfactory point of other schools one by one in this book. You must study these matters deeply to appreciate the benefit of my Ni To Ichi school.

Other Schools Using Extra-Long Swords

Some other schools have a liking for extra-long swords. From the point of view of my strategy these must been seen as weak schools. This is because they do not appreciate the principle of cutting the enemy by any means. Their preference is for the extra-long sword and, relying on the virtue of its length, they think to defeat the enemy from a distance.

In this world it is said, "One inch gives the hand advantage", but these are the idle words of one who does not know strategy. It shows the inferior strategy of a weak spirit that men should be dependent on the length of their sword, fighting from a distance without the benefit of strategy.

I expect there is a case for the school in question liking extra-long swords as part of its doctrine, but if we compare this to real life it is unreasonable. Surely we need not necessarily be defeated if we are using a short sword, and have no long sword?

It is difficult for these people to cut the enemy when at close quarters because of the length of the long sword. The blade path is large so the long sword is an encumbrance, and they are at a disadvantage compared to the man armed with a short companion sword.

From olden times it has been said: "Great and small go together.". So do not unconditionally dislike extra-long swords. What I dislike is the inclination towards the long sword. If we consider large-scale strategy, we can think of large forces in terms of long swords, and small forces as short swords. Cannot few me give battle against many? There are many instances of few men overcoming many.

Your strategy is of no account if when called on to fight in a confined space your heart is inclined to the long sword, or if you are in a house armed only with your companion sword. Besides, some men have not the strength of others.

In my doctrine, I dislike preconceived, narrow spirit. You must study this well.

The Strong Long Sword Spirit in Other Schools

You should not speak of strong and weak long swords. If you just wield the long sword in a strong spirit your cutting will be coarse, and if you use the sword coarsely you will have difficulty in winning.

If you are concerned with the strength of your sword, you will try to cut unreasonably strongly, and will not be able to cut at all. It is also bad to try to cut strongly when testing the sword. Whenever you cross swords with an enemy you must not think of cutting him either strongly or weakly; just think of cutting and killing him. Be intent solely upon killing the enemy. Do not try to cut strongly and, of course, do not think of cutting weakly. You should only be concerned with killing the enemy.

If you rely on strength, when you hit the enemy's sword you will inevitably hit too hard. If you do this, your own sword will be carried along as a result. Thus the saying, "The strongest hand wins", has no meaning.

In large-scale strategy, if you have a strong army and are relying on strength to win, but the enemy also has a strong army, the battle will be fierce. This is the same for both sides.

Without the correct principle the fight cannot be won.

The spirit of my school is to win through the wisdom of strategy, paying no attention to trifles. Study this well.

Use of the Shorter Long Sword in Other Schools

Using a shorter long sword is not the true Way to win.

In ancient times, tachi and katana meant long and short swords. Men of superior strength in the world can wield even a long sword lightly, so there is no case for their liking the short sword. They also make use of the length of spears and halberds. Some men use a shorter long sword with the intention of jumping in and stabbing the enemy at the unguarded moment when he flourishes his sword. This inclination is bad.

To aim for the enemy's unguarded moment is completely defensive, and undesirable at close quarters with the enemy. Furthermore, you cannot use the method of jumping inside his defense with a short sword if there are many enemies. Some men think that if they go against many enemies with a shorter long sword they can unrestrictedly frisk around cutting in sweeps, but they have to parry cuts continuously, and eventually become entangled with the enemy. This is inconsistent with the true Way of strategy.

The sure Way to win thus is to chase the enemy around in confusing manner, causing him to jump aside, with your body held strongly and straight. The same principle applies to large-scale strategy. The essence of strategy is to fall upon the enemy in large numbers and bring about his speedy downfall. By their study of strategy, people of the world get used to countering, evading and retreating as the normal thing. They become set in this habit, so can easily be paraded around by the enemy. The Way of strategy is straight and true. You must chase the enemy around and make him obey your spirit.

Other Schools with many Methods of using the Long Sword

Placing a great deal of importance on the attitudes of the long sword is a mistaken way of thinking. What is known in the world as "attitude" applies when there is no enemy. The reason is that this has been a precedent since ancient times, and there should be no such thing as "This is the modern way to do it" in dueling. You must force the enemy into inconvenient situations.

Attitudes are for situations in which you are not to be moved. That is, for garrisoning castles, battle array, and so on, showing the spirit of not being moved even by a strong assault. In the Way of dueling, however, you must always be intent upon taking the lead and attacking. Attitude is the spirit of awaiting an attack. You must appreciate this.

In duels of strategy you must move the opponent's attitude. Attack where his spirit is lax, throw him into confusion, irritate and terrify him. Take advantage of the enemy's rhythm when he is unsettled and you can win.

I dislike the defensive spirit know as "attitude". Therefore, in my Way, there is something called "Attitude-No Attitude".

In large-scale strategy we deploy our troops for battle bearing in mind our strength, observing the enemy's numbers, and noting the details of the battle field. This is at the start of the battle.

The spirit of attacking first is completely different from the spirit of being attacked. Bearing an attack well, with a strong attitude, and parrying the enemy's attack well, is like making a wall of spears and halberds. When you attack the enemy, your spirit must go to the extent of pulling the stakes out of a wall and using them as spears and halberds. You must examine this well.

Fixing the Eyes in Other Schools

Some schools maintain that the eyes should be fixed on the enemy's long sword. Some schools fix the eyes on the hands. Some fix the eyes on the face, and some fix the eyes on the feet, and so on. If you fix the eyes on these places your spirit can become confused and your strategy thwarted.

I will explain this in detail. Footballers do not fix their eyes on the ball, but by good play on the field they can perform well. When you become accustomed to something, you are not limited to the use of your eyes. People such as master musicians have the music score in front of their nose, or flourish swords in several ways when they have mastered the Way, but this does not mean that they fix their eyes on these things specifically, or that they make pointless movements of the sword. It means that they can see naturally.

In the Way of strategy, when you have fought many times you will easily be able to appraise the speed and position of the enemy's sword, and having mastery of the Way you will see the weight of his spirit. In strategy, fixing the eyes means gazing at the man's heart.

In large-scale strategy the area to watch is the enemy's strength. "Perception" and "sight" are the two methods of seeing. Perception consists of concentrating strongly on the enemy's spirit, observing the condition of the battlefield, fixing the gaze strongly, seeing the progress of the fight and the changes of advantages. This is the sure way to win.

In single combat you must not fix the eyes on the details. As I said before, if you fix your eyes on details and neglect important things, your spirit will become bewildered, and victory will escape you. Research this principle well and train diligently.

Use of the Feet in Other Schools

There are various methods of using the feet: floating foot, jumping foot, springing foot, treading foot, crow's foot, and such nimble walking methods. From the point of view of my strategy, these are all unsatisfactory.

I dislike floating foot because the feet always tend to float during the fight. The Way must be trod firmly.

Neither do I like jumping foot, because it encourages the habit of jumping, and a jumpy spirit. However much you jump, there is no real justification for it; so jumping is bad.

Springing foot causes a springing spirit which is indecisive.

Treading foot is a "waiting" method, and I especially dislike it.

Apart from these, there are various fast walking methods, such as crow's foot, and so on.

Sometimes, however, you may encounter the enemy on marshland, swampy ground, river valleys, stony ground, or narrow roads, in which situations you cannot jump or move the feet quickly.

In my strategy, the footwork does not change. I always walk as I usually do in the street. You must never lose control of your feet. According to the enemy's rhythm, move fast or slowly, adjusting you body not too much and not too little.

Carrying the feet is important also in large-scale strategy. This is because, if you attack quickly and thoughtlessly without knowing the enemy's spirit, your rhythm will become deranged and you will not be able to win. Or, if you advance too slowly, you will not be able to take advantage of the enemy's disorder, the opportunity to win will escape, and you will not be able to finish the fight quickly. You must win by seizing upon the enemy's disorder and derangement, and by not according him even a little hope of recovery. Practice this well.

Speed in Other Schools

Speed is not part of the true Way of strategy. Speed implies that things seem fast or slow, according to whether or not they are in rhythm. Whatever the Way, the master of strategy does not appear fast.

Some people can walk as fast as a hundred or a hundred and twenty miles in a day, but this does not mean that they run continuously from morning till night. Unpracticed runners may seem to have been running all day, but their performance is poor.

In the Way of dance, accomplished performers can sing while dancing, but when beginners try this they slow down and their spirit becomes busy. The "old pine tree" melody beaten on a leather drum is tranquil, but when beginners try this they slow down and their spirit becomes busy. Very skilful people can manage a fast rhythm, but it is bad to beat hurriedly. If you try to beat too quickly you will get out of time. Of course, slowness is bad. Really skilful people never get out of time, and are always deliberate, and never appear busy. From this example, the principle can be seen.

What is known as speed is especially bad in the Way of strategy. The reason for this is that depending on the place, marsh or swamp and so on, it may not be possible to move the body and legs together quickly. Still less will you be able to cut quickly if you have a long sword in this situation. If you try to cut quickly, as if using a fan or short sword, you will not actually cut even a little. You must appreciate this.

In large-scale strategy also, a fast busy spirit is undesirable. The spirit must be that of holding down a pillow, then you will not be even a little late.

When your opponent is hurrying recklessly, you must act contrarily and keep calm. You must not be influenced by the opponent. Train diligently to attain this spirit.

"Interior" and "Surface" in Other Schools

There is no "interior" nor "surface" in strategy.

The artistic accomplishments usually claim inner meaning and secret tradition, and "interior" and "gate", but in combat there is no such thing as fighting on the surface, or cutting with the interior. When I teach my Way, I first teach by training in techniques which are easy for the pupil to understand, a doctrine which is easy to understand. I gradually endeavor to explain the deep principle, points which it is hardly possible to comprehend, according to the pupil's progress. In any event, because the way to understanding is through experience, I do not speak of "interior" and "gate".

In this world, if you go into the mountains, and decide to go deeper and yet deeper, instead you will emerge at the gate. Whatever the Way, it has an interior, and it is sometimes a good thing to point out the gate. In strategy, we cannot say what is concealed and what is revealed.

Accordingly I dislike passing on my Way through written pledges and regulations. Perceiving the ability of my pupils, I teach the direct Way, remove the bad influence of other schools, and gradually introduce them to the true Way of the warrior.

The method of teaching my strategy is with a trustworthy spirit. You must train diligently.

I have tried to record an outline of the strategy of other schools in the above nine sections. I could now continue by giving a specific account of these schools one by one, from the "gate" to the "interior", but I have intentionally not named the schools or their main points. The reason for this is that different branches of schools give different interpretations of the doctrines. In as much as men's opinions differ, so there must be differing ideas on the same matter. Thus no one man's conception is valid for any school.

I have shown the general tendencies of other schools on nine points. If we look at them from an honest viewpoint, we see that people always tend to like long swords or short swords, and become concerned with strength in both large and small matters. You can see why I do not deal with the "gates" of other schools.

In my Ichi school of the long sword there is neither gate nor interior. There is no inner meaning in sword attitudes. You must simply keep your spirit true to realize the virtue of strategy.

The Book of the Void

The Ni To Ichi Way of strategy is recorded in this the Book of the Void.

What is called the spirit of the void is where there is nothing. It is not included in man's knowledge. Of course the void is nothingness. By knowing things that exist, you can know that which does not exist. That is the void.

People in this world look at things mistakenly, and think that what they do not understand must be the void. This is not the true void. It is bewilderment. In the Way of strategy, also, those who study as warriors think that whatever they cannot understand in their craft is the void. This is not the true void.

To attain the Way of strategy as a warrior you must study fully other martial arts and not deviate even a little from the Way of the warrior. With your spirit settled, accumulate practice day by day, and hour by hour. Polish the twofold spirit heart and mind, and sharpen the twofold gaze perception and sight. When your spirit is not in the least clouded, when the clouds of bewilderment clear away, there is the true void.

Until you realize the true Way, whether in Buddhism or in common sense, you may think that things are correct and in order. However, if we look at things objectively, from the viewpoint of laws of the world, we see various doctrines departing from the true Way. Know well this spirit, and with forthrightness as the foundation and the true spirit as the Way. Enact strategy broadly, correctly and openly.

Then you will come to think of things in a wide sense and, taking the void as the Way, you will see the Way as void. In the void is virtue, and no evil. Wisdom has existence, principle has existence, the Way has existence, spirit is nothingness.

Twelfth day of the fifth month, second year of Shoho (1645)

大石主税藤原良金

無祿　群屋住

良雄の嫡男にして母は但州
豊岡の藩石束源五
兵衛の女なり良金
十四すふて國難ふあひ
父の命に立さろって優
嬉書の刈ふ入り翌年
九月小野寺と共ふ武刕川崎さて
元服し一討入の時ハ
裏手の首長として
まいる力働をふう
死さる時十六才辞世
梅よのたいひと動をことに
ろ仙泡をそくて四十八人

刃上樹劔信士

Hagakure

The Way of the Samurai

by

Yamamoto Tsunetomo

Preface

Hagakure is the essential book of the Samurai. Written by Yamamoto Tsunetomo, who was a Samurai in the early 1700s, it is a book that combines the teachings of both Zen and Confucianism. These philosophies are centered on loyalty, devotion, purity and selflessness, and Yamamoto places a strong emphasis on the notion of living in the present moment with a strong and clear mind. The Samurai were knights who defended and fought for their lords at a time when useful farming land was scarce and in need of protection. They believed in duty, and gave themselves completely to their masters. The Samurai believed that only after transcending all fear could they obtain peace of mind and yield the power to serve their masters faithfully and loyally even in the face of death. The word Hagakure literally translates as hidden beneath the leaves and also fallen leaves. Perhaps it was named this because at the time that it was written, the way of the samurai was becoming obsolete.

The Hagakure has been rewritten in modern terms by one of Japan's famous writers, Yukio Mishima. His own views were very similar to those of Yamamoto, particularly the philosophy of cultivating the self. His characters all had self sufficiency in common, and did not rely upon anyone else for completion.

Although the Hagakure was written centuries ago for a breed of warriors that no longer exist, the philosophies and wisdom within are still practical, even in our modern times.

SELECTIONS

From the 1ˢᵗ Chapter

Although it stands to reason that a samurai should be mindful of the Way of the Samurai, it would seem that we are all negligent. Consequently, if someone were to ask, "What is the true meaning of the Way of the Samurai?" the person who would be able to answer promptly is rare. This is because it has not been established in one's mind beforehand. From this, one's unmindfulness of the Way can be known.

Negligence is an extreme thing.

The Way of the Samurai is found in death. When it comes to either/or, there is only the quick choice of death. It is not particularly difficult. Be determined and advance. To say that dying without reaching one's aim is to die a dog's death is the frivolous way of sophisticates. When pressed with the choice of life or death, it is not necessary to gain one's aim.

We all want to live. And in large part we make our logic according to what we like. But not having attained our aim and continuing to live is cowardice. This is a thin dangerous line. To die without gaming one's aim is a dog's death and fanaticism. But there is no shame in this. This is the substance of the Way of the Samurai. If by setting one's heart right every morning and evening, one is able to live as though his body were already dead, he pains freedom in the Way. His whole life will be without blame, and he will succeed in his calling.

A man is a good retainer to the extent that he earnestly places importance in his master. This is the highest sort of retainer. If one is born into a prominent family that goes back for generations, it is sufficient to deeply consider the matter of obligation to one's ancestors, to lay down one's body and mind, and to earnestly esteem one's master. It is further good fortune if, more than this, one has wisdom and talent and can use them appropriately. But even a person who is good for nothing and exceedingly clumsy will be a reliable retainer if only he has the determination to think earnestly of his master. Having only wisdom and talent is the lowest tier of usefulness.

According to their nature, there are both people who have quick intelligence, and those who must withdraw and take time to think things over. Looking into this thoroughly, if one thinks selflessly and adheres to the four vows of the Nabeshima samurai, surprising wisdom will occur regardless of the high or low points of one's nature.'

People think that they can clear up profound matters if they consider them deeply, but they exercise perverse thoughts and come to no good because they do their reflecting with only self-interest at the center.

It is difficult for a fool's habits to change to selflessness. In confronting a matter, however, if at first you leave it alone, fix the four vows in your heart, exclude self-interest, and make an effort, you will not go far from your mark.

Because we do most things relying only on our own sagacity we become self-interested, turn our backs on reason, and things do not turn out well. As seen by other people this is sordid, weak, narrow and inefficient. When one is not capable of true intelligence, it is good to consult with someone of good sense. An advisor will fulfill the Way when he makes a decision by selfless and frank intelligence because he is not personally involved. This way of doing things will certainly be seen by others as being strongly rooted. It is, for example, like a large tree with many roots. One man's intelligence is like a tree that has been simply stuck in the ground.

We learn about the sayings and deeds of the men of old in order to entrust ourselves to their wisdom and prevent selfishness. When we throw off our own bias, follow the sayings of the ancients, and confer with other people, matters should go well and without mishap. Lord Katsushige borrowed from the wisdom of Lord Naoshige. This is mentioned in the Ohanashikikigaki. We should be grateful for his concern.

Moreover, there was a certain man who engaged a number of his younger brothers as retainers, and whenever he visited Edo or the Kamigata area, he would have them accompany him. As he consulted with them everyday on both private and public matters, it is said that he was without mishap.

Sagara Kyuma was completely at one with his master and served him as though his own body were already dead. He was one man in a thousand.

Once there was an important meeting at Master Sakyo's Mizugae Villa, and it was commanded that Kyuma was to commit seppuku. At that time in Osaki there was a teahouse on the third floor of the suburban residence of Master Taku Nut. Kyuma rented this, and gathering together all the good-for-nothings in Saga he put on a puppet show, operating one of the puppets himself, carousing and drinking all day and night. Thus, overlooking Master Sakyo's villa, he carried on and caused a great disturbance. In instigating this disaster he gallantly thought only of his master and was resolved to committing suicide.

Being a retainer is nothing other than hemp a supporter of one's lord, entrusting matters of good and evil to him, and renouncing self-interest. If there are but two or three men of this type, the fief will be secure.

If one looks at the world when affairs are going smoothly, there arc many who go about putting in their appearance, being useful by their wisdom, discrimination and artfulness. However, if the lord should retire or go into seclusion, there are many who will quickly turn their backs on him and ingratiate themselves to the man of the day. Such a thing is unpleasant even to think about. Men of high position, low position, deep wisdom and artfulness all feel that they are the ones who are working righteously, but when it comes to the point of throwing away one's life for his lord, all get weak in the knees. This is rather disgraceful. The fact that a useless person often becomes a matchless warrior at such times is because he has already given up his life and has become one with his lord. At the time of Mitsushige's death there was an example of this. His one resolved attendant was I alone. The others followed in my wake. Always the pretentious, self-asserting notables turn their backs on the man just as his eyes are closing in death.

Loyalty is said to be important in the pledge between lord and retainer. Though it may seem unobtainable, it is right before your eyes. If you once set yourself to it, you will become a superb retainer at that very moment.

To give a person one's opinion and correct his faults is an important thing. It is compassionate and comes first in matters of service. But the way of doing this is extremely difficult. To discover the good and bad points of a person is an easy thing, and to give an opinion concerning them is easy, too. For the most part, people think that they are being kind by saying the things that others find distasteful or difficult to say. But if it is not received well, they think that there is nothing more to be done. This is completely worthless. It is the same as brining shame to a person by slandering him. It is nothing more than getting it off one's chest.

To give a person an opinion one must first judge well whether that person is of the disposition to receive it or not. One must become close with him and make sure that he continually trusts one's word. Approaching subjects that are dear to him, seek the best way to speak and to be well understood. Judge the occasion, and determine whether it is better by letter or at the time of leave-taking. Praise his good points and use every device to encourage him, perhaps by talking about one's own faults without touching on his, but so that they will occur to him. Have him receive this in the way that a man would drink water when his throat is dry, and it will be an opinion that will correct faults.

This is extremely difficult. If a person s fault is a habit of some years prior, by and large it won't be remedied. I have had this experience myself. To be intimate with alt one's comrades, correcting each other's faults, and being of one mind to be of use to the master is the great compassion of a retainer. By bringing shame to a person, bow could one expect to make him a better man?

It is bad taste to yawn in front of people. When one unexpectedly has to yawn, if he rubs his forehead in an upward direction, the sensation will stop. If that does not work, he can lick his lips while keeping his mouth closed, or simply hide it with his hand or his sleeve in such a way that no one will know what he is doing. It is the same with sneezing. One will appear foolish. There are other things besides these about which a person should use care and training.

When a certain person was saying that present matters of economy should be detailed, someone replied that this is not good at all.

It is a fact that ash will not live where the water is too clear. But if there is duckweed or something, the fish will hide under its shadow and thrive. Thus, the lower classes will live in tranquillity if certain matters are a bit overlooked or left unheard. This fact should be understood with regard to people's conduct.

Once when Lord Mitsushige was a little boy and was supposed to recite from a copybook for the priest Kaion, he called the other children and acolytes and said, "Please come here and listen. It's difficult to read if there are hardly any people listening." The priest was impressed and said to the acolytes, "That's the spirit in which to do everything."

Every morning one should first do reverence to his master and parents and then to his patron deities and guardian Buddhas. If he will only make his master first in importance, his parents will rejoice and the gods and Buddhas will give their assent. For a warrior there is nothing other than thinking of his master. If one creates this resolution within himself, he will always be mindful of the master's person and will not depart from him even for a moment.

Moreover, a woman should consider her husband first, just as he considers his master first.

According to a certain person, a number of years ago Matsuguma Kyoan told this story:

In the practice of medicine there is a differentiation of treatment according to the Yin and Yang of men and women. There is also a difference in pulse. In the last fifty years, however, men's pulse has become the same as women's. Noticing this, in the treatment of eye disease I applied women's treatment to men and found it suitable. When I observed the application of men's treatment to men, there was no result. Thus I knew that men's spirit had weakened and that they had become the same as women, and the end of the world had come. Since I witnessed this with certainty, I kept it a secret.

When looking at the men of today with this in mind, those who could be thought to have a woman's pulse are many indeed, and those who seem like real men few. Because of this, if one were to make a little effort, he would be able to take the upper hand quite easily. That there are few men who arc able to cut well in beheadings is further proof that men's courage has waned. And when one comes to speak of kaishaku, it has become an age of men who are prudent and clever at making excuses. Forty or fifty years ago, when such things as matanuki were considered manly, a man wouldn't show an unscarred thigh to his fellows, so he would pierce it himself.

All of man's work is a bloody business. That fact, today, is considered foolish, affairs are finished cleverly with words alone, and jobs that require effort are avoided. I would like young men to have some understanding of this.

The priest Tannen used to say, "People come to no understanding because priests teach only the doctrine of 'No Mind.' What is called 'No Mind' is a mind that is pure and lacks complication.' This is interesting.

Lord Sanenori said, "In the midst of a single breath, where perversity cannot be held, is the Way. " If so, then the Way is one. But there is no one who can understand this clarity at first. Purity is something that cannot be attained except by piling effort upon effort.

There is nothing that we should be quite so grateful for as the last line of the poem that goes, "When your own heart asks." It can probably be thought of in the same way as the Nembutsu, and previously it was on the lips of many people.

Recently, people who are called "clever" adorn themselves with superficial wisdom and only deceive others. For this reason they are inferior to dull-wilted folk. A dull-wilted person is direct. If one looks deeply into his heart with the above phrase, there will be no hidden places. It is a good examiner. One should be of the mind that, meeting this examiner, he will not be embarrassed.

The word gen means "illusion" or "apparition." In India, a man who uses conjury is called a genjutsushi ["a master of illusion technique"]. Everything in this world is but a marionette show. Thus we use the word gen.

To hate injustice and stand on righteousness is a difficult thing. Furthermore, to think that being righteous is the best one can do and to do one's utmost to be righteous will, on the contrary, brig many mistakes. The Way is in a higher place then righteousness. This is very difficult to discover, but it is the highest wisdom. When seen from this standpoint, things like righteousness are rather shallow. If one does not understand this on his own, it cannot be known. There is a method of getting to this Way, however, even if one cannot discover it by himself. This is found in consultation with others. Even a person who has not attained this Way sees others front the side. It is like the saying from the game of go: "He who sees from the side has eight eyes." The saying, "Thought by thought we see our own mistakes," also means that the highest Way is in discussion with others. Listening to the old stories and reading books are for the purpose of sloughing off one's own discrimination and attaching oneself to that of the ancients.

A certain swordsman in his declining years said the following:

In one's life. there are levels in the pursuit of study. In the lowest level, a person studies but nothing comes of it, and he feels that both he and others are unskillful. At this point he is worthless. In the middle level he is still useless but is aware of his own insufficiencies and can also see the insufficiencies of others. In a higher level he has pride concerning his own ability, rejoices in praise from others, and laments the lack of ability in his fellows. This man has worth. In the highest level a man has the look of knowing nothing.

These are the levels in general;. But there is one transcending level, and this is the most excellent of all. This person is aware of the endlessness of entering deeply into a certain Way arid never thinks of himself as having finished. He truly knows his own insufficiencies and never in his whole life thinks that he has succeeded. He has no thoughts of pride but with self-abasement knows the Way to the end. It is said that Master Yagyu once remarked, "I do not know the way to defeat others, but the way to defeat myself. "

Throughout your life advance daily, becoming more skillful than yesterday, more skillful than today. This is never-ending.

Among the maxims on Lord Naoshige's wall there was this one: "Matters of great concern should be treated lightly." Master lttei commented, "Matters of small concern should be treated seriously." Among one's affairs there should not be more than two or three matters of what one could call great concern. If these are deliberated upon during ordinary times, they can be understood. Thinking about things previously and then handling them lightly when the time comes is what this is all about. To face an event anew solve it lightly is difficult if you are not resolved beforehand, and there will always be uncertainty in hitting your mark. However, if the foundation is laid previously, you can think of the saying, "Matters of great concern should be treated lightly," as your own basis for action.

A certain person spent several years of service in Osaka and then returned home. When he made his appearance at the local bureau, everyone was put out and he was made a laughingstock because he spoke in the Kamigata dialect. Seen in this light, when one spends a long time in ado or the Kamigata area, he had better use his native dialect even more than usual.

When in a more sophisticated area it is natural that one s disposition be affected by different styles. But it is vulgar and foolish to look down upon the ways of one's own district as being boorish, or to be even a bit open to the persuasion of the other place's ways and to think about giving up one's own. That one's own district is unsophisticated and unpolished is a great treasure. Imitating another style is simply a sham.

A certain man said to the priest Shungaku, "The Lotus Sutra Sect's character is not good because it's so fearsome." Shungaku replied, "It is by reason of its fearsome character that it is the Lotus Sutra Sect. If its character were not so, it would be a different sect altogether." This is reasonable.

At the time when there was a council concerning the promotion of a certain man, the council members were at the point of deciding that promotion was useless because of the fact that the man had previously been involved in a drunken brawl. But someone said, "If we were to cast aside every man who had made a mistake once, useful men could prob- ably not be come by. A man who makes a mistake once will be considerably more prudent and useful because of his repentance. I feet that he should be promoted."

Someone else then asked, "Will you ;guarantee him?" The man replied, "Of course I will."

The others asked, "By what will you guarantee him?"

And he replied, "I can guarentee him by the fact that he is a man who has erred once. A man who bas never once erred is dangerous." This said, the man was promoted.

At the time of a deliberation concerning criminals, Nakane Kazuma proposed making the punishment one degree lighter than what would be appropriate. This is a treasury of wisdom that only he was the possessor of. At that time, though there were several men in attendance, if it had not been for Kazuma alone, no one would have opened his mouth. For this reason he is called Master Commencement and Master Twenty-five Days.

A certain person was brought to shame because he did not take revenge. The way of revenge lies in simply forcing one's way into a place and being cut down. There is no shame in this. By thinking that you must complete the job you will run out of time. By considering things like how many men the enemy has, time piles up; in the end you will give up. No matter if the enemy has thousands of men, there is fulfillment in simply standing them off and being determined to cut them all down, starting from one end. You will finish the greater part of it.

Concerning the night assault of Lord Asano's ronin, the fact that they did not commit seppuku at the Sengakuji was an error, for there was a long delay between the time their lord was struck down and the time when they struck down the enemy. If Lord Kira had died of illness within that period, it would have been extremely regrettable. Because the men of the Kamigata area have a very clever sort of wisdom, they do well at praiseworthy acts but cannot do things indiscriminately, as was done in the Nagasaki fight.

Although all things are not to be judged in this manner, I mention it in the investigation of the Way of the Samurai. When the time comes, there is no moment for reasoning. And if you have not done your inquiring beforehand, there is most often shame. Reading books and listening to people's talk are for the purpose of prior resolution.

Above all, the Way of the Samurai should be in being aware that you do not know what is going to happen next, and in querying every item day and night. Victory and defeat are matters of the temporary force of circumstances. The way of avoiding shame is different. It is simply in death.

Even if it seems certain that you will lose, retaliate. Neither wisdom nor technique has a place in this. A real man does not think of victory or defeat. He plunges recklessly towards an irrational death. By doing this, you will awaken from your dreams.

There are two things that will blemish a retainer, and these are riches and honor. If one but remains in strained circumstances, he will not be marred.

Once there was a certain man who was very clever, but it was his character to always see the negative points of his jobs. In such a way, one will be useless. If one does not get it into his head from the very beginning that the world is full of unseemly situations, for the most part his demeanor will be poor and he will not be believed by others. And if one is not believed by others, no matter how good a person he may be, he will not have the essence of a good person. This can also be considered as a blemish.

There was a man who said, "Such and such a person has a violent disposition, but this is what I said right to his face... This was an unbecoming thing to say, and it was said simply because he wanted to be known as a rough fellow. It was rather low, and it can be seen that he was still rather immature. It is because a samurai has correct manners that he is admired. Speaking of other people in this way is no different from an exchange between low class spearmen. It is vulgar.

It is not good to settle into a set of opinions. It is a mistake to put forth effort and obtain some understanding and then stop at that. At first putting forth great effort to be sure that you have grasped the bastes, then practicing so that they may come to fruition is something that will never stop for your whole lifetime. Do not rely on following the degree of understanding that you have discovered, but simply think, "This is not enough."

One should search throughout his whole life how best to follow the Way. And he should study, setting his mind to work without putting things off. Within this is the Way.

These are from the recorded sayings of Yamamoto Jin'-emon:

If you can understand one affair, you will understand eight.

An affected laugh shows lack of self-respect in a man and lewdness in a woman.

Whether speaking formally or informally, one should look his listener in the eye. A polite greeting is done at the beginning and finished. Speaking with downcast eyes is carelessness.

It is carelessness to go about with one's hands inside the slits in the sides of his hakama.

After reading books and the like, it is best to burn them or throw them away. It is said that reading books is the work of the Imperial Court, but the work of the House of Nakano is found in military valor, grasping the staff of oak.

A samurai with no group and no horse is not a samurai at all.

A kusemono is a man to rely upon.

It is said that one should rise at four in the morning, bathe and arrange his hair daily, eat when the sun comes up, and retire when it becomes dark.

A samurai will use a toothpick even though he has not eaten. Inside the skin of a dog, outside the hide of a tiger.

How should a person respond when he is asked, "As a human being, what is essential in terms of purpose and discipline?" First, let us say, "It is to become of the mind that is right now pure and lacking complications." People in general all seem to be dejected. When one has a pure and uncomplicated mind, his expression will be lively. When one is attending to matters, there is one thing that comes forth from his heart. That is, in terms of one's lord, loyalty; in terms of one's parents, filial piety; in martial affairs, bravery ; and apart from that, something that can be used by all the world.

This is very difficult to discover. Once discovered, it is again difficult to keep in constant effect. There is nothing outside the thought of the immediate moment.

Every morning, the samurai of fifty or sixty years ago would bathe, shave their foreheads, put lotion in their hair, cut their fingernails and toenails rubbing them with pumice and then with wood sorrel, and without fail pay attention to their personal appearance. It goes without saying that their armor in general was kept free from rust, that it was dusted, shined, and arranged.

Although it seems that taking special care of one's appearance is similar to showiness, it is nothing akin to elegance. Even if you are aware that you may be struck down today and are firmly resolved to an inevitable death, if you are slain with an unseemly appearance, you will show your lack of previous resolve, will be despised by your enemy, and will appear unclean. For this reason it is said that both old and young should take care of their appearance.

Although you say that this is troublesome and time-consuming, a samurai's work is in such things. It is neither busy-work nor time-consuming. In constantly hardening one's resolution to die in battle, deliberately becoming as one already dead, and working at one's job and dealing with military affairs, there should be no shame. But when the time comes, a person will be shamed if he is not conscious of these things even in his dreams, and rather passes his days in self- interest and self-indulgence. And if he thinks that this is not shameful, and feels that nothing else matters as long as he is comfortable, then his dissipate and discourteous actions will be repeatedly regrettable.

The person without previous resolution to inevitable death makes certain that his death will be in bad form. But if one is resolved to death beforehand, in what way can he be despicable? One should be especially diligent in this concern.

Furthermore, during the last thirty years customs have changed; now when young samurai jeer together, if there is not just talk about money matters, loss and gain, secrets, clothing styles or matters of sex, there is no reason to gather together at all. Customs are going to pieces. One can say that formerly when a man reached the age of twenty or thirty, he did not carry despicable things in his heart, and thus neither did such words appear. If an elder unwittingly said something of that sort, he thought of it as a sort of injury. This new custom probably appears because people attach importance to being beautiful before society and to household finances. What things a person should be able to accomplish if he had no haughtiness concerning his place in society!

It is a wretched thing that the young men of today are so contriving and so proud of their material possessions. Men with contriving hearts are lacking in duty. Lacking in duty, they will have no self-respect. According to Master lttei, even a poor penman will become substantial in the art of calligraphy if he studies by imitating a good model and puts forth effort. A retainer should be able to become substantial too, if he takes a good retainer as his model.

Today, however, there are no models of good retainers. In light of this, it would be good to make a model and to learn from that. To do this, one should look at many people and choose from each person his best point only. For example, one person for politeness, one for bravery, one for the proper way of speaking, one for correct conduct and one for steadiness of mind. Thus will the model be made.

An apprentice will not be up to his teacher's good points in the world of the arts either but will receive and imitate only his bad ones. This is worthless. There are people who are good at manners but have no uprightness. In imitating someone like this, one is likely to ignore the politeness and imitate only the lack of uprightness. If one perceives a person's good points, he will have a model teacher for anything.

When delivering something like an important letter or other written materials, grasp it firmly in your hand as you go and do not release it once, but hand it over directly to the recipient.

A retainer is a man who remains consistently undistracted twenty-four hours a day, whether he is in the presence of his master or in public. If one is careless during his rest period, the public will see him as being only careless.

Regardless of class, a person who does something beyond his social standing will at some point commit mean or cowardly acts. In the lower classes there are even people who will run away. One should be careful with menials and the like.

From the 2ⁿᵈ Chapter

It is said that much sake, self-pride and luxury are to be avoided by a samurai, There is no cause for anxiety when you are unhappy, but when you become a little elated, these three things become dangerous. Look at the human condition. It is unseemly for a person to become prideful and extravagant when things are going well. Therefore, it is better to have some unhappiness while one is still young, for if a person does not experience some bitterness, his disposition will not settle down. A person who becomes fatigued when unhappy is useless. Meeting with people should be a matter of quickly grasping their temperament and reacting appropriately to this person and that. Especially with an extremely argumentative person, after yielding considerably one should argue him down with superior logic, but without sounding harsh, and in a fashion that will allow no resentment to be left afterwards. This is a function of both the heart and words. This was an opinion given by a priest concerning personal encounters.

Dreams are truthful manifestations. When I occasionally have dreams of dying in battle or committing seppuku, if I brace myself with courage, my frame of mind within the dream gradually changes.

This concerns the dream I had on the night of the twenty- seventh day of the fifth month.

If one were to say in a word what the condition of being a samurai is, its basis lies first in seriously devoting one's body and soul to his master. And if one is asked what to do beyond this, it would be to fit oneself inwardly with intelligence, humanity and courage.' The combining of these three virtues may seem unobtainable to the ordinary person, but it is easy. Intelligence is nothing more than discussing things with others. Limitless wisdom comes from this. Humanity is something done for the sake of others, simply comparing oneself with them and putting them in the fore. Courage is gritting one' s teeth ; it is simply doing that and pushing ahead, paying no attention to the circumstances. Anything that seems above these three is not necessary to be known.

As for outward aspects, there are personal appearance, one's way of speaking and calligraphy. And as all of these are daily matters, they improve by constant practice. Basically, one should perceive their nature to be one of quiet strength. If one has accomplished all these things, then he should have a knowledge of our area's history and customs. After that he may study the various arts as recreation. If you think it over, being a retainer is simple. And these days, if you observe people who are even a bit useful, you will see that they have accomplished these three outward aspects.

A certain priest said that if one thoughtlessly crosses a river of unknown depths and shallows, he will die in its currents without ever reaching the other side or finishing his business. This is the same as when one is indiscriminately eager in being a retainer without understanding the customs of the times or the likes and dislikes of the master and, as a result, is of no use and brings ruin upon himself. To try to enter the good graces of the master is unbecoming. One should consider first stepping back and getting some understanding of the depths and shallows and then work without doing anything the master dislikes.

If you attach a number of bags of cloves to your body, you will not be affected by inclemency or colds. Some years ago Nakano Kazuma returned to this province as a messenger by horse in the dead of winter, and though he was an old man, he was not the least bit in pain. It is said that that was because of his having used cloves. Furthermore, drinking a decoction of the feces from a dappled horse is the way to stop bleeding from an injury received by falling off a horse.

A faultless person is one who withdraws from affairs. This must be done with strength.

There is surely nothing other than the single purpose of the present moment. A man's whole life is a succession of moment after moment. If one fully understands the present moment, there will be nothing else to do, and nothing else to pursue. Live being true to the single purpose of the moment.

Everyone lets the present moment slip by, then looks for it as though he thought it were somewhere else. No one seems to have noticed this fact. But grasping this firmly, one must pile experience upon experience. And once one has come to this understanding he will be a different person from that point on, though he may not always bear it in mind.

When one understands this settling into single-mindedness well, his affairs will thin out. Loyalty is also contained within this single-mindedness.

It is said that what is called "the spirit of an ape' ' is seine- thing to which one cannot return. That this spirit gradually dissipates is due to the world's coming to an end. In the same way, a single year does not have just spring or summer. A single day, too, is the same.

For this reason, although one would like to change today's world back to the spirit of one hundred years or more ago, it cannot be done. Thus it is important to make the best out of every generation. This is the mistake of people who are attached to past generations. They have no understanding of this point.

On the other hand, people who only know the disposition of the present day and dislike the ways of the past are too lax.

Be true to the thought of the moment and avoid distraction. Other than continuing to exert yourself, enter into nothing else, but go to the extent of living single thought by single thought.

The brave men of old times were for the most part rowdies. As they were of the disposition to be out running amuck, their vitality was strong and they were brave. When I had doubts about this and asked, Tsunetomo said, "It is understandable that since their vitality was strong they were generally rough and went about running amuck. These days rowdiness is nonexistent because man's vitality has weakened. Vitality has fallen behind, but man's character has improved. Valor is yet a different thing. Although men have become gentle these days because of the lack of vitality, this does not mean that they are inferior in being crazy to die. That has nothing to do with vitality."

Concerning the military tactics of Lord Naoshige, Ushida Shoemon said that it was characteristic of his retainers to face a situation with no previous knowledge of what was to happen, and for him to freely bring everything to a finish by a single word. When he was at the point of passing from this world, he said nothing, even when his chief retainers came to see him.

Once Lord Ieyasu gamed nothing in a battle, but in a later judgment it was said, "Ieyasu is a general of great courage. Of his retainers who died in battle, not one of them died with his back turned. They all died facing the enemy lines." Since a warrior' s daily frame of mind is manifested even after death, it is something that can bring shame to him.

As Yasuda Ukyo said about offering up the last wine cup, only the end of things is important. One's whole life should be like this. When guests are leaving, the mood of being reluctant to say farewell is essential. If this mood is lacking, one will appear bored and the day and evening's conversation will disappear. In all dealings with people it is essential to have a fresh approach. One should constantly give the impression that he is doing something exceptional. It is said that this is possible with but a little understanding.

Our bodies are given life from the midst of nothingness. Existing where there is nothing is the meaning of the phrase, "Form is emptiness." That all things are provided for by nothingness is the meaning of the phrase, "Emptiness is form."' One should not think that these are two separate things.

Uesugi Kenshin said, "I never knew about winning from beginning to end, but only about not being behind in a situation." This is interesting. A retainer will be dumbfounded if he is behind in a situation. In each and every instance one's function or responsiveness will not be shallow if he is not behind.

One should be wary of talking on end about such subjects as learning, morality or folklore in front of elders or people of rank. It is disagreeable to listen to.

In the Kamigata area they have a sort of tiered lunch box they use for a single day when flower viewing. Upon returning, they throw them away, trampling them underfoot. As might be expected, this is one of my recollections of the capital [Kyoto]. The end is important in all things.

While walking along the road together, Tsunetomo said, "Is not man like a well-operated puppet? It is a piece of dexterous workmanship that he can run, jump, leap, and even talk though there are no strings attached. Will we not be guests at next year's Ben Festival? This world is vanity indeed. People always forget this."

It was once said to one of the young lords that "right now" is "at that time, " and "at that time" is "right now." One will miss the occasion if he thinks that these two are different. For example, if one were called before the master to explain something right away, he would most likely be perplexed. This is proof that he understands the two to be different. If, however, a person makes "right now" and "at that time" one, though he will never be an advisor to the master, still he is a retainer, and in order to be able to say something clearly, whether it be in front of the master, the elders or even the shogun at Edo Castle, it should be practiced beforehand in the corner of one's bedroom.

All things are like this. Accordingly, one should inquire into things carefully. It is the same for martial training as for official business. When one attempts to concentrate things in this manner, won't daily negligence and today's lack of resolve be understood?

Even though one has made some blunder in governmental work, it can probably be excused by pleading clumsiness or inexperience. But what kind of excuse may be given for the failure of the men who were involved in this recent unexpected event?" Master Jin'emon always used to say, "It is enough if a warrior is simply a stalwart," and this is just such a case. If one felt that such a failure were a mortification, it would be the least he could do to cut open his stomach, rather than live on in shame with a burning in his breast and the feeling that he had no place to go, and, as his luck as a warrior had run out, he was no longer able to function quickly and had been given a bad name. But if one regretted losing his life and reasoned that he should live because such a death would be useless, then for the next five, ten or twenty years of his life, he would be pointed at from behind and covered with shame. After his death his corpse would be smeared with disgrace, his guiltless descendants would receive his dishonor for having been born in his line, his ancestors' name would be dragged down, and all the members of his family would be blemished. Such circumstances are truly regrettable.

If one has no earnest daily intention, does not consider what it is to be a warrior even in his dreams, and lives through the day idly, he can be said to be worthy of punishment.

Presumably it can be said that a man who has been cut down was lacking in ability and had run out of luck as a warrior. The man who cut him down, compelled by unavoidable circumstances and feeling that there was nothing else to be done, also put his life on the line, and thus there should be no evidence of cowardice. Being short-tempered is inappropriate, but it cannot be said that two men who face each other are cowards. In this recent event, however, the men who lived and covered themselves with shame were not true warriors.

One should every day think over and make an effort to implant in his mind the saying, "At that time is right now." It is said that it is strange indeed that anyone is able to pass through life by one means or another in negligence. Thus, the Way of the Samurai is, morning after morning, the practice of death, considering whether it will be here or be there, imagining the most sightly way of dying, and putting one's mind firmly in death. Although this may be a most difficult thing, if one will do it, it can be done. There is nothing that one should suppose cannot be done.

Moreover, the influence of words is important in military affairs. It would have been best for stopping the man in this recent event, too. When the situation is too much, one may either cut the man down, or, if the man is escaping, yell something like, "Don't run I Only cowards run!" and thus, according to what the situation demands, achieve one's goals by the influence of words. There was a certain man who was said to be good at judging men's dispositions and formerly had everyone's attention, and he was able to handle such cases. This is proof that "right now" is no different from "when the time comes." The position of yokoza no yari is another example of this.* It is something that should be made one's aim beforehand.

The things to be deeply considered beforehand are many. If there is someone who has killed a man in the lord's mansion and has managed to escape, as one does not know whether he may still be swinging his sword and advancing toward the room next to the lord's, he should cut the man down. Indeed, one may be blamed later in an investigation as a confederate of the killer, or as someone who had a grudge against him. But at that time one should think only of cutting the man down and not anticipate later blame.

Even if one's head were to be suddenly cut off, he should be able to do one more action with certainty. The last moments of Nitta Yoshisada are proof of this. Had his spirit been weak, he would have fallen the moment his head was severed. Recently, there is the example of Ono Doken. These actions occurred because of simple determination. With martial valor, if one becomes like a revengeful ghost and shows great determination, though his head is cut off, he should not die.

Whether people be of high or low birth, rich or poor, old or young, enlightened or confused, they are all alike in that they will one day die. It is not that we don't know that we are going to die, but we grasp at straws. While knowing that we will die someday, we think that all the

Hagakure - The Way of the Samurai

others will die before us and that we will be the last to go. Death seems a long way oft.

Is this not shallow thinking? It is worthless and is only a joke within a dream. It will not do to think in such a way and be negligent. insofar as death is always at one's door, one should make sufficient effort and act quickly.

It is good to carry some powdered rouge in one's sleeve. It may happen that when one is sobering up or waking from sleep, his complexion may be poor. At such a time it is good to take out and apply some powdered rouge.

There are times when a person gets carried away and talks on without thinking much. But this can be seen by observers when one's mind is flippant and lacking truth. After such an occasion it is best to come face to face with the truth and express it. The truth will then be arrived at in one's own heart too. Even when greeting someone lightly, one should consider the circumstances and after deliberation speak in a way that will not injure the man's feelings.

Furthermore, if there is a person who is criticizing the Way of the Samurai or one's own province, one should speak with him severely, without the least bit of ceremony. One must be resolved in advance.

Although a person who excels in an art regards others as competitors, last year Hyodo Sachu gave up the title of Master of Renga to Yamaguchi Shochin. A praiseworthy act.

The priest Tannen used to hang up wind-bells but said, "It's not because I like the sound. I hang them in order to know the wind conditions in the event of fire, for that is the only worry in having a large temple." When the wind blew, he himself walked about at night. Throughout his whole life the fire in his brazier was never out, and he always put a paper lantern and lighter by his pillow. He said, ' 'People are flustered during an emergency, and there is no one to quickly strike a light."

If one makes a distinction between public places and one's sleeping quarters, or between being on the battlefield and on the tatami, when the moment comes there will not be time for making amends. There is only the matter of constant awareness. If it were not for men who demonstrate valor on the tatami, one could not find them on the battlefield either.

Bravery and cowardice are not things that can be conjectured in times of peace. They are in different categories.

Though it may be said that the gods dislike impurity, if one thinks a bit, he will see that he has not been negligent in his daily worship. Thus, one's previous faithfulness has been exactly for the sake of praying for good fortune in such times as when one is barbed in blood and climbing over the dead. At such a time, if it is a god that turns back when one is defiled, then one should know clearly that praying is ineffective and should worship regardless of defilement.

times of great trouble or disaster, one word will suffice. At times of happiness, too, one word will be enough. And when meeting or talking with others, one word will do. One should think well and then speak. This is clear and firm, and one should learn it with no doubts. It is a matter of putting forth one's whole effort and having the correct attitude previously. This is very difficult to explain but is something that everyone should work on in his heart. If a person has not learned this in his heart, it is not likely that he will understand it.

Human life is truly a short affair. It is better to live doing the things that you like. It is foolish to live within this dream of a world seeing unpleasantness and doing only things that you do not like. But it is important never to tell this to young people as it is something that would be harmful if incorrectly understood.

Personally, I like to sleep. And I intend to appropriately confine myself more and more to my living quarters and pass my life away sleeping.

I had a dream on the night of the twenty-eighth day of the twelfth month in the third year of Shotoku. The content of the dream changed gradually to the extent that I strengthened my will. The condition of a person is revealed by his dreams. It would be good to make companions of your dreams and to put forth effort.

Shame and repentance are like upsetting a pot of water. When a certain friend of mine listened to the way that a man who had stolen his sword ornament confessed, he felt compassion. If one will rectify his mistakes, their traces will soon disappear.

According to what the Buddhist priest Kaion said, a person becomes more and more prideful if he gains a little understanding because he thinks he knows his own limits and weak points. However, it is a difficult thing to truly know one's own limits and weak points.

At a glance, every individual's own measure of dignity is manifested just as it is. There is dignity in personal appearance. There is dignity in a calm aspect. There is dignity in a paucity of words. There is dignity in flawlessness of manners. There is dignity in solemn behavior. And there is dignity in deep insight and a clear perspective.

These are all reflected on the surface. But in the end, their foundation is simplicity of thought and tautness of spirit.

Covetousness, anger and foolishness are things to sort out well. When bad things happen in the world, if you look at them comparatively, they are not unrelated to these three things. Looking comparatively at the good things, you will see that they are not excluded from wisdom, humanity and bravery.

This is according to what Nakano Kazuma Toshiaki said. There are people who feel that using old utensils for the Tea Ceremony is coarse, and that it is better to use new, clean utensils. There are also people who are wont to use old materials because of their lack of gaudiness. Both are mistaken. Old utensils, although they are things that are used by the humble, are also used by the higher classes because of their value. Their value is revered.

A retainer is just like this. A person rises from the humble to the higher classes because he has value. At the same time, to feel that a person of no family cannot do the same work as one of higher family, or that a man who has heretofore been only a foot soldier should not be allowed to become a leader, is entirely wrong thinking. As for a person who has risen from the humble, his value should be prized and especially respected, even more than that of a person who was born into his class.

My father Jin'emon said that when he was young he was taken from time to time to the entrance of the Chinese settlement in order to be exposed to the atmosphere of the city and to become used to people. From the time he was five years old he was sent as family representative to various people's homes, and in order to make him strong he was made to put on a warrior's straw sandals and visit the temples of his ancestors from the time he was seven.

It is said that one will not be able to do great works if he does not behave with some reserve towards his master, the chief retainers and elders. What is done casually and freely will not work out well. It is a matter of attitude.

It is unfitting that one be ignorant of the history and origins of his clan and its retainers. But there are times when extensive knowledge becomes a hindrance. One should use discretion. Knowing the circumstances can be an obstruction in everyday affairs, too. One should use discretion.

It is written that the priest Shungaku said, "In just refusing to retreat from something one gains the strength of two men." This is interesting. Something that is not done at that time and at that place will remain unfinished for a lifetime. At a time when it is difficult to complete matters with the strength of a single man, one will bring it to a conclusion with the strength of two. If one thinks about it later, he will be negligent all his life.

"Stamp quickly and pass through a wall of iron" is another interesting phrase. To quickly break in and stamp through directly is the first step of celerity. In connection with this, Hideyoshi can be thought of as the only man who has grasped solidly the chance of a lifetime since the creation of Japan.

People who talk on and on about matters of little importance probably have some complaint in the back of their mind. But in order to be ambiguous and to hide this they repeat what they are saving over and over. To hear something like this causes doubt to arise in one's breast.

One should be careful and not say things that are likely to cause trouble at the time. When some difficulty arises in this world, people get excited, and before one knows it the matter is on everyone's lips. This is useless. If worse comes to worse, you may become the subject of gossip, or at least you will have made enemies by saying somethinp unnecessary and will have created ill will. It is said that at such a time it is better to stay at home and think of poetry. To tallc about other people's affairs is a great mistake. To praise them, too, is unfttting. In any event, it is best to know your own ability well, to put forth effort in your endeavors, and to be discreet in speech.

The heart of a virtuous person has settled down and he does not rush about at things. A person of little merit is not at peace but walks about making trouble and is in conflict with all.

It is a good viewpoint to see the world as a dream. When you have something like a nightmare, you will wake up and tell yourself that it was only a dream. It is said that the world we live in is not a bit different from this.

People with intelligence will use it to fashion things both true and false and will try to push through whatever they want with their clever reasoning. This is injury from intelligence. Nothing you do will have effect if you do not use truth.

In affairs like law suits or even in arguments, by losing quickly one will lose in fine fashion. It is like sumo [wrestling]. If one thinks only of winning, a sordid victory will be worse than a defeat. For the most part, it becomes a squalid defeat.

Feeling deeply the difference between oneself and others, bearing ill will and falling out with people--these things come from a heart that lacks compassion. If one wraps up everything with a heart of compassion, there will be no coming into conflict with people.

A person who knows but a little will put on an air of knowledpe. This is a matter of inexperience. When someone knows something well, it will not be seen in his manner. This person is genteel.

When going someplace for a talk or something similar, it is best to let the person know ahead of time, and then go. To go without knowing whether the other party is busy, or when he has some particular anxiety, is awkward. There is nothing that surpasses not going where you have not been invited. Good friends are rare. Even if someone is invited somewhere, he should use understanding. It is difficult to feel deeply the sensitivities of people other than those who go out only rarely. Fiascos at pleasure gatherings are numerous.

However, you should not be brusque towards a person who has come to visit, even if you are busy.

It is bad to carry even a good thing too far. Even concerning things such as Buddhism, Buddhist sermons, and moral lessons, talking too much will bring harm.

The late Jin'emon said that it is better not to bring up daughters. They are a blemish to the family name and a shame to the parents. The eldest daughter is special, but it is better to disregard the others.

The priest Keiho related that Lord Aki once said that martial valor is a matter of becoming a fanatic. I thought that this was surprisingly in accord with my own resolve and thereafter became more and more extreme in my fanaticism.

The late Nakano Kazuma said that the original purpose of the Tea Ceremony is to cleanse the six senses. For the eyes there are the hanging scroll and flower arrangement. For the nose there is the incense. For the ears there is the sound of the hot water. For the mouth there is the taste of the tea. And for the hands and feet there is the correctness of term. When the five senses have thus been cleansed, the mind will of itself be purified. The Tea Ceremony will cleanse the mind when the mind is clogged up. I do not depart from the heart of the Tea Ceremony for twenty-four hours a day, yet this is absolutely not a matter of tasteful living. Moreover, the tea utensils are something that should be in accord with one's social position.

In the poem, "Under the deep snows in the last village/ Last night numerous branches of plum blossomed," the opulence of the phrase "numerous branches" was changed to "a single branch." It is said that this "single branch" contains true tranquillity.

From the 3ʳᵈ Chapter

Lord Naoshige once said, "There is nothing felt quite so deeply as giri. There are times when someone like a cousin dies and it is not a matter of shedding tears. But we may hear of someone who lived fifty or a hundred years ago, of whom we know nothing and who has no family ties with us whatsoever, and yet from a sense giri shed tears." When Lord Naoshige was passing by a place called Chiriku, someone said to him, ' 'In this place there lives a man who is over ninety years old. Since this man is so fortunate, why don't you stop and see him?" Naoshige heard this and said, "How could anyone be more pitiful than this man? How many of his children and grandchildren do you suppose he has seen fall before his very eyes? Where is the good fortune in that?"

It seems that he did not stop to see the man.

When Lord Naoshige was speaking to his grandson, Lord Motoshige, he said, "No matter whether one be of high or low rank, a family line is something that will decline when its trine has come. If one tries to keep it from going to ruin at that time, it will have an unsightly finish. If one thinks that the time has come, it is best to let it go down with good grace. Doing so, he may even cause it to be maintained."

It is said that Motoshige's younger brother heard this from him.

From the 4ᵗʰ Chapter

When Nabeshima Tadanao was fifteen years old, a manservant in the kitchen committed some rude act and a foot soldier was about to beat him, but in the end the servant cut the soldier down. The clan elders deemed the death sentence appropriate, saying that the man had in the first place erred in matters concerning the ranks of men, and that he had also shed the blood of his opponent. Tadanao heard this and said, "Which is worse, to err in matters concerning the ranks of men or to stray from the Way of the Samurai ?"

The elders were unable to answer. Then Tadanao said, "I have read that when the crime itself is unclear, the punishment should be light. Put him in confinement for a while." Once, when Lord Katsushige was hunting at Shiroishi, he shot a large boar. Everyone came running up to see it and said, "Well, well. You have brought down an uncommonly large one!" Suddenly the boar got up and dashed into their midst. All of them fled in confusion, but Nabeshima Matabet drew his sword and finished it off. At that point Lord Katsushige covered his face with his sleeve and said, "It sure is dusty." This was presumably because he did not want to see the spectacle of his flustered men.

When Lord Katsushige was young, he was instructed by his father, Lord Naoshige, "For practice in cutting, execute some men who have been condemned to death." Thus, in the place that is now within the western gate, ten men were lined up, and Katsushige continued to decapitate one after another until he had executed nine of them. When he came to the tenth, he saw that the man was young and healthy and said, "I'm tired of cutting now. I'll spare this man's life." And the man's life was saved.

Lord Katsushige always used to say that there are four kinds of retainers. They are the "quick, then lapping," the "lagging, then quick," the "continually quick," and the "continually lagging."

The "continually quick" are men who when given orders will undertake their execution quickly and settle the matter well. Fukuchi Kichizaemon and the like resemble this type.

The "lagging, then quick" are men who, though lacking in understanding when given orders, prepare quickly and bring the matter to a conclusion. I suppose that Nakano Kazuma and men similar are like this.

The "quick, then lagging" are men who when given orders seem to be going to settle things but in their preparation take time and procrastinate. There are many people like this.

Other than these, one could say that the rest are "continually lagging."

From the 6th Chapter

When Lord Takanobu was at the Battle of Bungo, a messenger came from the enemy camp bearing sake and food. Takanobu wanted to partake of this quickly, but the men at his side stopped him, saying, "Presents from the enemy are likely to be poisoned. This is not something that a general should eat."

Takanobu heard them out and then said, "Even if it is poisoned, how much of an effect would that have on things? Call the messenger here!" He then broke open the barrel right in front of the messenger, drank three large cups of sake, offered the messenger one too, gave him a reply, and sent him back to his camp. Takagi Akifusa turned against the Ryuzoji clan, appealed to Maeda Iyo no kami Iesada, and was sheltered by him. Akifusa was a warrior of matchless valor and was an accomplished and agile swordsman. His retainers were Ingazaemon and Fudozaemon, stalwarts in no way inferior, and they left Akifusa's side neither day nor night. Thus it happened that a request was sent from Lord Takanobu to Iesada to kill Akifusa. At one point, when Akifusa was seated on the veranda having Ingazaemon wash his feet, Iesada came running up behind him and struck off his head, Before his head fell, Akifusa drew out his short sword and turned to strike, but cut off Ingazaemon's head. The two heads fell into the wash basin together. Akifusa's head then rose into the midst of those present. This was the sort of magic technique that he consistently had.

The priest Tannen used to say in his daily talks that: A monk cannot fulfill the Buddhist Way if he does not manifest compassion without and persistently store up courage within. And if a warrior does not manifest courage on the outside and hold enough compassion within his heart to burst his chest, he cannot become a retainer. Therefore, the monk pursues courage with the warrior as his model, and the warrior pursues the compassion of the monk.

I traveled about for many years and met men of wisdom but never found the means to the pursuit of knowledge. Therefore, whenever I heard of a man of courage in one place or another, I would go and look for him regardless of the hardships on the way. I have learned clearly that these stories of the Way of the Samurai have been an aid on the road to Buddhism. Now a warrior with his armor will rush into the enemy camp, making that armor his strength. Do you suppose that a monk with a single rosary can dash into the midst of spears and long swords, armed with only meekness and compassion? If he does not have great courage, he will do no dashing at all. As proof of this, the priest offering the incense at a great Buddhist memorial service may tremble, and this is because he has no courage.

Things like kicking a man back from the dead, or pulling all living creatures out of hell, are all matters of courage. Nevertheless, monks of recent times all entertain false ideas and desire to become laudably gentle ; there are none who complete the Way. Furthermore, among warriors there are some cowards who advance Buddhism. These are regrettable matters. It is a great mistake for a young samurai to learn about Buddhism. The reason is that he will see things in two ways. A person who does not set himself in just one direction will be of no value at all. It is fine for retired old men to learn about Buddhism as a diversion, but if a warrior makes loyalty and filial piety one load, and courage and compassion another, and carries these twenty-four hours a day until his shoulders wear out, he will be a samurai.

In one's morning and evening worship, and as one goes about his day, he had best recite the name of his master. It is not a bit different from the Buddha's names and holy words. Furthermore, one should be in harmony with his family gods. These are matters of the strength of one's fate. Compassion is like a mother who nurtures one's fate. Examples of the ruin of merciless warriors who were brave alone are conspicuous in both past and present.

There was a certain point in the conversation when a retainer of Lord Nabeshima Naohiro said, "There are no men here upon whom the master can truly rely. Although I am consistently useless, I am the only one who would throw away his life for you."

It is said that Lord Naohiro got outrageously angry, saying, "Among our retainers there is not a one who holds his life in regret! You are talking arrogance!" and he was at the point of striking him when the man was pulled away by others who were there.

Once when Master Tanesada, the founder of the China family, was coming by sea to the island of Shikoku, a strong wind began blowing and the boat was damaged. The boat was saved from sinking by abalone gathering together and covering over the damaged sections. From that time on none of the China family nor any of its retainers ate abalone. If one of them mistakenly ate one, it is said that his body was covered with boils in the shape of abalone.

At the fall of the castle at Arima, on the twenty-eighth day in the vicinity of the inmost citadel, Mitsuse Gender sat down on a levee between the fields. When Nakano Shintohi passed by and asked the reason for this, Mitsuse replied, "I have abdominal pains and can't go a step farther. I have sent the members of my group ahead, so please take command." This situation was reported by the overseer, pronounced to be a case of cowardice, and Mitsuse was ordered to commit seppuku.

Long ago, abdominal pains were called "cowardice grass." This is because they come suddenly and render a person immobile.

At the time of Lord Nabeshima Naohiro's death, Lord Mitsushige forbade Naohiro 's retainers the practice of tsuifuku. His messenger went to Naohiro's mansion and made the declaration, but those who received this news could in no way agree to it. From their midst Ishimaru Uneme (later called Seizaemon) spoke from the lowest seat, "It is improper for me as a younger person to speak out, but I think that what Lord Katsushige has said is reasonable. As a person who received the master's care when I was young, I had whole- heartedly decided on tsuifuku. But hearing Lord Katsushige's dictum and being convinced of his reasoning, no matter what the others may do, I am giving up the idea of tsuifuku and will serve the master's successor." Hearing this, the others all followed suit.

Once Lord Masaie was playing shogi with Lord Hideyoshi and there were a number of daimyo watching. When it came time to withdraw, although Lord Masaie could stand, his feet were numb and he could not walk. He made his withdrawal crawling away, causing everyone to laugh. Because Lord Masaie was big and obese he was not ordinarily able to be on his knees. After this event he thought it would not be fitting to he in attendance anymore and began refusing such duties.

Nakano Uemonnosuke Tadaaki was killed on the twelfth day of the eighth month in the sixth year of Eiroku, at the time of the fight between Master Goto and Master Hirai of Suko on the island of Kabashima in the Kishima district. When Uemonnosuke was leaving for the front lines, he emgraced his son Shikibu (later called Jin'emon) in the garden and, although Shikibu was very young, said, "When you grow up, win honor in the Way of the Samurai!"

Even when the children in his family were very young, Yamamoto Jin'emon would draw near to them and say, "Grow up to be a great stalwart, and be of good use to your master." He said, "It is good to breathe these things into their ears even when they are too young to understand."

When Ogawa Toshikiyo's legitimate son Sahei Kiyoji died as a youth, there was one young retainer who galloped up to the temple and committed seppuku.

When Taku Nagato no kami Yasuyori passed away, Kola Yataemon said that he had been unable to repay the master's kindness and committed seppuku.

From the 7ᵗʰ Chapter

Narutomi Hyogo said, "What is called winning is defeaing one's allies. Defeating one's allies is defeating oneself, and defeating oneself is vigorously overcoming one's own body.

"It is as though a man were in the midst of ten thousand allies but not a one were following him. If one hasn't previously mastered his mind and body, he will not defeat the enemy." During the Shimabara Rebellion, his armor being still at the encampment, Shugyo Echizen no kami Tanenao participated in the fight dressed only in hakama and haori. It is said that he died in battle in this attire.

At the time of the attack on the castle at Shimabara, Tazaki Geki was wearing very resplendent armor. Lord Katsushige was not pleased by this, and after that every time he saw something showy he would say, "That's just like Geki's armor."

In the light of this story, military armor and equipment that are showy can be seen as being weak and having no strength. By them one can see through the wearer's heart.

When Nabeshima wizen no kami Tadanao died, his attendant Ezoe Kinbei took his remains and had them consecrated at Mt. Kola. Then, confining himself in a hermitage, he carved a statue of his master and another of himself doing reverence before the master. On the first anniversary of Tadanao's death, he returned to his home and committed tsuifuku. Later the statue was taken from Mt. Koya and was placed at the Kodenji.

In the generation of Lord Mitsushige, Oishi Kosuke was at first a foot soldier serving at the side of his master. Whenever Lord Mitsushige was making the trip for his alternate- year residence in Edo, Kosuke would make the rounds around the sleeping quarters of his master, and if he thought a certain area to be insecure, he would spread a straw mat and pass through the night awake by himself. In rainy weather he would simply wear a bamboo hat and an oilpaper raincoat and would stand watch while being pelted by the rain. It is said that to the end he never spent a single night in negligence.

When Oishi Kosuke was an uchitonin, a mysterious person sneaked into the area of the maids' chambers late at night.' There was a great commotion from upstairs to down and men and women of all ranks were running about; only Kosuke was not to be seen. While the senior ladies-in- waiting were searching about, Kosuke yanked his sword from its scabbard and waited quietly in the room next to the master's bedchamber. As all was in confusion, he had felt apprehension for the master and was there to protect him. Because of this it was said that his viewpoint was quite different.

The man who had sneaked in was Narutomi Kichibei. He and his accomplice Hamada Ichizaemon were condemned to death for adultery.

Once when Lord Katsushige was hunting at Nishime, for some reason he got very angry. He drew his sword from his obi, scabbard and all, and began beating Soejima Zennojo with it, but his hand slipped and his sword fell into a ravine. Zennojo, in order to stay with the sword, fumbled down into the ravine and picked it up. This done, he stuck the sword in his lapel, crawled up the precipice, and just as he was, offered the sword to his master. In terms of quick- mindedness and reserve this was matchless resource.

Once when Master Sane Ukyo was crossing over the Takao River, the bridge was being repaired and there was one large piling that could not be pulled up. Master Ukyo dismounted, grasped the piling firmly, pave a shout, and began to pull it up. There was a tremendous sound, and although he was able to pull it up to his own height, it would go no further and thereupon sank. After he returned home he became sick and suddenly died.

At the time of the funeral at the temple in Jobaru, when the funeral procession crossed the Takao Bridge, the corpse leapt from the casket and fell into the river. A sixteen-year- old acolyte from the Shufukuji immediately jumped into the river and took hold of the dead body. Everyone then ran down into the river and pulled up the corpse. The head monk was very impressed and instructed the other acolytes to be guided by this young man. It is said that he later became a very famous monk.

Yamamoto Kichizaemon was ordered by his father Jin'-emon to cut down a dog at the age of five, and at the age of fifteen he was made to execute a criminal. Everyone, by the time they were fourteen or fifteen, was ordered to do a beheading without fail. When Lord Katsushige was young, he was ordered by Lord Naoshige to practice killing with a sword. It is said that at that time he was made to cut down more than ten men successively.

A long time ago this practice was followed, especially in the upper classes, but today even the children of the lower classes perform no executions, and this is extreme negligence. To say that one can do without this sort of thing, or that there is no merit in killing a condemned man, or that it is a crime, or that it is defiling, is to make excuses. In short, can it not be thought that because a person's martial valor is weak, his attitude is only that of trimming his nails and being attractive?

If one investigates into the spirit of a man who finds these things disagreeable, one sees that this person gives himself over to cleverness and excuse making not to kill because he feels unnerved. But Naoshige made it his orders exactly because this is something that must be done.

Last year I went to the Kase Execution Grounds to try my hand at beheading, and I found it to be an extremely good feeling. To think that it is unnerving is a symptom of cowardice.

Among the pageboys in forelocks in Lord Mitsushige's retinue, one Tomoda Shozaemon was in attendance. A rather wanton fellow, he fell in love with a leading actor of the theater by the name of Tamon Shozaemon and changed both his name and his crest to that of the actor. Completely abandoning himself to this affair, he spent everything he had and lost all his clothing and furnishings. And at length, when he had exhausted all his means, he stole Mawatari Rokubei's sword and had a spearman take it to a pawnshop.

The spearman, however, spoke up about this matter, and in the investigation both he and Shozaemon were condemned to death. The investigator was Yamamoto Gorozaemon. When he read the report, he spoke in a loud voice and said, "The man who accuses the defendant is Spearman so-and- so."

Mitsushige responded quickly, "Put him to death."

When it came time to announce his fate to Shozaemon, Gorozaemon came in and said, "There is now nothing left to be done for you. Prepare yourself for your place of death."

Shozaemon settled himself and said, "Very well. I understand what you have said and am grateful for your words." Due to somebody's trickery, however, while a kaishaku was introduced to Shozaemon, it was arranged that a foot soldier, Naozuka Rokuuemon, was to step from the side and decapitate him.

Repairing to the execution grounds, where the kaishaku stood opposite him, Shozaemon saluted him with extreme calm. But just then, seeing Naozuka drawing his sword, he jumped up and said, "Who are you? I'll never let you cut off my head!" From that point on his peace of mind was shattered and he showed terrible cowardice. Finally he was brought to the ground, stretched out, and decapitated.

Gorozaemon later said secretly, ' 'If he hadn't been deceiv- ed, he would have probably met his death well."

Noda Kizaemon said about the function of kaishaku, "When a man who has come to his place of death loses his wits and is crawling about, it is likely seine damage will be done when it comes time to perform kaishak. At such a time first wait a bit and by some means gather your strength. Then if you cut by standing firm and not missing the chance, you will do well."

In the generation of Lord Katsushige there were retainers who, regardless of high or low rank, were requested to work before the master from the time they were young. When Shiba Kizaemon was doing such service, once the master was clipping his nails and said, "Throw these away." Kizaemon held them in his hand but did not stand up, and the master said, "What's the matter?" Kizaemon said, "There's one missing." The master said, ' 'Here it is," and banded over the one that he had hidden.

Sawabe Heizaemon was ordered to commit seppuku on the eleventh day of the eleventh month in the second year of Tenna. As this became known to him on the night of the tenth, he sent a request to Yamamoto Gonnojo [Tsunetomo] to be kaishaku. The following is a copy of Yamamoto's reply. (Tsunetomo was twenty-four years old at this time.)

I am in accord with your resolution and accept your request for me to function as kaishaku. I instinctively felt that I should decline, but as this is to take place tomorrow there is no time for making excuses and I will undertake the job. The fact that you have chosen me from among many people is a great personal satisfaction to me. Please set your mind at ease concerning all that must follow. Although it is now late at night, I will come to your house to talk over the particulars.

When Heizaemon saw this reply, it is said that he remarked, "This is a matchless letter."

From ages past it has been considered ill-omened by samurai to be requested as kaishaku. The reason for this is that one pains no fame even if the job is well done. And if by chance one should blunder, it becomes a lifetime disgrace.

Once when Tanaka Yahei was attending to affairs in Edo, one of his menials was rather insolent and Yahei scolded him severely. Late that night Yahei heard the noise of someone coming up the stairs. He felt this to be suspicious and quietly got up. With short sword in hand he asked who was there, and it turned out to be the menial whom he had scolded previously, secretly holding a short sword. Yahei leapt down and with a single stroke cut the man down. I heard many people later state that he had had good luck.

A certain Master Tokuhisa was born quite different from other people and looked to be a bit moronic. Once, a guest was invited and mudfish salad was served. At that time everyone said, "Master Tokuhisa's mudfish salad," and laughed. Later when he was in attendance and a certain person made fun of him by quoting the above remark, Tokuhisa pulled out his sword and cut the man down. This event was investigated and it was stated to Lord Naoshige, "Seppuku is recommended because this was a matter of rashness within the palace."

When Lord Naoshige heard this, he said, ' 'To be made fun of and remain silent is cowardice. There is no reason to overlook this fact because one is within the palace. A man who makes fun of people is himself a fool. It was his own fault for being cut down."

Once when Nakano Mokunosuke bearded a small boat on the Sumida River to enjoy the coolness, a rogue got in too and committed all manner of rude acts. When Mokunosuke saw that the rogue was relieving himself over the side of the boat, he cut the man's head off and it fell into the river. So that people would not notice this, he quickly covered the body with various things. He then said to the boatman, "This matter should not become known. Row up to the upper reaches of the river and bury the corpse. I shall naturally pay you well."

The boatman did as he was told, but in the lagoon where the body was buried Mokunosuke cut off the head of the boatman and returned directly. It is said that this fact never became known publicly. At that time there was also one young homosexual male prostitute riding in the boat. Mekunosuke said, "That fellow was a man too. It is best to learn how to cut a man while one is still young," and so the man cut the corpse once. Because of that the young man said nothing later on.

It is said that every time Oki Hyobu's group gathered and after all their affairs were finished he would say, "Young men should discipline themselves rigorously in intention and courage. This will be accomplished if only courage is fixed in one's heart. If one's sword is broken, he will strike with his hands. If his hands are cut off, he will press the enemy down with his shoulders. If his shoulders are cut away, he will bite through ten or fifteen enemy necks with his teeth. Courage is such a thing."

Shida Kichinosuke said, "At first it is an oppressive thing to run until one is breathless. But it is an extraordinarily good feeling when one is standing around after the running. More than that, it is even better to sit down. More than that, it is even better to lie down. And more than that, to put down a pillow and sleep soundly is even better. A man's whole life should be like this. To exert oneself to a great extent when one is young and then to sleep when he is old or at the point of death is the way it should be. But to first sleep and then exert oneself... To exert oneself to the end, and to end one's whole life in toil is regrettable." Shimomura Rokurouemon told this story.

A saying of Kichinosuke's that is similar to this is, "A man's life should be as toilsome as possible."

When Ueno Rihei was overseer of accounting in Edo, he had a young assistant whom he treated in a very intimate way. On the first night of the eighth month he went drinking with Hashimoto Taemon, an overseer of foot soldiers, and got so drunk that he lost good sense. He accompanied his young assistant back home, babbling on in a drunken manner, and when they arrived there, Rihei said that he was going to cut the assistant down. The assistant pushed away the tip of Rihei's scabbard. They grappled and both fell into the gutter with the assistant on top pushing Rihei down. At this time, Rihei's servant ran up and asked, "Is Master Rihei on the top or on the bottom?"

When Rihei replied, "I'm on the bottom!" the servant stabbed the assistant once. The assistant got up and, as his wound was light, ran away.

When the affair was brought under investigation, Rihei was put into confinement at the Naekiyama prison and was condemned to capital punishment by beheading. Before this, when he was positioned in Edo and living in a rented house in the merchants' district, a servant had opposed him and he had cut him down. But he had acted in a good way at that time, and people said that he had acted like a man. This time, however, his actions were outrageous and were certainly unnecessary.

If one thinks about this well from beginning to end, to get so drunk as to draw one's sword is both cowardice and lack of resolve. Rihei's servant was a man from Taku, but his name is not remembered. Though he was a member of the lower classes, he was a brave man. It is said that Taemon committed suicide during the investigation.

In the twelfth section of the fifth chapter of the Ryoankyo there is this story:

In the Province of wizen there was a certain man from Take who, although he had contracted smallpox, was considering joining the forces attacking the castle at Shimabara. His parents earnestly tried to get him to desist, saying, "With such a grave illness, even if you should get there, how could you be of any use?"

He replied, "It would be to my satisfaction to die on the way. After having received the warm benevolence of the master, should I tell myself that I will be of no use to him now?" And he left for the front. Although it was winter camp and the cold was extreme, he did not pay any attention to his health, and neither put on many layers of clothing nor took off his armor day or night. Moreover, he did not avoid uncleanliness, and in the end recovered quickly and was able to fulfill his loyalty completely. So to the contrary of what you would expect, it cannot be said that one is to despise uncleanliness.

When the teacher, Suzuki Shozo, heard this, he said, "Was it not a cleansing act to throw away his life for his master? For a man who will cut of his life for the sake of righteousness, there is no need to call upon the god of smallpox. All the gods of heaven will protect him. "

Lord Katsushige said, "Whether a man of Hizen holds death in regret or not is not a matter of concern. What I worry about is that people will not take to heart the command to keep the rules of manners and etiquette correctly. I am afraid that the entire clan, our relatives and elders, out of too much earnestness, will feel that the command to keep correct etiquette is an exaggeration. Up to now there have existed men who were used to these things, and even if etiquette was slightly wrong, they could remember the correct way, and the matter was settled. I have given this command because people are negligent in affairs of this sort."

During the Genroku period there was a samurai of low rank from the Province of Ise by the name of Suzuki Rokubei. He was ill with a severe fever, and his consciousness became dim. At that time a certain male nurse was unexpectedly stricken with greed and was about to open up the inkbox and steal the money that was kept in it. Just then the sick man suddenly stirred, took the sword from the base of his pillow, and in a sudden attack cut the man down with one blow. With that, the sick man fell back and died. By this act, Rokubei seemed to be a man of principled disposition.

I heard this story in Edo, but later when I was serving in the same province with a Dr. Nagatsuka, who was also from the Province of Ise, I asked him about it, and indeed he knew the story and said that it was true.

From the 8th Chapter

On the night of the thirteenth day of the ninth month in the fourth year of Teikyo, there was a group of ten No actors moon-viewing at the house of Nakayama Mosuke, a foot soldier, in Sayanomoto. Beginning with Naotsuka Kanzaemon they all began to make fun of the foot soldier Araki Kyozaemen because he was so short. Araki became angry, killed Kanzaemon with his sword, and then began striking at the others.

Though he suffered a severed hand, Matsumoto Rokuzaemon came down into the garden, seized Araki from behind with his other hand, and said, "As for the likes of you, I'll twist your head off with one hand!" Grabbing away Araki's sword, he pushed him to the doorsill and pressed him down with his knee, but as he seized him by the neck he became faint and was quickly overpowered.

Araki quickly sprang back and again began to strike at those around him, but now Master Hayata (later known as Jirozaemon) met him with a spear. In the end he was overpowered by a number of men. Following this, Araki was made to commit seppuku, and the others who were involved were all made ronin on account of their indiscretion, but Hayata was later pardoned.

As Tsunetomo does not remember this story clearly, one should ask around about it. Some years ago there was a sutra reading at the Jissoin in Kawakami. Five or six men from Kon'yamachi and the area of Tashiro had gone to the service, and on their way home passed some time drinking. Among them was one of Kizuka Kyuzaemon's retainers who, having some reason for doing so, turned down his companions' invitation to join them and returned borne before nightfall. The others, however, later pot into a fight with some men and cut them all down.

Kyuzaemon's retainer heard of this late that night and went quickly to his companions' quarters. He listened to the details and then said, "In the end I suppose you will have to submit a statement. When you do, you should say that I was there also and assisted in cutting down those men. When I return, I will say as much to Kyuzaemon. Since a fight is a matter involving all concerned, I should meet the same death sentence as you. And that is my deepest desire. The reason is that even if I were to explain to my master that I had returned home early, he would never accept it as the truth. Kyuzaemon has always been a severe man, and even if I were cleared by the investigators, he would probably have me executed as a coward right before his eyes. In such a case, dying with the bad reputation of having run away from a place would be extremely regretful.

"Since the fate of dying is the same, I would like to die being blamed for having killed a man. If you are not in agreement with this, I will cut my stomach open right here."

Having no alternative, his companions spoke as he had requested. Presently, during the inquiry, although the circumstances were explained in the above manner, it became known that the retainer had returned home early. All the investigators were impressed and in fact praised the man.

This matter was transmitted to me only in outline, so I will look into the details at a later date.

Once when Nabeshima Aki no kami Shigetake was halfway through his meal, a guest suddenly came to see him and he left his tray just as it was. Later, a certain retainer of his sat down at the tray and began eating the fried fish that was on it. Just then Lord Aki came back and saw him, and the man became flustered and ran off. Lord Aki yelled out, "What a low-life slave you are to eat something that someone else has been eating!" and sat down and finished what was left.

This is one of Jin'emon's stories. It is said that this retainer was one of those who committed tsuifuku for the master.

Yamamoto Jin'emon always said to his retainers, "Go ahead and gamble and lie. A person who will not tell you seven lies within a hundred yards is useless as a man. " Long ago people spoke in this fashion because they were only concerned with a man's attitude towards military matters and considered that a man who was "correct" would never do great works. They also ignored the misconduct of men and dismissed such matters by saying, "They do good works, too..."

Men like Sagara Kyoma also excused retainers who had committed theft and adultery and trained them gradually. He said, "If it weren't for such persons, we would have no useful men at all."

Ikumo Oribe said, "If a retainer will just think about what he is to do for the day at hand, he will be able to do anything. If it is a single day's work, one should be able to put up with it. Tomorrow, too, is but a single day."

At the time when Lord Nabeshima Tsunashige had still not taken over as heir, he was converted by the Zen priest Kurotakiyama Choon and learned Buddhism from him. Since he had had an enlightenment, the priest was going to confer the seal upon him, and this became known throughout the mansion. At that time Yamamoto Gorozaemon had been ordered to be both Tsunashige's attendant and overseer. When he heard of this, he knew that it absolutely would not do and planned to make a request to Choon, and if he did not assent, kill him. He went to the priest's house in Edo and entered; the priest, thinking that he was someone on a pilgrimage, met him in a dignified manner.

Gorozaemon drew near him and said, ' 'I have some secret thing to tell you directly. Please send out your attendant priests.

"It is said that you will soon award Tsunashige the seal because of his cleverness in Buddhism. Now as you are from Hizen, you should know in large part the customs of the Ryuzoji and Nabeshima clans. Our country is ruled with harmony between high and low because, unlike others, it has had continuous heirs for successive generations. There has never been the taking of a Buddhist seal by the daimyo for ages past. If you present the seal now, Tsunashige will probably think of himself as enlightened and regard what his retainers say as so much dirt. A great man will become vain. Absolutely do not give this award.

If you do not agree to this, I too am resolved. This he said with determination.

The priest's color changed, but he said, "Well, well. You have trustworthy intentions, and I see that you under- stand the affairs of your clan well. You are a loyal retainer... "

But Gorozaemon said, "No! I understand that ploy. I didn't come here to be praised. Without adding anything else, let me hear clearly whether you plan to cancel the seal or not."

Choon said, "What you say is reasonable. I will definitely not award the seal."

Gorozaemon made sure of this and returned. Tsunetomo heard this story directly from Gorozaemon.

A group of eight samurai all took the same road for some merrymaking. Two of them, Komori Eijun and Otsubo Jin'-emon, went into a teahouse in front of the Kannon temple at Asakusa, got into an argument with the male employees there, and were soundly beaten. This could be heard by the others, who were in an excursion boat, and Mute Rokuemen said, "We should go back and take revenge." Yoshii Yoichiemon and Ezoe Jinbei both agreed to this.

The others, however, dissuaded them, saying, "This will cause trouble for the clan," and they all returned home. When they arrived at the mansion, Rokuemon again said, "We should definitely take revenge!" but the others disuaded him. Although they sustained heavy wounds on their arms and legs, Eijian and Jin'emon cut the teahouse men down, and those who had returned were taken to task by the master.

In due course some thought was given to the details of this event. One person said, "By waiting to ;get the agreement of others, a matter like taking revenge will never be brought to a conclusion. One should have the resolution to go alone and even to be cut down. A person who speaks vehemently about taking revenge but does nothing about it is a hypocrite. Clever people, by using their mouths alone, are taking care of their reputations for a later date. But a real stalwart is a man who will go out secretly, saying nothing, and die. It is not necessary to achieve one's aim ; one is a stalwart in being cut down. Such a person will most likely achieve his pur- pose."

Ichiyuken was a low class servant in the kitchen of Lord Takanobu. Because of some grudge he had over a matter of wrestling, he cut down seven or eight men and was hence ordered to commit suicide. But when Lord Takanobu heard of this he pardoned the man and said, "In these strife-torn times of our country, brave men are important. This man would seem to be a man of bravery." Consequently, at the time of the action around the Uji River, Lord Takanobu took Ichiyuken along, and the latter earned unrivaled fame, advancing deep into the lead and plundering the enemy every time.

At the battle of Takagi, Ichiyuken went so far into the enemy lines that Lord Takanobu felt regret and called him back. Since the vanguard had been unable to advance, only by quickly dashing out was he able to grab Ichiyuken by the sleeve of his armor. At that time Ichiyuken's head had suffered many wounds, but he had stopped them up with preen leaves which he bound with a thin towel.

On the first clay of the attack on Hara Caste, Tsuruta Yashichibei went as a messenger from Lord Mimasaka to Oki Hyobu, but as he was delivering the message, he was shot through the pelvic region by a bullet fired from the castle and instantly fell on his face. He got up again and delivered the rest of the message, was felled a second time, and died. Yashichibei's body was carried back by Taira Chihyoei. When Chihyoei was returning to Hyobu's camp, he too was struck by a rifle ball and died.

Dense was born in Taku, and the members of his family living at this time were his elder brother Jirbei, his younger brother and his mother. Around the ninth month Denko's mother took Jirobei's son with her to hear a sermon. When it was time to go home, the child, as he was putting on his straw sandals, accidentally stepped on the foot of the man next to him. The man rebuked the child, and in the end they pot into a vehement argument and the man unsheathed his short sword and killed him. Jirobei's mother was dumb struck. She clung to the man, and he killed her too. Having done this, the man returned to his house.

This man's name was Gorouemon, and he was the son of a ronin by the name of Nakajima Moan. His younger brother was the mountain ascetic, Chuzobo. Moan was an advisor to Master Mimasaka, and Gorouemon had been given a stipend also.

When the circumstances became known at Jirobei's home, his younger brother set out for Gorouemon's place. Finding that the door was locked from within and that no one would come out, he disguised his voice, pretending to be a visitor. When the door was opened, he shouted his real name and crossed swords with his enemy. Both men fumbled into the rubbish heap, but in the end Gorouemon was killed. At this point, Chuzobo dashed in and cut down Jirobei's younger brother.

Hearing of this incident, Dense went immediately to Jirobei's place and said, "Of our enemies only one has been killed, while we have lost three. This is extremely regret- table, so why don't you strike at Chuzobo?" Jirobei, however, would not comply.

Denko felt that this was indeed shameful, and although a Buddhist priest, he decided on striking at the enemy of his mother, younger brother and nephew. He knew, nevertheless, that since he was simply an ordinary priest, there was likely to be a reprisal from Master Mimasaka and therefore worked hard, finally gaining eminence as the chief priest of the Ryuunji. He then went to the sword maker Iyonojo and asked him to make both a long and a short sword, offered to be his apprentice, and was even allowed to take part in the work.

By the twenty-third day of the ninth month of the follow- ing year, he was ready to make his departure. By chance a guest had come at this time. Giving orders for food to be served, Denko secretly slipped out of the chief priest's headquarters disguised as a layman. He then went to taku and, upon asking about Chuzobo, learned that he was with a large group of people who had gathered to watch the moonrise, and that therefore nothing much could be done. Unwilling to let time pile up, he felt that it would be fulfilling his basic desire to strike at the father, Moan. Going to Moan's house, he forced his way into the sleeping chambers, announced his name, and when the man began to get up, stabbed and killed him. When the people of the neighborhood came running and surrounded him, he explained the situation, threw away both long and short swords, and returned home. News of this preceded him to Saga, and a good number of Denko's parishioners came out quickly and accompanied him on his return.

Master Mimasaka was quite outraged, but as Denko was the chief priest of a Nabeshima clan temple, there was nothing to be done. Finally, through the offices of Nabeshima Toneri, he sent word to Tannen, the chief priest of the Kodenji, saying, "When a priest has killed a man, he should be given a sentence of death." Tannen's reply was, "The punishment for one within the religion will be in accordance with the feelings of the Kodenji. Kindly do not interfere."

Master Mimasaka became even angrier and asked, "What sort of punishment will this be?" Tannen replied, "Although it is profitless for you to know, you are forcing the question, so I will give you an answer. The [Buddhist] Law is that an apostate priest is deprived of his robes and driven out."

Denko's robes were taken from him at the Kodenji, and when he was to be driven out, some novices put on their long and short swords, and a great number of parishioners came to protect him, accompanying him as far as Todoroki. On the road a number of men who looked like hunters appeared and asked if the party had come from Taku. Thereafter Denko lived in Chikuzen, was well received by all, and was on friendly terms with samurai as well. This story was widely circulated, and it is said that he was treated kindly everywhere.

Horie San'emon's misdeed was robbing the Nabeshima warehouse in Edo of its money and fleeing to another prov ince. He was caught and confessed. Thus it was pro nounced, "Because this is a grave crime he should be tortured to death, " and Nakano Daigaku was ordered to be the official who verified the execution. At first all the hairs on his body were burner off and his fingernails were pulled out. His tendons were then cut, he was bored with drills and sub jected to various other tortures. Throughout, he did not flinch once, nor did his face change color. In the end his back was split, he was boiled in soy sauce, and his body was bent back in two.

Once when Fukuchi Rokurouemon was leaving the castle, the palanquin of what appeared to be a rather upper class woman was passing in front of Master Taku's mansion, and a man who was standing there made the proper salutation. A halberd carrier who was with the palanquin procession, however, said to the man, "You didn't bow low enough," and struck him on the head with the handle of his halberd. When the man wiped his head, he found that he was bleeding. In just that condition he stood up and said, "You have committed an outrageous act, even though I was courteous. A regrettable piece of luck." So saying, he cut the halberd carrier down with a single blow. The palanquin continued on to wherever it was going, but Rokurouemon unsheathed his spear, stood before the man, and said. "Put away your sword. Within the castle grounds it is forbidden to go about holding a naked blade." The man said, "What happened now was unavoidable, and I was compelled by the circumstances. Certainly you could see that this was so. Although I would like to sheathe my sword, it is difficult to do so due to the tone of your words. It is unpleasant, but I shall be glad to accept your challenge."

Rokurouemon immediately threw down his spear and said courteously, "What you have said is reasonable. My name is Fukuchi Rokurouemon. I will bear witness that your conduct was quite admirable. Moreover, I will back you up even if it means forfeiting my life. Now put away your sword."

"With pleasure," the man said, and sheathed his sword. On being asked where he was from, the man replied that he was a retainer of Taku Nagato no kami Yasuyori. Therefore Rokurouemon accompanied him and explained the circumstances. Knowing that the woman in the palanquin was the wife of a nobleman, however, Lord Nagato ordered his retainer to commit seppuku.

Rokurouemon came forward and said, "Because I have given the promise of a samurai, if this man is ordered to commit seppuku, then I will commit seppuku first."

It is said that the affair was thus finished without mishap.

Lord Shima sent a messenger to his father, Lord Aki, saying, "I would like to make a pilgrimage to the Atago Shrine in Kyoto." Lord Aki asked, "For what reason?" and the messenger replied, "Since Atago is the pod of archery, my intentions are for the sake of fortune in war." Lord Aki became angry and answered. "That is absolutely worthless! Should the vanguard of the Nabeshimas be making requests to Atago? If the incarnation of Atago were fighting on the enemy's side, the vanguard should be equal to cutting him neatly in two."

Dohaku lived in Kurotsuchibaru. His son was named Gorobei. Once when Gorobei was carrying a load of rice, a ronin of Master Kumashiro Sakyo's by the name of Iwamura Kyunai was coming from the other direction. There was a grudge between the two of them from some former incident, and now Gorobei struck Kyunai with his load of rice, started an argument, beat him and pushed him into a ditch, and then returned home. Kyunai yelled some threat at Gorobei and returned to his home where he related this event to his older brother Gen'emon. The two of them then went off to Gorobei's to take revenge.

When they got there the door was open just a bit, and Gorobei was waiting behind it with drawn sword. Not knowing this, Gen'emon entered and Gorobei struck at him with a sweep from the side. having received a deep wound, Gen'emon used his sword as a staff and hobbled back outside. Then Kyunai rushed in and struck at Dohaku's son-in-law Katsuemon, who was sitting by the hearth. His sword glanced off the pot hanger, and he cut off half of Katsuemen's face. Dohaku, together with his wife, grabbed the sword away from Kyunai.

Kyunai apologized and said, "I have already achieved my purpose. Please give me back my sword and I will accompany my brother home. But when Dohaku banded it back to him, Kyunai cut him once in the back and severed his neck halfway through. He then crossed swords with Gorobei again and both went outside and fought an even match until he cut off Gorobei's arm.

At this point Kyunai, who also suffered many wounds, shouldered his elder brother Gen'emon and returned home. Gen'emon, however, died on the way back.

Gorobei's wounds were numerous. Although he stopped the bleeding, he died on account of drinking some water. Dohaku's wife suffered some severed fingers. Dohaku's wound was a severed neck bone, and since only his throat remained intact, his head hung down in front. Now boosting his head up with his own hands, Dohaku went off to the surgeon 's.

The surgeon s treatment was like this: First he rubbed a mixture of pine resin and oil on Dohaku's jaw and bound it in ramie. He then attached a rope to the top of his head and tied it to a beam, sewed the open wound shut, and buried his body in rice so that he would not be able to move.

Dohaku never lost consciousness nor did he change from his everyday attitude, nor did he even drink ginseng. It is said that only on the third day when there was a hemorrhage did he use a little medicinal stimulant. In the end the bones mended, and he recovered without incident.

When Lord Mitsushige contracted smallpox at Shimonoseki, Ikushima Sakuan gave him some medicine. It was an exceptionally heavy case of smallpox, and his attendants both high and low were rather tense. Suddenly his scabs turned black. The men who were nursing him lost heart and secretly informed Sakuan, who came immediately. He said, "Well, this is something to be thankful for. The scabs are healing. He should soon make a complete recovery with no complications. I give you my guarantee."

The people who were at Lord Mitsushige's side heard this and thought, "Sakuan looks a little deranged. This has become all the more hopeless. "

Sakuan then set folding screens around, came out after a while, and fed Lord Mitsushige one packet of medicine. Very quickly the patient's scabs healed, and he made a complete recovery. Sakuan later confided to someone, "I gave the master that one packet of medicine resolved that, as I was undertaking this treatment alone, if he did not recover I would quickly cut open my stomach and die with him."

When Nakano Takumi was dying, his whole house garthered and he said, "You should understand that there are three conditions to the resolution of a retainer. They are the condition of the master's will, the condition of vitality, and the condition of one's death."

Once when a number of men had gathered on the platform of the inner citadel of the castle, a certain man said to Uchida Shouemon, "It is said that you are a teacher of the sword, but judging by your everyday attitude, your teaching must be very wild indeed. If you were requested to perform kaishaku, I can imagine that instead of cutting the neck you'd probably cut the top of the man's head."

Shouemon rejoined, "Such is not the case. Draw a little ink spot on your own neck, and I'll show you that I can cut without being off by a hair."

Nagayama Rokurozaemon was going down the Tokaido and was at Hamamatsu. As he passed by an inn, a beggar faced his palanquin and said, "I am a ronin from Echigo. I am short of money and in difficulties. We are both warriors. Please help me out."

Rokurozaemon got angry and said, "It is a discourtesy to mention that we are both warriors. If I were in your state of affairs, I'd cut my stomach open. Rather than being out of money for the road and exposing yourself to shame, cut your stomach open right where you are!" It is said that the beggar moved off.

In Makiguchi Yohei's life he was kaishaku for many men. When a certain Kanahara was to commit seppuku, Yohei consented to be kaishaku. Kanahara thrust the sword into his belly, but at the point of pulling it across he was unable to go further. Yohei approached his side, yelled "Ei!" and stamped his foot. From this impetus, Kanahara was able to pull his sword straight across his belly. After finishing the kaishaku, it is said that Yohei shed tears and said, "Even though he was formerly a good friend of mine... " This is a story of Master Sukeemon's.

At the time of a certain person's seppuku, when the kaishaku a cut off his head, a little bit of skin was left hanging and the head was not entirely separated from the body. The official observer said, "There's some left." The kaishaku got angry, took hold of the head, and cutting it completely off, held it above eye level and said, "Take a look!" It is said that it was rather chilling. This is a story of Master Sukeemon's.

In the practice of past times, there were instances when the head flew off. It was said that it is best to cut leaving a little skin remaining so that it doesn't fly oft in the direction of the verifying officials. However, at present it is best to cut clean through.

A man who had cut off fifty heads once said, "According to the head, there are cases when even the trunk of a body will bring some reaction to you. Cutting off just three heads, at first there is no reaction and you can cut well. But when you pet to four or five, you feel quite a bit of reaction. At any rate, since this is a very important matter, if one always plans on bringing the head to the ground there should be no mistakes."

When Lord Nabeshima Tsunashige was a child, Iwamura Kuranosuke was ordered to the position of elder. On one occasion Kuranosuke saw that there were gold coins before the young Tsunashige and asked the attending retainer, "For what reason have you brought these out before the young master?" The attendant replied, "The master just now heard that a gift had been brought for him. He said that he had not yet seen it, so I brought it out for him." Kuranosuke scolded the man severely, saying, "To place such base things before a person of importance is the extremity of careless ness. You may also consider them something not to be put before the lord's son. Attending retainers should henceforth be very mindful of this."

Another time, when Lord Tsunashige was about twenty years old, he once went to the mansion at Naekiyama for some diversion. As the party neared the mansion, he asked for a walking stick. His sandal carrier, Miura Jibuzaemon, fashioned a stick and was about to give it to the young lord. Kuranosake saw this, quickly took the stick from Jibuzaemon, and scolded him severely, saying, ' 'Will you make our important young lord a sluggard ? Even if he should ask for a stick, it should not be given to him. This is carelessness on the part of the attending retainer."

Jibuzaernon was later promoted to the rank of teakiyari, and Tsunetomo heard this story directly from him.

From the 9th Chapter

When Shimomura Shoun was on service at the castle, Lord Naoshige said, "How wonderful it is that Katsushige is so vigorous and powerful for his age. In wrestling with his peers he even beat those who are older than he is."

Shoun replied, "Even though I'm an old man, I'll bet I'm best at seated wrestling." So saying, he jerked up Katsushige and threw him so forcefully that it hurt. He then said, "To be prideful about your strength while your mettle is not yet established is likely to bring you shame in the midst of people. You are weaker than you look." Then he withdrew. At the time when Matsuda Yohei was an intimate friend of Ishii Jinku's, there developed some bad feeling's between the former and Nozoe Jinbei. Yohei sent word to Jinbei saying, "Please come and I will settle this matter once and for all." Then he and Jinku set out together and, coming to the Yamabushi mansion at Kihara, they crossed the only bridge there was and destroyed it. Talking over the circumstances of the discord, they examined them from all sides and found no reason to fight. But when they decided to turn around and go home, there was, of course, no bridge

While they were looking for an appropriate way of crossing the moat, the men whom the two had challenged could be seen approaching stealthily. Yohei and Jinku saw this and said, "We have passed the point of no return, and may as well fight rather than be disgraced at a later date. " The battle lasted for some time. Seriously wounded, Yohei fell down between two fields. Jinbei also received a deep wound, and with blood flowing into his eyes was unable to find Yohei. While Jinbei thus searched about blindly, Yohei was able to hold him off from his prone position and in the end cut him down. But when he attempted to deliver the finishing blow, having no strength left in his hand, he pierced Jinbei's neck by pushing the sword with his foot.

At this point, friends arrived and accompanied Yohei back. After his wounds healed he was ordered to commit seppuku. At that time he called his friend Jinku, and they drank a farewell cup together.

Okubo Toemon of Shioda ran a wineshop for Nabeshima Kenmotsu. Lord Okura, the son of Nabeshima Kai no kami, was a cripple and confined indoors in a place called Mine. He harbored wrestlers and liked rowdies. The wrestlers would often go to nearby villages and cause disturbances. One time they went to Toemon's place, drank sake and talked unreasonably, bringing Toemon into an argument. He met them with a halberd, but as there were two of them he was cut down.

His son, Kannosuke, was fifteen years old and was in the midst of studies at the Jozeiji when he was informed of the incident. Galloping off, he took a short sword about sixteen inches in length, joined combat with the two big men, and in a short time finished them both off. Although Kannosuke received thirteen wounds, he recovered. Later he was called Doko and is said to have become very adept at massage.

It is said that Tokunaga Kichizaemon repeatedly com- plained, "I've grown so old that now, even if there were to be a battle, I wouldn't be able to do anything. Still, I would like to die by galloping into the midst of the enemy and being struck down and killed. It would be a shame to do nothing more than to die in one's bed."

It is said that the priest Gyojaku heard this when he was an acolyte. Gyojaku's master was the priest Yemen, who was Kichizaemon's youngest child.

When Sagara Kyuma was requested to become a chief retainer, he said to Nabeshima Heizaemon, "For some reason I have been increasingly well treated by the master and now have been requested to take a high rank. Not having a good retainer, my affairs are liable to be in disorder. It is my request that you give me your retainer, Takase Jibusaemon." Heizaemon listened to him and consented, saying, "It is very gratifying that you have kept an eye on my retainer. I will therefore do as you ask."

But when he related this to Jibusaemon, the latter said, "I should reply directly to Master Kyuma." He then went to Kyuma's place and talked with him. Jibusaemon told Kyuma, "I know it is a great honor that you have thought well of me and have made this request. But a retainer is a person who cannot change masters. As you are of high rank, if I were to become your retainer my life would be replete, but that repleteness would be a vexation to me. Because Her zaemon is of low rank and is hard pressed, we live by eating cheap rice gruel. Yet that is sweet enough. Please think this over."

Kyuma was extremely impressed.

A certain man went of somewhere and on returning home late at night, found that a strange man had slipped into the house and was committing adultery with his wife. He thereupon killed the man. He then broke down a wall and propped up a bale of rice, and by this arrangement submitted to the authorities that he had killed a thief. Thus it went without mishap. After some time had passed he divorced his wife and the affair was finished.

When a certain person returned home from some place or other, he found his wife committing adultery with a retainer in the bedroom. When he drew near the two, his retainer fled through the kitchen. He then went into the bedroom and slew his wife.

Calling the maidservant, he explained what had happened and said, "Because this would bring shame to the children, it should be covered up as death by illness and I will need considerable help. If you think that this is too much for you, I may as well kill you too for your part in this serious crime."

She replied, "If you will spare my life, I will go on as if I don't know anything. " She rearranged the room and set out the corpse in its nightclothes. Then, after sending a man to the doctor's place two or three times saying that there was a sudden illness, they sent a last messenger saying that it was too late and there was no longer any need to come. The wife's uncle was called in and told about the illness, and he was convinced. The entire affair was passed oft as death by illness, and to the end no one knew the truth. At a later date the retainer was dismissed. This affair happened in Edo.

At New Year's in the third year of Keicho at a place in Korea called Yolsan, when the armies of the Ming appeared by the hundreds of thousands, the Japanese troops were amazed and watched with bated breath. Lord Naoshige said, "Well, well. That's a great number of men! I wonder how many hundreds of thousands there are?"

Jin'emon said, "In Japan, for something that's numberless we say 'as many as the hairs on a three-year-old calf.' This would certainly live up to the number of hairs on a three-year-old calf!" It is said that everybody laughed and regained their spirits.

Later, Lord Katsushige was hunting at MI. Shiroishi and told Nakano Matabei about this. ' 'Except for your father who spoke in such a way, there was no one who said even a word."

Nakano Jin'emon constantly said, "A person who serves when treated kindly by the master is not a retainer. But one who serves when the master is being heartless and unreasonable is a retainer. You should understand this principle well."

When Yamamoto Jin'emon was eighty years old, he be- came ill. At one point, he seemed to be on the verge of groaning, and someone said to him, "You'll feel better if you groan. Go ahead. *' But he replied, "Such is not the case. The name of Yamamoto Jin'emon is known by everyone, and I have shown up well throughout a whole lifetime. To let people hear my groaning voice in my last moments would never do." It is said that he did not let out a groan to the very end.

A certain son of Mori Monbei got into a fight and returned home wounded. Asked by Monbei, "What did you do to your opponent?" his son replied, "I cut him down."

When Monbei asked, "Did you deliver the coup de grace?" his son replied, "Indeed I did."'

Then Monbei said, "You have certainly done well, and there is nothing to regret. Now, even if you fled you would have to commit seppuku anyway. When your mood improves, commit seppuku, and rather than die by another's hand, you can die by your father's. " And soon after he performed kaishaku for his son.

A man in the same group as Aiura Genzaemon committed some nefarious deed, and so the group leader gave him a note, condemning him to death, which was to be taken to Genzaemon's place. Genzaemon perused the note and then said to the man, "It says here that I should kill you, so I will do away with you on the eastern bank. Previously you have practiced such things as swordsmanship.... Now fight with all you've got."

The man replied, "I will do as you say," and with Genzaemon alone accompanying him, they left the house. They had gone about twenty yards along the edge of the moat when a retainer of Genzaernon's yelled out, "Hey, Hey!" from the other side. As Genzaemon was turning around, the condemned man attacked him with his sword. Genzaemon ducked backwards, drew his sword, and cut the man down. He then returned home.

He put the clothes he had been wearing at that time into a chest and locked them up, never showing them to anyone for the rest of his life. After he died the clothes were examined, and it was seen that they were rent. This was told by his son, Genzaemon.

Okubo Doko is said to have remarked:

Everyone says that no masters of the arts will appear as the world comes to an end. This is something that I cannot claim to understand. Plants such as peonies, azaleas and camellias will be able to produce beautiful flowers, end of the world or not. If men would give some thought to this fact, they would understand. And if people took notice of the masters of even these times, they would be able to say that there are masters in the various arts. But people become imbued with the idea that the world has come to an end and no longer put forth any effort. This is a shame. There is no fault in the times.

While Fukahori Magoroku was still living as a dependent second son, he once went hunting at Fukahori, and his retainer, mistaking him for a wild boar in the darkness of the undergrowth, fired the rifle, wounding him in the knee and causing him to fall from a great height. The retainer, greatly upset, stripped himself to the waist and was about to commit seppuku. Magoroku said, "You can cut your stomach open later. I don't feel well, so bring me some water to drink." The retainer ran about and obtained some water for his master to drink and in the process calmed down. After that the retainer was again about to commit seppuku, but Magoroku forcibly stopped him. Upon returning they checked in with the man on guard, and Magoroku asked his father, Kanzaemen, to forgive the retainer.

Kanzaemon said to the retainer, "It was an unexpected mistake, so do not be worried. There is no need for reservation. Continue with your work."

A man by the name of Takagi got into an argument with three farmers in the neighborhood, was soundly beaten out in the fields, and returned home. His wife said to him, "Haven't you forgotten about the matter of death?" "Definitely not!" he replied.

His wife then retorted, "At any rate, a man dies only once. Of the various ways of dying -dying of disease, being cut down in battle, seppuku or being beheaded--to die ignominiously would be a shame," and went outside. She soon returned, carefully put the two children to bed, prepared some torches, dressed herself for battle after nightfall, and then said, "When I went out to survey the scene a bit earlier, it seemed that the three men went into one place for a discussion. Now is the right time. Let's go quickly!" So saying, they went out with the husband in the lead, burning torches and wearing short swords. They broke into their opponents' place and dispersed them, both husband and wife slashing about and killing two of the men and wounding the other. The husband was later ordered to commit seppuku.

From the 10th Chapter

There was a certain retainer of Ikeda Shingen's who started an argument with a man, grappled him to the ground, thrashed him soundly, and trampled on him until his companions ran up and pulled them apart. The elders conferred over this and said, "The man who was trampled should be punished." Shingen heard this and said, "A fight is something that goes to the finish. A man who forgets the Way of the Samurai and does not use his sword will be forsaken by the gods and Buddhas. As an example to subsequent retainers, both men should be crucified." The men who had pulled them apart were banished. In Yui Shosetsu's military instructions, "The Way of the Three Ultimates," there is a passage on the character of karma.' He received an oral teaching of about eighteen chapters concerning the Greater Bravery and the Lesser Bravery. He neither wrote them down nor committed them to memory but rather forgot them completely. Then, in facing real situations, he acted on impulse and the things that he had learned became wisdom of his own. This is the character of karma.

When faced with a crisis, if one puts some spittle on his earlobe and exhales deeply through his nose, he will overcome anything at hand. This is a secret matter. Furthermore, when experiencing a rush of blood to the head, if one puts spittle on the upper part of one's ear, it will soon go away.

Tzu Ch'an was on the point of death when someone asked him how to govern the country. He replied:

There is nothing that surpasses ruling with benevolence. However, to put into practice enough benevolent governing to rule the country is difficult. To do this lukewarmly will result in neglect. If governing with benevolence is difficult, then it is best to govern strictly. To govern strictly means to be strict before things have arisen, and to do things in such a way that evil will not arise. To be strict after the evil has arisen is like laying a snare. There are few people who will make mistakes with fire after having once been burned. Of people who regard water lightly, many have been drowned.

A certain man said, "I know the shapes of Reason and of Woman." When asked about this, he replied, "Reason is four-cornered and will not move even in an extreme situation. Woman is round. One can say that she does not distinguish between good and evil or right and wrong and tum- bles into any place at all."

The basic meaning of etiquette is to be quick at both the beginning and end and tranquil in the middle. Mitani Chizaemon heard this and said, "That's just like being a kaishaku.

Fukae Angen accompanied an acquaintance of his to the priest Tesshu of Osaka, and at first said privately to the priest, "This man aspires to study Buddhism and hopes to receive your teaching. He is a man of rather high determination."

Soon after the interview the priest said, "Angen is a man who does harm to others. He said that this man is a good man, but wherein is his goodness? There was no goodness visible to Tesshu's eyes. It is not a good idea to praise people carelessly. When praised, both wise and foolish become prideful. To praise is to do harm."

When Hotta Kaga no kami Masamori was a page to the shogun, he was so headstrong that the shogun wished to test what was at the bottom of his heart. To do this, the shogun heated a pair of tongs and placed them in the hearth. Masamori's custom was to go to the other side of the hearth, take the tongs, and greet the master. This time, when he unsuspectingly picked up the tongs, his hands were immediately turned. As he did obeisance in his usual manner, however, the shogun quickly pot up and took the tongs from him.

A certain person said, "When a castle is being surrendered, as long as there are one or two men within it who are determined to hold on, the defending forces will not be of one accord, and in the end no one will hold the castle. "In the taking of the castle, if when the man who is to receive it approaches and the one or two men who are determined to hold on to it lightly fire on him from the shadows, the man will be alarmed and the battle will be on. In such a case, even though it is unwillingly done, the castle will have to be stormed. This is called being forced to besiege a castle by those besieged."

The Buddhist priest Ryozan wrote down some generalities concerning Takanobu's battles. A certain priest saw this and criticized him, saying, "It is inappropriate for a priest to write about a military commander. No matter how successful his writing style may be, since he is not acquainted with military things, he is liable to be mistaken in understanding a famous general's mind. It is irreverent to pass on misconceptions concerning a famous general to later generations."

A certain person said, "In the Saint's mausoleum there is a poem that goes:

> *If in one's heart*
> *He follows the path of sincerity,*
> *Though he does not pray*
> *Will not the gods protect him?*

What is this path of sincerity?"

A man answered him by saying, "You seem to like poetry. I will answer you with a poem.

> *As everything in this world is but a shame,*
> *Death is the only sincerity.*

It is said that becoming as a dead man in one's daily living is the following of the path of sincerity."

If you cut a face lengthwise, urinate on it, and trample on it with straw sandals, it is said that the skin will come off. This was heard by the priest Gyojaku when he was in Kyoto. It is information to be treasured.

One of Matsudaira Sagami no kami's retainers went to Kyoto on a matter of debt collection and took up lodgings by renting living quarters in a townhouse. One day while standing out front watching the people go by, he heard a passer-by say, "They say that Lord Matsudaira's men are involved in a fight right now." The retainer thought, "How worrisome that some of my companions are involved in a fight. There are some men to relieve those at Edo staying here. Perhaps these are the men involved." He asked the passer-by of the location, but when he arrived out of breath, his companions had already been cut down and their adver- saries were at the point of delivering the coup de grace. He quickly let out a yell, cut the two men down, and returned to his lodgings.

This matter was made known to an official of the shogunate, and the man was called up before him and questioned. "You gave assistance in your companions' fight and thus disregarded the government's ordinance. This is true beyond a doubt, isn't it?"

The man replied, "I am from the country, and it is difficult for me to understand everything that Your Honor is saying. Would you please repeat that?"

The official got angry and said, "Is there something wrong with your ears? Didn't you abet a fight, commit bloodshed, disregard the government's ordinance, and break the law?"

The man then replied, "I have at length understood what you are saying. Although you say that I have broken the law and disregarded the government's ordinance, I have by no means done so. The reason for this is that all living things value their lives, and this goes without saying for human beings. I, especially, value my life. However, I thought that to hear a rumor that one's friends are involved in a fight and to pretend not to hear this is not to preserve the Way of the Samurai, so I ran to the place of action. To shamelessly return home after seeing my friends struck down would surely have lengthened my life, but this too would be disregarding the Way. In observing the Way, one will throw away his own precious life. Thus, in order to preserve the Way of the Samurai and not to disregard the Samurai Ordinances, I quickly threw away my life at that place. I beg that you execute me immediately."

The official was very impressed and later dismissed the matter, communicating to Lord Matsudaira, "You have a very able samurai in your service. Please treasure him."

This is among the sayings of the priest Banker. "Not to borrow the strength of another, nor to rely on one's own strength ; to cut off past and future thoughts, and not to live within the everyday mind... then the Great Way is right before one's eyes."

Lord Soma's family genealogy, called the Chiken marokashi, was the best in Japan. One year when his mansion suddenly caught fire and was burning to the ground, Lord Soma said, "I feel no regret about the house and all its furnishings, even if they burn to the very last piece, because they are things that can be replaced later on. I only regret that I was unable to take out the genealogy, which is my family's most precious treasure."

There was one samurai among those attending him who said, "I will go in and take it out."

Lord Soma and the others all laughed and said, "The house is already engulfed in flames. How are you going to take it out?"

Now this man had never been loquacious, nor had he been particularly useful, but being a man who did things from beginning to end, he was engaged as an attendant. At this point he said, "I have never been of use to my master because I'm so careless, but I have lived resolved that someday my life should be of use to him. This seems to be that time." And he leapt into the flames.

After the fire had been extinguished the master said, "Look for his remains. What a pity!"

Looking everywhere, they found his burnt corpse in the garden adjacent to the living quarters. When they turned it over, blood flowed out of the stomach. The man had cut open his stomach and placed the genealogy inside and it was not damaged at all. From this time on it was called the "Blood Genealogy.'

According to a certain person's story, "In the tradition of the I Ching, it is a mistake to think that it is something for divination. Its essence is non-divination. This can be seen by the tact that the Chinese character 'I' is read as 'change.' Although one divines good fortune, if he does evil it will become bad fortune. And although he divines bad fortune, if he does good it will become good fortune.

"Confucius' saying, 'By setting myself to the task for many years and in the end learning change [I], I should make no big mistakes,' is not a matter of learning the I Ching. It means by studying the essence of change and conducting oneself for many years in the Way of Good, one should make no mistakes."

Hirano Gonbei was one of the Men of Seven Spears who advanced straight up the hill at the battle of Shizugadake. At a later date he was invited to become one of Lord Ieyasu's hatamoto. Once he was being entertained at Master Hosekawa's. The master said, "Master Gonbei's bravery is not a hidden matter in Japan. It is truly a shame that such a man of bravery has been placed in a low rank such as you are in now. This must be contrary to your wishes. If you were to become a retainer of mine, I would give you half the domain."

Giving no answer at all, Gonbei suddenly pot up from his seat, went out to the veranda, stood facing the house, and urinated. Then he said, "If I were the master's retainer, it would never do to urinate from here."

When the priest Daiyu from Sanshu was making a sick call at a certain place, he was told, "The man has just now died." Daiyu said, "Such a thing shouldn't have happened at this time. Didn't this occur from insufficient treatment? What a shame!"

Now the doctor happened to be there at that time and heard what was said from the other side of the shoji. He got extraordinarily angry and came out and said, "I heard Your Reverence say that the man died from insufficient treatment. Since I am a rather bungling doctor, this is probably true. I have heard that a priest embodies the power of the Buddhist Law. Let me see you bring this dead man back to life, for without such evidence Buddhism is worthless."

Daiyu was put out by this, but he felt that it would be un- pardonable for a priest to put a blemish on Buddhism, so he said, "I will indeed show you how to bring his life back by prayer. Fleas' wait a moment. I must go prepare myself," and returned to the temple. Soon he came back and sat in meditation next to the corpse. Pretty soon the dead man began to breathe and then completely revived. It is said that he lived on for another half a year. As this was something told directly to the priest Tannen, there is nothing mistaken about it.

When telling of the way he prayed, Daiyu said, "This is something not practiced in our sect, so I didn't know of any way of prayer. I simply set my heart for the sake of the Buddhist Law, returned to the temple, sharpened a short sword that had been given as an offering to the temple, and put it in my robe. Then I faced the dead man and prayed, 'If the strength of the Buddhist Law exists, come back to life immediately. ' Since I was thus committed, if he hadn't come back to life, I was resolved to the point of cutting open my stomach and dying embracing the corpse."

When Yamamoto Gorozaemon went to the priest Tetsugyu in Edo wanting to hear something about Buddhism, Tetsugyo said, "Buddhism gets rid of the discriminating mind. It is nothing more than this. I can give you an illustration in terms of the warrior. The Chinese character for "cowardice" is made by adding the character for "meaning" to the character radical for "mind". Now "meaning" is "discrimination, " and when a man attaches discrimination to his true mind, he becomes a coward. In the Way of the Samurai can a man be courageous when discrimination arises? I suppose you can get the idea from this."

According to what one of the elders said, taking an enemy on the battlefield is like a hawk taking a bird. Even though it enters into the midst of a thousand of them, it gives no attention to any bird other than the one that it has first marked.

Moreover, what is called a tezuke no kubi is a head that one has taken after having made the declaration, "I will take that warrior wearing such and such armor."

In the Kiyogunkan one person said, "When facing the enemy, I feel as if I have just entered darkness. Because of this I get heavily wounded. Although you have fought with many famous men, you have never been wounded. Why is that?"

The other man answered, "When I have faced the enemy, of course it is like being in the dark. But if at that time I tranquilize my mind, it becomes like a night lit by a pale moon. If I begin my attack from that point, I feel as though I will not be wounded. " This is the situation at the moment of truth.

A rifle ball hitting the water will ricochet. It is said that if one marks it with a knife or dents it with his teeth, it will pass through the water. Moreover, when the master is hunting or some such thing, if one marks the ball with a sign, it will come in handy in case of a mishap.

When Master Owari, Master Kit and Master Mite were around the age of ten, one day Lord Ieyasu was with them in the garden and knocked down a big wasps' nest. A great number of wasps flew out, and Master Owari and Master Kit were frightened and ran away. But Master Mite picked off the wasps that were on his face, threw them away one by one, and did not run away.

Another time, when Lord Ieyasu was roasting a great number of chestnuts in a large hearth, he invited the boys to join him. When the chestnuts got sufficiently hot, they all started to pop out at once. Two of the boys were frightened and moved away. Master Mite, however, not the least bit frightened, picked up the ones that had popped out and threw them back into the hearth.

In order to study medicine Eguchi Than went to old Yoshida lchian's place in the Bancho area of Edo. At that time, there was in the neighborhood a teacher of swordsmanship, to whom he used to go for training from time to time. There was a ronin pupil there who one day came up to toan and said as a parting remark, "I am now going to realize a longcherished ambition, one I have had for many years. I am informing you of this because you have always been friendly to me." Then he walked away. Than felt uneasy about this, and when he followed him, he could see a man wearing a braided hat coming from the opposite direction.

Now the sword teacher was about eight or ten yards ahead of the ronin, and in passing by the man with the hat he soundly struck the man's scabbard with his own. When the man looked around, the ronin knocked off' the man's hat and announced in a loud voice that his purpose was revenge. With the man's attention being distracted by the confusion, he was easily cut down. A tremendous amount of congratulations came from the nearby mansions and townhouses. It is said that they even brought out money for him. This was a favorite story of Toan's.

Once when the priest Ungo of Matsushima was passing through the mountains at night, he was set upon by mountain bandits. Ungo said, "I am a man of this area, not a pilgrim. I have no money at all, but you can have these clothes if you like. Please spare my life."

The bandits said, "Well, our efforts have been in vain. We don't need anything like clothes," and passed on. They had gone about two hundred yards when Ungo turned back and called to them, "I have broken the commandment against lying. In my confusion I forgot that I had one piece of silver in my moneybag. I am truly regretful I said that I had nothing at all. I have it here now, so please take it." The mountain bandits were deeply impressed, cut off their hair right there, and became his disciples.

In Edo four or five hatamoto gathered together one night for a game of go. At one point one of them got up to go to the toilet, and while he was gone an argument broke out. One man was cut down, the lights were extinguished, and the place was in an uproar. When the man came running back, he yelled, "Everybody calm down I This is really over nothing at all. Put the lamps back on and let me handle this." After the lamps had been relighted and everyone had calmed down, the man suddenly struck off the head of the other man involved in the argument. He then said, "My luck as a samurai having run out, I was not present at the fight. If this were seen as cowardice, I would be ordered to commit seppuku. Even if that didn't happen, I would have no excuse if it were said that I had fled to the toilet, and I would still have no recourse other than seppuku. I have done this thing because I thought I would die having cut down an adversary rather than die having shamed myself alone." When the shogun heard of this matter, he praised the man.

Once a group of ten blind masseuses were traveling together in the mountains, and when they began to pass along the top of a precipice, they all became very cautious, their legs shook, and they were in general struck with terror. Just then the leading man stumbled and fell of the cliff. Those that were left all wailed, "Ahh, ahh I How piteous!" But the masseuse who had fallen veiled up from below, "Don't be afraid. Although I fell, it was nothing. I am now rather at ease. Before falling I kept thinking 'What will I do if I fall?' and there was no end to my anxiety. But now I've settled down. If the rest of you want to be at ease, fall quickly!"

Hojo Awa no kami once gathered together his disciples in the martial arts and called in a physiognomist, who was popular in Edo at the time, to have him determine whether they were brave men or cowards. He had them see the man one by one, telling them, "If he determines 'bravery,' you should strive all the more. If it is 'cowardice,' you should strive by throwing away your life. It's something that you're born with, so there's no shame in it."

Hirose Denzaemon was then about twelve or thirteen years old. When he sat down in front of the physiognomist, he said in a bristling voice, "if you read cowardice in me, I'll cut you down with a single blow!"

When there is something to be said, it is better if it is said right away. If it is said later, it will sound like an excuse. Moreover, it is occasionally good to really overwhelm your opponent. Also, in addition to having spoken sufficiently it is the highest sort of victory to teach your opponent some- thing that will be to his benefit. This is in accordance with the Way.

The priest Ryoi said: The samurai of old were mortified by the idea of dying in bed; they hoped only to die on the battlefield. A priest, too, will be unable to fulfill the Way unless he is of this disposition. The man who shuts himself away and avoids the company of men is a coward. Only evil thoughts allow one to imagine that something good can be done by shutting oneself away. For even if one does some good thing by shutting himself away, he will be unable to keep the way open for future generations by promulgating the clan traditions.

Takeda Shingen's retainer, Amari Bizen no kami, was killed in action and his son, Tozo, at the age of eighteen took over his father's position as an armed horseman attached to a general. Once a certain man in his group received a deep wound, and since the blood would not clot, Tozo ordered him to drink the feces of a red-haired horse mixed with water. The wounded man said, "Life is dear to me. How can I drink horse feces?' Tozo heard this and said, "What an admirably brave warrior! What you say is reasonable. However, the basic meaning of loyalty requires us to preserve our lives and gain victory for our master on the battlefield. Well, then, I'll drink some for you." Then he drank some himself and banded over the cup to the man who took the medicine gratefully and recovered.

From the 11th Chapter

In the "Notes on Martial Laws" it is written that:

The phrase, "Win first, fight later, " can be summed up in the two words, "Win beforehand." The resourcefulness of times of peace is the military preparation for times of war. With five hundred allies one can defeat an enemy force of ten thousand.

When advancing on the enemy's castle and then pulling back, do not retreat by the main road, but rather by the side roads.

One should lay one's dead and wounded allies face down in the direction of the enemy.

It is a matter of course that a warrior's attitude should be to be in the vanguard during an attack and in the rear during a retreat. In approaching for the attack he does not forget to wait for the right moment. In waiting for the right moment he never forgets the attack. A helmet is usually thought to be very heavy, but when one is attacking a castle or something similar, and arrows, bullets, large rocks, great pieces of wood and the like are corning down, it will not seem the least bit so.

Once when Master Yagyu was before the shogun on some business, a number of bamboo swords fell from the ceiling. He quickly clasped his hands above his head and was not struck.

Again, at a certain time when he was summoned, the shogun was waiting behind cover with a bamboo sword ready to strike him. Master Yagyu called out in a loud voice, "This is for your own discipline. Don't look!" As the shogun turned around, Master Yagyu stepped up and took the sword out of his hand.

A person who does not want to be struck by the enemy s arrows will have no divine protection. For a man who does not wish to be hit by the arrows of a common soldier, but rather by those of a warrior of fame, there will be the protection for which he has asked.

Wind-bells are things that are used during campaigns in order to know the direction of the wind. For night attacks, fire can be set windward while the attack can be carried out from the opposite direction. Your allies should be mindful of this also. One should always hang wind-bells in order to know the direction of the wind.

Lord Aki declared that he would not have his descendants learn military tactics. He said, "On the battlefield, once discretion starts it cannot be stopped. One will not break through to the enemy with discretion. Indiscretion is most important when in front of the tiger's den. Therefore, if one were informed of military tactics, he would have many doubts, and there will be no end to the matter. My descendants will not practice military tactics.'

According to Lord Naoshige's words:

There is something to which every young samurai should pay attention. During times of peace when listening to stories of battle, one should never say, "In facing such a situation, what would a person do?" Such words are out of the question. How will a man who has doubts even in his own room achieve anything on the battlefield? There is a saying that goes, "No matter what the circumstances might be, one should be of the mind to win. One should be holding the first spear to strike." Even though you have put your life on the line, there is nothing to be done when the situation doesn't go as planned.

Takeda Shingen once said, "If there was a man who could kill Lord Ieyasu, I would give him a handsome reward." Hearing this, a boy of thirteen entered into the service of Lord Ieyasu and one night when he saw that Ieyasu had retired, took a stab at his bedding. Lord Ieyasu was actually in the next room silently reading a sutra, but he quickly grabbed the boy.

When the investigation was held, the boy related the facts honestly, and Lord Ieyasu said, "You seemed to be an excellent young man, so I employed you on friendly terms. Now, however, I am even more impressed by you." He then sent the lad back to Shingen.

One night some samurai from Karatsu gathered together and were playing go. Master Kitabatake was watching the game, and when he offered a suggestion, one man attacked him with a sword. After the people around them had stopped the man, Master Kitabatake pinched out the light of the candle and said, "It was nothing more than my own indiscretion, and I apologize. The sword hit the go case; I was not the least bit wounded."

Then the candle was relighted, but when the man came to reconciliate and offer him a sake cup, Kitabatake cut the man's head off with one blow. Presently he said, "My thigh having been cut through, it was difficult to offer any resistance, but by binding my leg with my coat and supporting myself with the go board, I have done this thing." Having said this, he expired.

There is nothing so painful as regret. We would all like to be without it. However, when we are very happy and become elated, or when we habitually jump into something thoughtlessly, later we are distraught, and it is for the most part because we did not think ahead and are now regretful. Certainly we should try not to become dejected, and when very happy should calm our minds.

These are teachings of Yamamoto Jin'emon:

Singlemindedness is all-powerful.

Tether even a roasted chicken.

Continue to spur a running horse.

A man who will criticize you openly carries no connivance.

A man exists for a generation, but his name lasts to the end of time.

Money is a thing that will be there when asked for. A good man is not so easily found.

Walk with a real man one hundred yards and he'll tell you at least seven lies.

To ask when you already know is politeness. To ask when you don't know is the rule.

Wrap your intentions in needles of pine.

One should not open his mouth wide or yawn in front of another. Do this behind your fan or sleeve.

A straw hat or helmet should be worn tilled toward the front.

It is a principle of the art of war that one should simply lay down his life and strike. If one's opponent also does the same, it is an even match. Defeating one's opponent is then a matter of faith and destiny.

One should not show his sleeping quarters to other people. The times of deep sleep and dawning are very important. One should be mindful of this. This is from a story by Nagahama lnosuke.

When one departs for the front, he should carry rice in a bag. His underwear should be made from the skin of a badger. This way he will not have lice. In a long campaign, lice are troublesome.

When meeting with the enemy, there is a way to determine his strength. If he has his head cast down, he will appear black and is strong. If he is looking upward, he will appear white and is weak. This is from a story by Natsume Toneri.

If a warrior is not unattached to life and death, he will be of no use whatsoever. The saying that "All abilities come from one mind" sounds as though it has to do with sentient matters, but it is in fact a matter of being unattached to life and death. With such non-attachment one can accomplish any feat. Martial arts and the like are related to this insofar as they can lead to the Way.

To calm one's mind, one swallows his saliva. This is a secret matter. When one becomes angry, it is the same. Putting spittle on one's forehead is also good. In the Yoshida school of archery, swallowing one's spittle is the secret principle of the art.

A certain general said, "For soldiers other than officers, if they would test their armor, they should test only the front. Furthermore, while ornamentation on armor is unnecessary, one should be very careful about the appearance of his helmet. It is something that accompanies his head to the enemy's camp."

Nakano Jin'emon said, "Learning such things as military tactics is useless. If one does not strike out by simply closing his eyes and rushing into the enemy, even if it is only one step, he will be of no use." This was also the opinion of Iyanaga Sasuke.

In Natsume Toneri's "Military Stories" it is written: "Look at the soldiers of recent times! Even in long battles there are hardly one or two occasions when blood is washed with blood. One should not be negligent." Toneri was a ronin from the Kamigata area.

To have execution grounds in a place where travelers come and go is useless. The executions in Edo and the Kamigala area are meant to be an example for the whole country. But the executions in one province are only for an example in that province. If crimes are many, it is a province's shame. How would this look to other provinces?

With the passing of time, the criminal will forget the reason for his crime ; it is best to execute him on the spot.

Matsudaira Izu no kami said to Master Mizuno Kenmotsu, "You're such a useful person, it's a shame that you're so short."

Kenmotsu replied, "That's true. Sometimes things in this world don't go the way we would like. Now if I were to cut off your head and attach it to the bottom of my feet, I would be taller. But that's something that couldn't be done."

A certain person was passing by the town of Yae when suddenly his stomach began to hurt. He stopped at a house on a side street and asked to use the toilet. There was only a young woman there, but she took him to the back and showed him where it was. Just as he was taking off his hakama and going into the toilet, the woman's husband came home and accused them both of adultery. In the end, it became a public matter.

Lord Naoshige heard the case and said, "Even if this is not a matter of adultery, it is the same as adultery to take off one's hakama without hesitation in a place where there is an unaccompanied woman, and in the woman's case to allow someone to disrobe while her husband is absent from home."

It is said that they were both condemned to death for this act.

In assessing the enemy's castle there is a saying that goes, "Smoke and mist are like looking at a spring mountain. After the rain is like viewing a clear day." There is weakness in perfect clarity.

Among the words spoken by great generals, there are some that were said offhandedly. One should not receive these words in the same manner, however.

People who have an intelligent appearance will not be outstanding even if they do something good, and if they do something normal, people will think them lacking. But if a person who is thought of as having a gentle disposition does even a slightly good thing, he will be praised by people.

On the fourteenth day of the seventh month in the third year of Shotoku, there were some cooks in the midst of preparations for the

Ben Festival in the outer citadel of the castle. One of them, Hara Jurozaemon, unsheathed his sword and cut off the head of Sagara Genzaemon. Mawatari Rokuuemon, Aiura Tarobei, Kola Kinbei and Kakihara Riemen all ran away in confusion. When Jurozaemon sighted Kinbei and started chasing him, the latter fled to the foot soldiers' gathering area. There, the daimyo's palanquin attendant, Tanaka Takeuemon, stood against Jurozaemon and took away his still drawn sword. Ishirnaru San'emon chased Jurozaemon, and when they came to the foot soldiers' area, assisted Takeuemon.

The punishment was given on the twenty-ninth day of the eleventh month in the same year. Jurozaemon was bound with rope and beheaded. Rokuuemon, Tarobei, Kinbei and Riemon were banished, and San'emon was ordered to retire. Takeuemon was rewarded with three pieces of silver.

It was later said that Takeuemon had been slow to act, for he had not bound the man at that time.

Among Takeda Shingen's retainers there were men of matchless courage, but when Katsuyori was killed in the fight at Tenmokuzan, they all fled. Tsuchiya Sozo, a warrior who had been in disfavor for many years, came out alone, however, and said, "I wonder where all the men are who spoke so bravely every day? I shall return the master's favors to me." And he fell alone in battle.

The essentials of speaking are in not speaking at all. If you think that you can finish something without speaking, finish it without saying a single word. If there is something that cannot be accomplished without speaking, one should speak with few words, in a way that will accord well with reason.

To open one's mouth indiscriminately brings shame, and there are many times when people will turn their backs on such a person.

A devotee of the Nembutsu recites the Buddha's name with every incoming and outgoing breath in order never to forget the Buddha. A retainer, too, should be just like this in thinking of his master. Not to forget one's master is the most fundamental thing for a retainer.

Men who did well at the time of their death were men of real bravery. There are many examples of such. But people who talk in an accomplished fashion every day yet are agitated at the time of their death can be known not to have true bravery.

In the secret principles of Yagyu Tajima no kami Munenori there is the saying, "There are no military tactics for a man of great strength." As proof of this, there was once a certain vassal of the shogun who came to Master Yagyu and asked to become a disciple. Master Yagyu said, "You seem to be a man who is very accomplished in some school of martial art. Let us make the master-disciple contract after I learn the name of the school."

But the man replied, "I have never practiced one of the martial arts."

Master Yagyu said, "Have you come to make sport of Tajima no kami? Is my perception amiss in thinking that you are a teacher to the shogun?" But the man swore to it and Master Yagyu then asked, "That being so, do you not have some deep conviction?"

The man replied, "When I was a child, I once became suddenly aware that a warrior is a man who does not hold his life in regret. Since I have held that in my heart for many years, it has become a deep conviction, and today I never think about death. Other than that I have no special conviction."

Master Yagyu was deeply impressed and said, "My perceptions were not the least bit awry. The deepest principle of my military tactics is just that one thing. Lip until now, among all the many hundreds of disciples I have had, there is not one who is licensed in this deepest principle. It is not necessary for you to take up the wooden sword. I will initiate you right now." And it is said that he promptly banded him the certified scroll.

Hagakure - The Way of the Samurai

This is a story of Muragawa Soden's.

Meditation on inevitable death should be performed daily. Every day when one's body and mind are at peace, one should meditate upon being ripped apart by arrows, rifles, spears and swords, being carried away by surging waves, being thrown into the midst of a great fire, being struck by lightning, being shaken to death by a great earthquake, falling from thousand-foot cliffs, dying of disease or committing seppuku at the death of one's master. And every day without fail one should consider himself as dead.

There is a saying of the elders' that goes, "Step from under the eaves and you're a dead man. Leave the gate and the enemy is waiting." This is not a matter of being careful. It is to consider oneself as dead beforehand.

People will become your enemies if you become eminent too quickly in life, and you will be ineffectual. Rising slowly in the world, people will be your allies and your happiness will he assured.

In the long run, whether you are fast or slow, as long as you have people's understanding there will be no danger. It is said that fortune that is urged upon you from others is the most effective.

The warriors of old cultivated mustaches, for as proof that a man had been slain in battle, his ears and nose would be cut off and brought to the enemy's camp. So that there would be no mistake as to whether the person was a man or a woman, the mustache was also cut off with the nose. At such a time the head was thrown away if it had no mustache, for it might be mistaken for that of a woman. Therefore, growing a mustache was one of the disciplines of a samurai so that his head would not be thrown away upon his death. Tsunetomo said, "If one washes his face with water every morning, if he is slain his complexion will not change. "

The word "person of the north" comes from a tradition of the correct way of upbringing. A couple will put their pillows in the west, and the

The Samurai Series 143

man, lying on the south side, will face the north, while the woman, lying on the north side, will face the south.

In bringing up a boy, one should first encourage a sense of valor. From the time he is young the child should liken his parents to the master, and learn everyday politeness and etiquette, the serving of other people, the ways of speech, forbearance and even the correct way of walking down the street. The elders were taught in the same fashion. When he does not put effort into things, he should be scolded and made to go the entire day without eating. This is also one of the disciplines of a retainer.

As for a girl, it is most important to teach her chastity from the time she is a child. She should not be in the comany of a man at a distance of less than six feet, nor should she meet them eye to eye, nor should she receive things from them directly from hand to hand. Neither should she go sight-seeing or take trips to temples. A woman who has been brought up strictly and has endured suffering at her own borne will suffer no ennui after she is married.

In dealing with younger children one should use rewards and punishments. If one is lax in being sure that they do as they are told, young children will become self-interested and will later be involved in wrongdoings. It is something about which one should be very careful.

Late Night Idle Talk

As a retainer of the Nabeshima clan, one should have the intention of studying our province's history and traditions, but provincial studies are made light of nowadays. The basic reason for this study is to understand the foundation of our clan, and to know that the clan's forefathers established its perpetuity by means of their suffering and compassion. The fact that our clan has perpetually continued in an unrivaled manner up to this very day is due to the humanity and martial valor of Master Ryuzoji Iekane, the charity and faith of Master Nabeshima Kiyohisa, and the appearance of Lord Ryuzoji Takanobu and Lord Nabeshima Naoshige and their might.

I am at a complete loss when it comes to understanding why people of this generation have forgotten these things and respect the Buddhas of other places. Neither the Shakyamuni Buddha, nor Confucius, nor Kusunoki, nor Shingen were ever retainers of the Ryuzojis or the Nabeshimas; hence it cannot be said that they are in harmony with our clan's customs. In times of war or in times of peace it would be sufficient if both the upper and lower classes would worship our ancestors and study their teachings. One worships the head of whatever clan or discipline to which he belongs. Outside learning for retainers of our clan is worthless. One may think that it is fine to study other disciplines as a diversion after his provincial studies are replete. Yet if a person has a good understanding of provincial studies, he will see that there is nothing lacking in them.

Today, if someone from another clan were to ask about the origin of the Ryuzojis and the Nabeshimas, or why the fief was transferred from the former to the latter, or if they were to ask something like, "I have heard that the Ryuzojis and the Nabeshimas are the greatest in Kyushu for deeds of martial valor, but can you tell me some of the particulars?" I suppose that the man with no knowledge of provincial studies would not be able to answer a word.

For a retainer there should be nothing other than doing his own job. For the most part people dislike their own jobs, find those of others more interesting, cause misunderstanding, and bring on utter disasters. Good models of men who performed their duty in their work are Lord Naoshige and Lord Katsushige. The retainers of those times all performed their duties. From the upper classes, men who would be of good use were searched out, while from the lower classes men desired to be useful. The minds of the two classes were of mutual accord, and the strength of the clan was secure.

In all our generations of masters there has never been a bad or foolish one, and in the end there has never been one who ranked second or third among the daimyo of Japan. It is truly a wonderful clan; this is due to the faith of its founders. Moreover, they did not send the clan's retainers to other provinces. nor did they invite men from other provinces in. Men who were made ronin were kept within the province, as were the descendants of those who were made to commit seppuku. The wonder of being born into a clan with such a deep pledge between master and servant is an inexpressible blessing, passed down through the apes, for both farmer and townsman. This goes without saying for the retainer.

The foundation of a Nabeshima samurai should be in knowing this fact; in being deeply resolved to return this blessing by being useful ; in serving more and more selflessly when treated kindly by the master ; in knowing that being made a ronin or being ordered to commit seppuku are also forms of service ; and in aiming to be mindful of the clan forever, whether one is banished deep in the mountains or buried under the earth. Although it is unfitting for someone like me to say this, in dying it is my hope not to become a Buddha. Rather, my will is permeated with the resolution to help manage the affairs of the province, though I be reborn as a Nabeshima samurai seven times. One needs neither vitality nor talent. In a word, it is a matter of having the will to shoulder the clan by oneself.

How can one human being be inferior to another? In all matters of discipline, one will be useless unless he has great pride. Unless one is determined to move the clan by himself, all his discipline will come to naught. Although, like a tea kettle, it is easy for one's enthusiasm to cool, there is a way to keep this from happening. My own vows are the following:

Never to be outdone in the Way of the Samurai.
To be of good use to the master.
To be filial to my parents.
To manifest great compassion, and to act for the sake of Man.

If one dedicates these four vows to the gods and Buddhas every morning, he will have the strength of two men and will never slip backward. One must edge forward like the inchworrn, bit by bit. The gods and Buddhas, too, first started with a vow.

Bushido

The Soul of Japan

by

Inazo Nitobe

The Samurai Series

Bushido - The Soul of Japan

Preface

About ten years ago, while spending a few days under the hospitable roof of the distinguished Belgian jurist, the lamented M. de Laveleye, our conversation turned, during one of our rambles, to the subject of religion. "Do you mean to say," asked the venerable professor, "that you have no religious instruction in your schools?" On my replying in the negative he suddenly halted in astonishment, and in a voice which I shall not easily forget, he repeated "No religion! How do you impart moral education?" The question stunned me at the time. I could give no ready answer, for the moral precepts I learned in my childhood days, were not given in schools; and not until I began to analyze the different elements that formed my notions of right and wrong, did I find that it was Bushido that breathed them into my nostrils.

The direct inception of this little book is due to the frequent queries put by my wife as to the reasons why such and such ideas and customs prevail in Japan.

In my attempts to give satisfactory replies to M. de Laveleye and to my wife, I found that without understanding Feudalism and Bushido [*Pronounced Boó-shee-doh'. In putting Japanese words and names into English, Hepburn's rule is followed, that the vowels should be used as in European languages, and the consonants as in English.*], the moral ideas of present Japan are a sealed volume.

Taking advantage of enforced idleness on account of long illness, I put down in the order now presented to the public some of the answers given in our household conversation. They consist mainly of what I was taught and told in my youthful days, when Feudalism was still in force.

Between Lafcadio Hearn and Mrs. Hugh Fraser on one side and Sir Ernest Satow and Professor Chamberlain on the other, it is indeed discouraging to write anything Japanese in English. The only advantage I have over them is that I can assume the attitude of a personal defendant, while these distinguished writers are at best solicitors and attorneys. I have often thought,—"Had I their gift of language, I would present the cause of Japan in more eloquent terms!" But one who speaks in a borrowed tongue should be thankful if he can just make himself intelligible.

All through the discourse I have tried to illustrate whatever points I have made with parallel examples from European history and literature, believing that these will aid in bringing the subject nearer to the comprehension of foreign readers.

Should any of my allusions to religious subjects and to religious workers be thought slighting, I trust my attitude towards Christianity itself will not be questioned. It is with ecclesiastical methods and with the forms which obscure the teachings of Christ, and not with the teachings themselves, that I have little sympathy. I believe in the religion taught by Him and handed down to us in the New Testament, as well as in the law written in the heart. Further, I believe that God hath made a testament which maybe called "old" with every people and nation,—Gentile or Jew, Christian or Heathen. As to the rest of my theology, I need not impose upon the patience of the public.

In concluding this preface, I wish to express my thanks to my friend Anna C. Hartshorne for many valuable suggestions and for the characteristically Japanese design made by her for the cover of this book.

Inazo Nitobe
Malvern, PA
December 1899

Preface
To the Tenth and Revised Edition

Since its first publication in Philadelphia, more than six years ago, this little book has had an unexpected history. The Japanese reprint has passed through eight editions, the present thus being its tenth appearance in the English language. Simultaneously with this will be issued an American and English edition, through the publishing-house of Messrs. George H. Putnam's Sons, of New York.

In the meantime, *Bushido* has been translated into Mahratti by Mr. Dev of Khandesh, into German by Fräulein Kaufmann of Hamburg, into Bohemian by Mr. Hora of Chicago, into Polish by the Society of Science and Life in Lemberg,—although this Polish edition has been censured by the Russian Government. It is now being rendered into Norwegian and into French. A Chinese translation is under contemplation. A Russian officer, now a prisoner in Japan, has a manuscript in Russian ready for the press. A part of the volume has been brought before the Hungarian public and a detailed review, almost amounting to a commentary, has been published in Japanese. Full scholarly notes for the help of younger students have been compiled by my friend Mr. H. Sakurai, to whom I also owe much for his aid in other ways.

I have been more than gratified to feel that my humble work has found sympathetic readers in widely separated circles, showing that the subject matter is of some interest to the world at large. Exceedingly flattering is the news that has reached me from official sources, that President Roosevelt has done it undeserved honor by reading it and distributing several dozens of copies among his friends.

In making emendations and additions for the present edition, I have largely confined them to concrete examples. I still continue to regret, as I indeed have never ceased to do, my inability to add a chapter on Filial Piety, which is considered one of the two wheels of the chariot of Japanese ethics—Loyalty being the other. My inability is due rather to my ignorance of the Western sentiment in regard to this particular virtue, than to ignorance of our own attitude towards it, and I cannot draw comparisons satisfying to my own mind. I hope one day to enlarge upon this and other topics at some length. All the subjects that are touched upon in these pages are capable of further amplification and discussion; but I do not now see my way clear to make this volume larger than it is.

This Preface would be incomplete and unjust, if I were to omit the debt I owe to my wife for her reading of the proof-sheets, for helpful suggestions, and, above all, for her constant encouragement.

Inazo Nitobe
Kyoto
May 22, 1905

Bushido - The Soul of Japan

Contents

Bushido - The Soul of Japan

Bushido as an Ethical System

Chivalry is a flower no less indigenous to the soil of Japan than its emblem, the cherry blossom; nor is it a dried-up specimen of an antique virtue preserved in the herbarium of our history. It is still a living object of power and beauty among us; and if it assumes no tangible shape or form, it not the less scents the moral atmosphere, and makes us aware that we are still under its potent spell. The conditions of society which brought it forth and nourished it have long disappeared; but as those far-off stars which once were and are not, still continue to shed their rays upon us, so the light of chivalry, which was a child of feudalism, still illuminates our moral path, surviving its mother institution. It is a pleasure to me to reflect upon this subject in the language of Burke, who uttered the well-known touching eulogy over the neglected bier of its European prototype.

It argues a sad defect of information concerning the Far East, when so erudite a scholar as Dr. George Miller did not hesitate to affirm that chivalry, or any other similar institution, has never existed either among the nations of antiquity or among the modern Orientals. [*History Philosophically Illustrated*, (3rd Ed. 1853), Vol. II, p. 2.] Such ignorance, however, is amply excusable, as the third edition of the good Doctor's work appeared the same year that Commodore Perry was knocking at the portals of our exclusivism. More than a decade later, about the time that our feudalism was in the last throes of existence, Carl Marx, writing his "Capital," called the attention of his readers to the peculiar advantage of studying the social and political institutions of feudalism, as then to be seen in living form only in Japan. I would likewise invite the Western historical and ethical student to the study of chivalry in the Japan of the present.

Enticing as is a historical disquisition on the comparison between European and Japanese feudalism and chivalry, it is not the purpose of this paper to enter into it at length. My attempt is rather to relate, *firstly*, the origin and sources of our chivalry; *secondly*, its character and teaching; *thirdly*, its influence among the masses; and, *fourthly*, the continuity and permanence of its influence. Of these several points, the first will be only brief and cursory, or else I should have to take my readers into the devious paths of our national history; the second will be dwelt upon at greater length, as being most likely to interest students of International Ethics and Comparative Ethology in our ways of thought and action; and the rest will be dealt with as corollaries.

The Japanese word which I have roughly rendered Chivalry, is, in the original, more expressive than Horsemanship. *Bu-shi-do* means literally Military-Knight-Ways—the ways which fighting nobles should observe in their daily life as well as in their vocation; in a word, the "Precepts of Knighthood," the *noblesse oblige* of the warrior class. Having thus given its literal significance, I may be allowed henceforth to use the word in the original. The use of the original term is also advisable for this reason, that a teaching so circumscribed and unique, engendering a cast of mind and character so peculiar, so local, must wear the badge of its singularity on its face; then, some words have a national *timbre* so expressive of race characteristics that the best of translators can do them but scant justice, not to say positive injustice and grievance. Who can improve by translation what the German "*Gemüth*" signifies, or who does not feel the difference between the two words verbally so closely allied as the English *gentleman* and the French *gentilhomme*?

Bushido, then, is the code of moral principles which the knights were required or instructed to observe. It is not a written code; at best it consists of a few maxims handed down from mouth to mouth or coming from the pen of some well-known warrior or savant. More frequently it is a code unuttered and unwritten, possessing all the more the powerful sanction of veritable deed, and of a law written on the fleshly tablets of the heart. It was founded not on the creation of one brain, however able, or on the life of a single personage, however renowned. It was an organic growth of decades and centuries of military career. It, perhaps, fills the same position in the history of ethics that the English Constitution does in political history; yet it has had nothing to compare with the Magna Charta or the Habeas Corpus Act. True, early in the seventeenth century Military Statutes (*Buké Hatto*) were promulgated; but their thirteen short articles were taken up mostly with marriages, castles, leagues, etc., and didactic regulations were but meagerly touched upon. We cannot, therefore, point out any definite time and place and say, "Here is its fountain head." Only as it attains consciousness in the feudal age, its origin, in respect to time, may be identified with feudalism. But feudalism itself is woven of many threads, and Bushido shares its intricate nature. As in England the political institutions of feudalism may be said to date from the Norman Conquest, so we may say that in Japan its rise was simultaneous with the ascendency of Yoritomo, late in the twelfth century. As, however, in England, we find the social elements of feudalism far back in the period previous to William the Conqueror, so, too, the germs of feudalism in Japan had been long existent before the period I have mentioned.

Again, in Japan as in Europe, when feudalism was formally inaugurated, the professional class of warriors naturally came into prominence. These were known as *samurai*, meaning literally, like the old English *cniht* (knecht, knight), guards or attendants—resembling in character the *soldurii* whom Caesar mentioned as existing in Aquitania, or the *comitati*, who, according to Tacitus, followed Germanic chiefs in his time; or, to take a still later parallel, the *milites medii* that one reads about in the history of Mediaeval Europe. A Sinico-Japanese word *Bu-ké* or *Bu-shi* (Fighting Knights) was also adopted in common use. They were a privileged class, and must originally have been a rough breed who made fighting their vocation. This class was naturally recruited, in a long period of constant warfare, from the manliest and the most adventurous, and all the while the process of elimination went on, the timid and the feeble being sorted out, and only "a rude race, all masculine, with brutish strength," to borrow Emerson's phrase, surviving to form families and the ranks of the *samurai*. Coming to profess great honor and great privileges, and correspondingly great responsibilities, they soon felt the need of a common standard of behavior, especially as they were always on a belligerent footing and belonged to different clans. Just as physicians limit competition among themselves by professional courtesy, just as lawyers sit in courts of honor in cases of violated etiquette, so must also warriors possess some resort for final judgment on their misdemeanors.

Fair play in fight! What fertile germs of morality lie in this primitive sense of savagery and childhood. Is it not the root of all military and civic virtues? We smile (as if we had outgrown it!) at the boyish desire of the small Britisher, Tom Brown, "to leave behind him the name of a fellow who never bullied a little boy or turned his back on a big one." And yet, who does not know that this desire is the corner-stone on which moral structures of mighty dimensions can be reared? May I not go even so far as to say that the gentlest and most peace-loving of religions endorses this aspiration? This desire of Tom's is the basis on which the greatness of England is largely built, and it will not take us long to discover that *Bushido* does not stand on a lesser pedestal. If fighting in itself, be it offensive or defensive, is, as Quakers rightly testify, brutal and wrong, we can still say with Lessing, "We know from what failings our virtue springs."

Ruskin was one of the most gentle-hearted and peace loving men that ever lived. Yet he believed in war with all the fervor of a worshiper of the strenuous life. "When I tell you," he says in the *Crown of Wild Olive*, "that war is the foundation of all the arts, I mean also that it is the foundation of all the high virtues and faculties of men. It is very strange to me to discover this, and very dreadful, but I saw it to be quite an undeniable fact. I found in brief, that all great nations learned their truth of word and strength of thought in war; that they were nourished in war and wasted by peace, taught by war and deceived by peace; trained by war and betrayed by peace; in a word, that they were born in war and expired in peace."

Bushido - The Soul of Japan

Sources of Bushido

Sneaks and *cowards* are epithets of the worst opprobrium to healthy, simple natures. Childhood begins life with these notions, and knighthood also; but, as life grows larger and its relations many-sided, the early faith seeks sanction from higher authority and more rational sources for its own justification, satisfaction and development. If military interests had operated alone, without higher moral support, how far short of chivalry would the ideal of knighthood have fallen! In Europe, Christianity, interpreted with concessions convenient to chivalry, infused it nevertheless with spiritual data. "Religion, war and glory were the three souls of a perfect Christian knight," says Lamartine.

In Japan there were several sources of Bushido of which I may begin with Buddhism. It furnished a sense of calm trust in Fate, a quiet submission to the inevitable, that stoic composure in sight of danger or calamity, that disdain of life and friendliness with death. A foremost teacher of swordsmanship, when he saw his pupil master the utmost of his art, told him, "Beyond this my instruction must give way to Zen teaching." "Zen" is the Japanese equivalent for the Dhyâna, which "represents human effort to reach through meditation zones of thought beyond the range of verbal expression."[Lafcadio Hearn, *Exotics and Retrospectives*, p. 84.] Its method is contemplation, and its purport, as far as I understand it, to be convinced of a principle that underlies all phenomena, and, if it can, of the Absolute itself, and thus to put oneself in harmony with this Absolute. Thus defined, the teaching was more than the dogma of a sect, and whoever attains to the perception of the Absolute raises himself above mundane things and awakes, "to a new Heaven and a new Earth."

What Buddhism failed to give, Shintoism offered in abundance. Such loyalty to the sovereign, such reverence for ancestral memory, and such filial piety as are not taught by any other creed, were inculcated by the Shinto doctrines, imparting passivity to the otherwise arrogant character of the samurai. Shinto theology has no place for the dogma of "original sin." On the contrary, it believes in the innate goodness

The Samurai Series 161

and God-like purity of the human soul, adoring it as the adytum from which divine oracles are proclaimed. Everybody has observed that the Shinto shrines are conspicuously devoid of objects and instruments of worship, and that a plain mirror hung in the sanctuary forms the essential part of its furnishing. The presence of this article, is easy to explain: it typifies the human heart, which, when perfectly placid and clear, reflects the very image of the Deity. When you stand, therefore, in front of the shrine to worship, you see your own image reflected on its shining surface, and the act of worship is tantamount to the old Delphic injunction, "Know Thyself." But self-knowledge does not imply, either in the Greek or Japanese teaching, knowledge of the physical part of man, not his anatomy or his psycho-physics; knowledge was to be of a moral kind, the introspection of our moral nature. Mommsen, comparing the Greek and the Roman, says that when the former worshiped he raised his eyes to heaven, for his prayer was contemplation, while the latter veiled his head, for his was reflection.

Essentially like the Roman conception of religion, our reflection brought into prominence not so much the moral as the national consciousness of the individual. Its nature-worship endeared the country to our inmost souls, while its ancestor-worship, tracing from lineage to lineage, made the Imperial family the fountain-head of the whole nation. To us the country is more than land and soil from which to mine gold or to reap grain—it is the sacred abode of the gods, the spirits of our forefathers: to us the Emperor is more than the Arch Constable of a *Rechtsstaat*, or even the Patron of a *Culturstaat*—he is the bodily representative of Heaven on earth, blending in his person its power and its mercy. If what M. Boutmy [*The English People*, p. 188.] says is true of English royalty—that it "is not only the image of authority, but the author and symbol of national unity," as I believe it to be, doubly and trebly may this be affirmed of royalty in Japan.

The tenets of Shintoism cover the two predominating features of the emotional life of our race—Patriotism and Loyalty. Arthur May Knapp very truly says: "In Hebrew literature it is often difficult to tell whether the writer is speaking of God or of the Commonwealth; of heaven or of Jerusalem; of the Messiah or of the nation itself." ["*Feudal and Modern Japan*" Vol. I, p. 183.] A similar confusion may be noticed in the nomenclature of our national faith. I said confusion, because it will be so deemed by a logical intellect on account of its verbal ambiguity; still, being a framework of national instinct and race feelings, Shintoism never pretends to a systematic philosophy or a rational theology. This religion—or, is it not more correct to say, the race emotions which this religion expressed?—thoroughly imbued Bushido with loyalty to the sovereign and love of country. These acted more as impulses than as doctrines; for Shintoism, unlike the Mediaeval Christian Church, prescribed to its votaries scarcely any *credenda*, furnishing them at the same time with *agenda* of a straightforward and simple type.

As to strictly ethical doctrines, the teachings of Confucius were the most prolific source of Bushido. His enunciation of the five moral relations between master and servant (the governing and the governed), father and son, husband and wife, older and younger brother, and between friend and friend, was but a confirmation of what the race instinct had recognized before his writings were introduced from China. The calm, benignant, and worldly-wise character of his politico-ethical precepts was particularly well suited to the samurai, who formed the ruling class. His aristocratic and conservative tone was well adapted to the requirements of these warrior statesmen. Next to Confucius, Mencius exercised an immense authority over Bushido. His forcible and often quite democratic theories were exceedingly taking to sympathetic natures, and they were even thought dangerous to, and subversive of, the existing social order, hence his works were for a long time under censure. Still, the words of this master mind found permanent lodgment in the heart of the samurai.

The writings of Confucius and Mencius formed the principal text-books for youths and the highest authority in discussion among the old. A mere acquaintance with the classics of these two sages was held, however, in no high esteem. A common proverb ridicules one who has only an intellectual knowledge of Confucius, as a man ever studious but ignorant of *Analects*. A typical samurai calls a literary savant a book-smelling sot. Another compares learning to an ill-smelling vegetable that must be boiled and boiled before it is fit for use. A man who has read a little smells a little pedantic, and a man who has read much smells yet more so; both are alike unpleasant. The writer meant thereby that knowledge becomes really such only when it is assimilated in the mind of the learner and shows in his character. An intellectual specialist was considered a machine. Intellect itself was considered subordinate to ethical emotion. Man and the universe were conceived to be alike spiritual and ethical. Bushido could not accept the judgment of Huxley, that the cosmic process was unmoral.

Bushido made light of knowledge as such. It was not pursued as an end in itself, but as a means to the attainment of wisdom. Hence, he who stopped short of this end was regarded no higher than a convenient machine, which could turn out poems and maxims at bidding. Thus, knowledge was conceived as identical with its practical application in life; and this Socratic doctrine found its greatest exponent in the Chinese philosopher, Wan Yang Ming, who never wearies of repeating, "To know and to act are one and the same."

I beg leave for a moment's digression while I am on this subject, inasmuch as some of the noblest types of *bushi* were strongly influenced by the teachings of this sage. Western readers will easily recognize in his writings many parallels to the New Testament. Making allowance for the terms peculiar to either teaching, the passage, "Seek ye first the kingdom of God and his righteousness; and all these things shall be added unto you," conveys a thought that may be found on almost any page of Wan Yang Ming. A Japanese disciple [*Miwa Shissai.*] of his says—"The lord of heaven and earth, of all living beings, dwelling in the heart of man, becomes his mind (*Kokoro*); hence a mind is a living thing, and is ever luminous:" and again, "The spiritual light of our essential being is pure, and is not affected by the will of man. Spontaneously springing up in our mind, it shows what is right and wrong: it is then called conscience; it is even the light that proceedeth from the god of heaven." How very much do these words sound like some passages from Isaac Pennington or other philosophic mystics! I am inclined to think that the Japanese mind, as expressed in the simple tenets of the Shinto religion, was particularly open to the reception of Yang Ming's precepts. He carried his doctrine of the infallibility of conscience to extreme transcendentalism, attributing to it the faculty to perceive, not only the distinction between right and wrong, but also the nature of psychical facts and physical phenomena. He went as far as, if not farther than, Berkeley and Fichte, in Idealism, denying the existence of things outside of human ken. If his system had all the logical errors charged to Solipsism, it had all the efficacy of strong conviction and its moral import in developing individuality of character and equanimity of temper cannot be gainsaid.

Thus, whatever the sources, the essential principles which *Bushido* imbibed from them and assimilated to itself, were few and simple. Few and simple as these were, they were sufficient to furnish a safe conduct of life even through the unsafest days of the most unsettled period of our nation's history. The wholesome, unsophisticated nature of our warrior ancestors derived ample food for their spirit from a sheaf of commonplace and fragmentary teachings, gleaned as it were on the highways and byways of ancient thought, and, stimulated by the demands of the age, formed from these gleanings anew and unique type of manhood. An acute French *savant*, M. de la Mazelière, thus sums up his impressions of the sixteenth century:—"Toward the middle of the sixteenth century, all is confusion in Japan, in the government, in society, in the church. But the civil wars, the manners returning to barbarism, the necessity for each to execute justice for himself,—these formed men comparable to those Italians of the sixteenth century, in whom Taine praises 'the vigorous initiative, the habit of sudden resolutions and desperate undertakings, the grand capacity to do and to suffer.' In Japan as in Italy 'the rude manners of the Middle Ages made of man a superb animal, wholly militant and wholly resistant.' And this is why the sixteenth century displays in the highest degree the principal quality of the Japanese race, that great diversity which one finds there between minds (*esprits*) as well as between temperaments. While in India and even in China men seem to differ chiefly in degree of energy or intelligence, in Japan they differ by originality of character as well. Now, individuality is the sign of superior races and of civilizations already developed. If we make use of an expression dear to Nietzsche, we might say that in Asia, to speak of humanity is to speak of its plains; in Japan as in Europe, one represents it above all by its mountains."

Rectitude or Justice

To the pervading characteristics of the men of whom M. de la Mazelière writes, let us now address ourselves. I shall begin with rectitude or justice the most cogent precept in the code of the samurai. Nothing is more loathsome to him than underhand dealings and crooked undertakings. The conception of Rectitude may be erroneous, it may be narrow. A well-known bushi defines it as a power of resolution;—"Rectitude is the power of deciding upon a certain course of conduct in accordance with reason, without wavering;—to die when it is right to die, to strike when to strike is right."

Another speaks of it in the following terms: "Rectitude is the bone that gives firmness and stature. As without bones the head cannot rest on the top of the spine, nor hands move nor feet stand, so without rectitude neither talent nor learning can make of a human frame a samurai. With it the lack of accomplishments is as nothing." Mencius calls Benevolence man's mind, and Rectitude or Righteousness his path. "How lamentable," he exclaims, "is it to neglect the path and not pursue it, to lose the mind and not know to seek it again! When men's fowls and dogs are lost, they know to seek for them again, but they lose their mind and do not know to seek for it." Have we not here "as in a glass darkly" a parable propounded three hundred years later in another clime and by a greater Teacher, who called Himself *the Way* of Righteousness, through whom the lost could be found? But I stray from my point. Righteousness, according to Mencius, is a straight and narrow path which a man ought to take to regain the lost paradise.

Even in the latter days of feudalism, when the long continuance of peace brought leisure into the life of the warrior class, and with it dissipations of all kinds and gentle accomplishments, the epithet *Gishi* (a man of rectitude) was considered superior to any name that signified mastery of learning or art. The Forty-seven Faithfuls—of whom so much is made in our popular education—are known in common parlance as the Forty-seven *Gishi*.

Bushido - The Soul of Japan

Courage, the Spirit of Daring and Bearing

In times when cunning artifice was liable to pass for military tact and downright falsehood for *ruse de guerre*, this manly virtue, frank and honest, was a jewel that shone the brightest and was most highly praised. Rectitude is a twin brother to Valor, another martial virtue. But before proceeding to speak of Valor, let me linger a little while on what I may term a derivation from Rectitude, which, at first deviating slightly from its original, became more and more removed from it, until its meaning was perverted in the popular acceptance. I speak of *Gi-ri*, literally the Right Reason, but which came in time to mean a vague sense of duty which public opinion expected an incumbent to fulfil. In its original and unalloyed sense, it meant duty, pure and simple,—hence, we speak of the *Giri* we owe to parents, to superiors, to inferiors, to society at large, and so forth. In these instances *Giri* is duty; for what else is duty than what Right Reason demands and commands us to do. Should not Right Reason be our categorical imperative?

Giri primarily meant no more than duty, and I dare say its etymology was derived from the fact that in our conduct, say to our parents, though love should be the only motive, lacking that, there must be some other authority to enforce filial piety; and they formulated this authority in *Giri*. Very rightly did they formulate this authority— *Giri*—since if love does not rush to deeds of virtue, recourse must be had to man's intellect and his reason must be quickened to convince him of the necessity of acting aright. The same is true of any other moral obligation. The instant Duty becomes onerous. Right Reason steps in to prevent our shirking it.

Giri thus understood is a severe taskmaster, with a birch-rod in his hand to make sluggards perform their part. It is a secondary power in ethics; as a motive it is infinitely inferior to the Christian doctrine of love, which should be *the* law. I deem it a product of the conditions of an artificial society—of a society in which accident of birth and unmerited favour instituted class distinctions, in which the family was the social unit, in which seniority of age was of more account than superiority of talents, in which natural affections had often to succumb before arbitrary man-made customs. Because of this very artificiality, *Giri* in time degenerated into a vague sense of propriety called up to explain this and sanction that,—as, for example, why a mother must, if need be, sacrifice all her other children in order to save the first-born; or why a daughter must sell her chastity to get funds to pay for the father's dissipation, and the like. Starting as Right Reason, *Giri* has, in my opinion, often stooped to casuistry. It has even degenerated into cowardly fear of censure. I might say of *Giri* what Scott wrote of patriotism, that "as it is the fairest, so it is often the most suspicious, mask of other feelings." Carried beyond or below Right Reason, *Giri* became a monstrous misnomer. It harbored under its wings every sort of sophistry and hypocrisy. It might easily—have been turned into a nest of cowardice, if Bushido had not a keen and correct sense of courage, the spirit of daring and bearing to the consideration of which we shall now return. Courage was scarcely deemed worthy to be counted among virtues, unless it was exercised in the cause of Righteousness.

In his "Analects" Confucius defines Courage by explaining, as is often his wont, what its negative is. "Perceiving what is right," he says, "and doing it not, argues lack of courage." Put this epigram into a positive statement, and it runs, "Courage is doing what is right." To run all kinds of hazards, to jeopardize one's self, to rush into the jaws of death—these are too often identified with Valor, and in the profession of arms such rashness of conduct—what Shakespeare calls, "valor misbegot"—is unjustly applauded; but not so in the Precepts of Knighthood. Death for a cause unworthy of dying for, was called a "dog's death." "To rush into the thick of battle and to be slain in it," says a Prince of Mito, "is easy enough, and the merest churl is equal to the task; but," he continues, "it is true courage to live when it is right to live, and to die only when it is right to die," and yet the Prince had not even heard of the name of Plato, who defines courage as "the knowledge of things that a man should fear and that he should not fear." A distinction which is made in the West between moral and physical courage has long been recognized among us. What samurai youth has not heard of "Great Valor" and the "Valor of a Villein?"

Valor, Fortitude, Bravery, Fearlessness, Courage, being the qualities of soul which appeal most easily to juvenile minds, and which can be trained by exercise and example, were, so to speak, the most popular virtues, early emulated among the youth. Stories of military exploits were repeated almost before boys left their mother's breast. Does a little booby cry for any ache? The mother scolds him in this fashion: "What a coward to cry for a trifling pain! What will you do when your arm is cut off in battle? What when you are called upon to commit *harakiri*?" We all know the pathetic fortitude of a famished little boy-prince of Sendai, who in the drama is made to say to his little page, "Seest thou those tiny sparrows in the nest, how their yellow bills are opened wide, and now see! there comes their mother with worms to feed them. How eagerly and happily the little ones eat! but for a samurai, when his stomach is empty, it is a disgrace to feel hunger." Anecdotes of fortitude and bravery abound in nursery tales, though stories of this kind are not by any means the only method of early imbuing the spirit with daring and fearlessness. Parents, with sternness sometimes verging on cruelty, set their children to tasks that called forth all the pluck that was in them. "Bears hurl their cubs down the gorge," they said. Samurai's sons were let down the steep valleys of hardship, and spurred to Sisyphus-like tasks. Occasional deprivation of food or exposure to cold, was considered a highly efficacious test for inuring them to endurance. Children of tender age were sent among utter strangers with some message to deliver, were made to rise before the sun, and before breakfast attend to their reading exercises, walking to their teacher with bare feet in the cold of winter; they frequently—once or twice a month, as on the festival of a god of learning,—came together in small groups and passed the night without sleep, in reading aloud by turns. Pilgrimages to all sorts of uncanny places—to execution grounds, to graveyards, to houses reputed to be haunted, were favorite pastimes of the young. In the days when decapitation was public, not only were small boys sent to witness the ghastly scene, but they were made to visit alone the place in the darkness of night and there to leave a mark of their visit on the trunkless head.

Does this ultra-Spartan system of "drilling the nerves" strike the modern pedagogist with horror and doubt—doubt whether the tendency would not be brutalizing, nipping in the bud the tender emotions of the heart? Let us see what other concepts Bushido had of Valor.

The spiritual aspect of valor is evidenced by composure—calm presence of mind. Tranquillity is courage in repose. It is a statical manifestation of valor, as daring deeds are a dynamical. A truly brave man is ever serene; he is never taken by surprise; nothing ruffles the equanimity of his spirit. In the heat of battle he remains cool; in the midst of catastrophes he keeps level his mind. Earthquakes do not shake him, he laughs at storms. We admire him as truly great, who, in the menacing presence of danger or death, retains his self-possession; who, for instance, can compose a poem under impending peril or hum a strain in the face of death. Such indulgence betraying no tremor in the writing or in the voice, is taken as an infallible index of a large nature—of what we call a capacious mind (*Yoyū*), which, for from being pressed or crowded, has always room for something more.

It passes current among us as a piece of authentic history, that as Ōta Dokan, the great builder of the castle of Tokyo, was pierced through with a spear, his assassin, knowing the poetical predilection of his victim, accompanied his thrust with this couplet—

> "Ah! how in moments like these
> Our heart doth grudge the light of life;"

whereupon the expiring hero, not one whit daunted by the mortal wound in his side, added the lines—

> "Had not in hours of peace,
> It learned to lightly look on life."

There is even a sportive element in a courageous nature. Things which are serious to ordinary people, may be but play to the valiant. Hence in old warfare it was not at all rare for the parties to a conflict to exchange repartee or to begin a rhetorical contest. Combat was not solely a matter of brute force; it was, as, well, an intellectual engagement.

Of such character was the battle fought on the bank of the Koromo River, late in the eleventh century. The eastern army routed, its leader, Sadato, took to flight. When the pursuing general pressed him hard and called aloud—"It is a disgrace for a warrior to show his back to the enemy," Sadato reined his horse; upon this the conquering chief shouted an impromptu verse—

"Torn into shreds is the warp of the cloth" (*koromo*).

Scarcely had the words escaped his lips when the defeated warrior, undismayed, completed the couplet—

"Since age has worn its threads by use."

Yoshiie, whose bow had all the while been bent, suddenly unstrung it and turned away, leaving his prospective victim to do as he pleased. When asked the reason of his strange behavior, he replied that he could not bear to put to shame one who had kept his presence of mind while hotly pursued by his enemy.

Benevolence, the Feeling of Distress

The sorrow which overtook Antony and Octavius at the death of Brutus, has been the general experience of brave men. Kenshin, who fought for fourteen years with Shingen, when he heard of the latter's death, wept aloud at the loss of "the best of enemies." It was this same Kenshin who had set a noble example for all time, in his treatment of Shingen, whose provinces lay in a mountainous region quite away from the sea, and who had consequently depended upon the Hōjō provinces of the Tokaido for salt. The Hōjō prince wishing to weaken him, although not openly at war with him, had cut off from Shingen all traffic in this important article. Kenshin, hearing of his enemy's dilemma and able to obtain his salt from the coast of his own dominions, wrote Shingen that in his opinion the Hōjō lord had committed a very mean act, and that although he (Kenshin) was at war with him (Shingen) he had ordered his subjects to furnish him with plenty of salt—adding, "I do not fight with salt, but with the sword," affording more than a parallel to the words of Camillus, "We Romans do not fight with gold, but with iron." Nietzsche spoke for the samurai heart when he wrote, "You are to be proud of your enemy; then, the success of your enemy is your success also." Indeed valor and honor alike required that we should own as enemies in war only such as prove worthy of being friends in peace. When valor attains this height, it becomes akin to benevolence, the feeling of distress, love, magnanimity, affection for others, sympathy and pity, which were ever recognized to be supreme virtues, the highest of all the attributes of the human soul. Benevolence was deemed a princely virtue in a twofold sense;—princely among the manifold attributes of a noble spirit; princely as particularly befitting a princely profession. We needed no Shakespeare to feel—though, perhaps, like the rest of the world, we needed him to express it—that mercy became a monarch better than his crown, that it was above his sceptered sway. How often both Confucius and Mencius repeat the highest requirement of a ruler of men to consist in benevolence. Confucius would say, "Let but a prince cultivate virtue, people will flock to him; with people will come to him lands; lands will bring forth for him wealth; wealth will give him the benefit of right uses. Virtue is the root, and wealth an outcome."

Again, "Never has there been a case of a sovereign loving benevolence, and the people not loving righteousness," Mencius follows close at his heels and says, "Instances are on record where individuals attained to supreme power in a single state, without benevolence, but never have I heard of a whole empire falling into the hands of one who lacked this virtue." Also,—"It is impossible that any one should become ruler of the people to whom they have not yielded the subjection of their hearts." Both defined this indispensable requirement in a ruler by saying, "Benevolence—Benevolence is Man." Under the régime of feudalism, which could easily be perverted into militarism, it was to Benevolence that we owed our deliverance from despotism of the worst kind. An utter surrender of "life and limb" on the part of the governed would have left nothing for the governing but self-will, and this has for its natural consequence the growth of that absolutism so often called "oriental despotism,"—as though there were no despots of occidental history!

Let it be far from me to uphold despotism of any sort; but it is a mistake to identify feudalism with it. When Frederick the Great wrote that "Kings are the first servants of the State," jurists thought rightly that a new era was reached in the development of freedom. Strangely coinciding in time, in the backwoods of North-western Japan, Yozan of Yonézawa made exactly the same declaration, showing that feudalism was not all tyranny and oppression. A feudal prince, although unmindful of owing reciprocal obligations to his vassals, felt a higher sense of responsibility to his ancestors and to Heaven. He was a father to his subjects, whom Heaven entrusted to his care. In a sense not usually assigned to the term, Bushido accepted and corroborated paternal government—paternal also as opposed to the less interested avuncular government (Uncle Sam's, to wit!). The difference between a despotic and a paternal government lies in this, that in the one the people obey reluctantly, while in the other they do so with "that proud submission, that dignified obedience, that subordination of heart which kept alive, even in servitude itself, the spirit of exalted freedom." [Burke, *French Revolution*.] The old saying is not entirely false which called the king of England the "king of devils, because of his subjects' often insurrections against, and depositions of, their princes," and which made the French monarch the "king of asses, because of their infinite taxes and Impositions," but which gave the title of "the king of men" to the sovereign of Spain "because of his subjects' willing obedience." But enough!—

Virtue and absolute power may strike the Anglo-Saxon mind as terms which it is impossible to harmonize. Pobyedonostseff has clearly set before us the contrast in the foundations of English and other European communities; namely that these were organized on the basis of common interest, while that was distinguished by a strongly developed independent personality. What this Russian statesman says of the personal dependence of individuals on some social alliance and in the end of ends of the State, among the continental nations of Europe and particularly among Slavonic peoples, is doubly true of the Japanese. Hence not only is a free exercise of monarchical power not felt as heavily by us as in Europe, but it is generally moderated by parental consideration for the feelings of the people. "Absolutism," says Bismarck, "primarily demands in the ruler impartiality, honesty, devotion to duty, energy and inward humility." If I may be allowed to make one more quotation on this subject, I will cite from the speech of the German Emperor at Coblenz, in which he spoke of "Kingship, by the grace of God, with its heavy duties, its tremendous responsibility to the Creator alone, from which no man, no minister, no parliament, can release the monarch."

We knew Benevolence was a tender virtue and mother-like. If upright Rectitude and stern Justice were peculiarly masculine, Mercy had the gentleness and the persuasiveness of a feminine nature. We were warned against indulging in indiscriminate charity, without seasoning it with justice and rectitude. Masamuné expressed it well in his oft-quoted aphorism—"Rectitude carried to excess hardens into stiffness; Benevolence indulged beyond measure sinks into weakness."

Fortunately Mercy was not so rare as it was beautiful, for it is universally true that "The bravest are the tenderest, the loving are the daring." "*Bushi no nasaké*"—the tenderness of a warrior—had a sound which appealed at once to whatever was noble in us; not that the mercy of a samurai was generically different from the mercy of any other being, but because it implied mercy where mercy was not a blind impulse, but where it recognized due regard to justice, and where mercy did not remain merely a certain state of mind, but where it was backed with power to save or kill. As economists speak of demand as being effectual or ineffectual, similarly we may call the mercy of bushi effectual, since it implied the power of acting for the good or detriment of the recipient.

Priding themselves as they did in their brute strength and privileges to turn it into account, the samurai gave full consent to what Mencius taught concerning the power of Love. "Benevolence," he says, "brings under its sway whatever hinders its power, just as water subdues fire: they only doubt the power of water to quench flames who try to extinguish with a cupful a whole burning wagon-load of fagots." He also says that "the feeling of distress is the root of benevolence, therefore a benevolent man is ever mindful of those who are suffering and in distress." Thus did Mencius long anticipate Adam Smith who founds his ethical philosophy on Sympathy.

It is indeed striking how closely the code of knightly honor of one country coincides with that of others; in other words, how the much abused oriental ideas of morals find their counterparts in the noblest maxims of European literature. If the well-known lines,

> Hae tibi erunt artes—pacisque imponere morem,
> Parcere subjectis, et debellare superbos,

were shown a Japanese gentleman, he might readily accuse the Mantuan bard of plagiarizing from the literature of his own country. Benevolence to the weak, the downtrodden or the vanquished, was ever extolled as peculiarly becoming to a samurai. Lovers of Japanese art must be familiar with the representation of a priest riding backwards on a cow. The rider was once a warrior who in his day made his name a by-word of terror. In that terrible battle of Sumano-ura, (1184 A.D.), which was one of the most decisive in our history, he overtook an enemy and in single combat had him in the clutch of his gigantic arms. Now the etiquette of war required that on such occasions no blood should be spilt, unless the weaker party proved to be a man of rank or ability equal to that of the stronger. The grim combatant would have the name of the man under him; but he refusing to make it known, his helmet was ruthlessly torn off, when the sight of a juvenile face, fair and beardless, made the astonished knight relax his hold. Helping the youth to his feet, in paternal tones he bade the stripling go: "Off, young prince, to thy mother's side! The sword of Kumagaye shall never be tarnished by a drop of thy blood. Haste and flee o'er yon pass before thy enemies come in sight!" The young warrior refused to go and begged Kumagaye, for the honor of both, to despatch him on the spot. Above the hoary head of the veteran gleams the cold blade, which many a time before has sundered the chords of life, but his stout heart quails; there flashes athwart his mental eye the vision of his own boy, who this self-same day marched to the sound of bugle to try his maiden arms; the strong hand of the warrior quivers; again he begs his victim to flee for his life. Finding all his entreaties vain and hearing the approaching steps of his comrades, he exclaims: "If thou art overtaken, thou mayest fall at a more ignoble hand than mine. O, thou Infinite! receive his soul!" In an instant the sword flashes in the air, and when it falls it is red with adolescent blood. When the war is ended, we find our soldier returning in triumph, but little cares he now for honor or fame; he renounces his warlike career, shaves his head, dons a priestly garb, devotes the rest of his days to holy pilgrimage, never turning his back to the West, where lies the Paradise whence salvation comes and whither the sun hastes daily for his rest.

Critics may point out flaws in this story, which is casuistically vulnerable. Let it be: all the same it shows that Tenderness, Pity and Love, were traits which adorned the most sanguinary exploits of the samurai. It was an old maxim among them that "It becometh not the fowler to slay the bird which takes refuge in his bosom." This in a large measure explains why the Red Cross movement, considered peculiarly Christian, so readily found a firm footing among us. For decades before we heard of the Geneva Convention, Bakin, our greatest novelist, had familiarized us with the medical treatment of a fallen foe. In the principality of Satsuma, noted for its martial spirit and education, the custom prevailed for young men to practice music; not the blast of trumpets or the beat of drums,—"those clamorous harbingers of blood and death"—stirring us to imitate the actions of a tiger, but sad and tender melodies on the *biwa*, [*A musical instrument, resembling the guitar.*] soothing our fiery spirits, drawing our thoughts away from scent of blood and scenes of carnage. Polybius tells us of the Constitution of Arcadia, which required all youths under thirty to practice music, in order that this gentle art might alleviate the rigors of that inclement region. It is to its influence that he attributes the absence of cruelty in that part of the Arcadian mountains.

Nor was Satsuma the only place in Japan where gentleness was inculcated among the warrior class. A Prince of Shirakawa jots down his random thoughts, and among them is the following: "Though they come stealing to your bedside in the silent watches of the night, drive not away, but rather cherish these—the fragrance of flowers, the sound of distant bells, the insect humming of a frosty night." And again, "Though they may wound your feelings, these three you have only to forgive, the breeze that scatters your flowers, the cloud that hides your moon, and the man who tries to pick quarrels with you."

It was ostensibly to express, but actually to cultivate, these gentler emotions that the writing of verses was encouraged. Our poetry has therefore a strong undercurrent of pathos and tenderness. A well-known anecdote of a rustic samurai illustrates a case in point. When he was told to learn versification, and "The Warbler's Notes" [*The uguisu or warbler, sometimes called the nightingale of Japan.*] was given him for the subject of his first attempt, his fiery spirit rebelled and he *flung* at the feet of his master this uncouth production, which ran:

> "The brave warrior keeps apart
> The ear that might listen
> To the warbler's song."

His master, undaunted by the crude sentiment, continued to encourage the youth, until one day the music of his soul was awakened to respond to the sweet notes of the *uguisu*, and he wrote:

> "Stands the warrior, mailed and strong,
> To hear the uguisu's song,
> Warbled sweet the trees among."

We admire and enjoy the heroic incident in Körner's short life, when, as he lay wounded on the battle-field, he scribbled his famous "Farewell to Life." Incidents of a similar kind were not at all unusual in our warfare. Our pithy, epigrammatic poems were particularly well suited to the improvisation of a single sentiment. Everybody of any education was either a poet or a poetaster. Not infrequently a marching soldier might be seen to halt, take his writing utensils from his belt, and compose an ode,—and such papers were found afterward in the helmets or the breast-plates, when these were removed from their lifeless wearers.

Bushido - The Soul of Japan

Politeness

What Christianity has done in Europe toward rousing compassion in the midst of belligerent horrors, love of music and letters has done in Japan. The cultivation of tender feelings breeds considerate regard for the sufferings of others. Modesty and complaisance, actuated by respect for others' feelings, are at the root of politeness that courtesy and urbanity of manners which has been noticed by every foreign tourist as a marked Japanese trait. Politeness is a poor virtue, if it is actuated only by a fear of offending good taste, whereas it should be the outward manifestation of a sympathetic regard for the feelings of others. It also implies a due regard for the fitness of things, therefore due respect to social positions; for these latter express no plutocratic distinctions, but were originally distinctions for actual merit.

In its highest form, politeness almost approaches love. We may reverently say, politeness "suffereth long, and is kind; envieth not, vaunteth not itself, is not puffed up; doth not behave itself unseemly, seeketh not her own, is not easily provoked, taketh not account of evil." Is it any wonder that Professor Dean, in speaking of the six elements of Humanity, accords to Politeness an exalted position, inasmuch as it is the ripest fruit of social intercourse?

While thus extolling Politeness, far be it from me to put it in the front rank of virtues. If we analyze it, we shall find it correlated with other virtues of a higher order; for what virtue stands alone? While—or rather because—it was exalted as peculiar to the profession of arms, and as such esteemed in a degree higher than its deserts, there came into existence its counterfeits. Confucius himself has repeatedly taught that external appurtenances are as little a part of propriety as sounds are of music.

When propriety was elevated to the *sine qua non* of social intercourse, it was only to be expected that an elaborate system of etiquette should come into vogue to train youth in correct social behavior. How one must bow in accosting others, how he must walk and sit, were taught and learned with utmost care. Table manners grew to be a science. Tea serving and drinking were raised to a ceremony. A man of education is, of course, expected to be master of all these. Very fitly does Mr. Veblen, in his interesting book, [*Theory of the Leisure Class*, N.Y. 1899, p. 46.] call decorum "a product and an exponent of the leisure-class life."

I have heard slighting remarks made by Europeans upon our elaborate discipline of politeness. It has been criticized as absorbing too much of our thought and in so far a folly to observe strict obedience to it. I admit that there may be unnecessary niceties in ceremonious etiquette, but whether it partakes as much of folly as the adherence to ever-changing fashions of the West, is a question not very clear to my mind. Even fashions I do not consider solely as freaks of vanity; on the contrary, I look upon these as a ceaseless search of the human mind for the beautiful. Much less do I consider elaborate ceremony as altogether trivial; for it denotes the result of long observation as to the most appropriate method of achieving a certain result. If there is anything to do, there is certainly a best way to do it, and the best way is both the most economical and the most graceful. Mr. Spencer defines grace as the most economical manner of motion. The tea ceremony presents certain definite ways of manipulating a bowl, a spoon, a napkin, etc. To a novice it looks tedious. But one soon discovers that the way prescribed is, after all, the most saving of time and labor; in other words, the most economical use of force,—hence, according to Spencer's dictum, the most graceful.

The spiritual significance of social decorum,—or, I might say, to borrow from the vocabulary of the "Philosophy of Clothes," the spiritual discipline of which etiquette and ceremony are mere outward garments,—is out of all proportion to what their appearance warrants us in believing. I might follow the example of Mr. Spencer and trace in our ceremonial institutions their origins and the moral motives that gave rise to them; but that is not what I shall endeavor to do in this book. It is the moral training involved in strict observance of propriety, that I wish to emphasize.

I have said that etiquette was elaborated into the finest niceties, so much so that different schools advocating different systems, came into existence. But they all united in the ultimate essential, and this was put by a great exponent of the best known school of etiquette, the Ogasawara, in the following terms: "The end of all etiquette is to so cultivate your mind that even when you are quietly seated, not the roughest ruffian can dare make onset on your person." It means, in other words, that by constant exercise in correct manners, one brings all the parts and faculties of his body into perfect order and into such harmony with itself and its environment as to express the mastery of spirit over the flesh. What a new and deep significance the French word *biensèance* [Etymologically *well-seatedness*.] comes thus to contain!

If the premise is true that gracefulness means economy of force, then it follows as a logical sequence that a constant practice of graceful deportment must bring with it a reserve and storage of force. Fine manners, therefore, mean power in repose. When the barbarian Gauls, during the sack of Rome, burst into the assembled Senate and dared pull the beards of the venerable Fathers, we think the old gentlemen were to blame, inasmuch as they lacked dignity and strength of manners. Is lofty spiritual attainment really possible through etiquette? Why not?—All roads lead to Rome!

As an example of how the simplest thing can be made into an art and then become spiritual culture, I may take *Cha-no-yu*, the tea ceremony. Tea-sipping as a fine art! Why should it not be? In the children drawing pictures on the sand, or in the savage carving on a rock, was the promise of a Raphael or a Michael Angelo. How much more is the drinking of a beverage, which began with the transcendental contemplation of a Hindoo anchorite, entitled to develop into a handmaid of Religion and Morality? That calmness of mind, that serenity of temper, that composure and quietness of demeanor, which are the first essentials of *Cha-no-yu* are without doubt the first conditions of right thinking and right feeling. The scrupulous cleanliness of the little room, shut off from sight and sound of the madding crowd, is in itself conducive to direct one's thoughts from the world. The bare interior does not engross one's attention like the innumerable pictures and bric-a-brac of a Western parlor; the presence of *kakemono* [*Hanging scrolls, which may be either paintings or ideograms, used for decorative purposes.*] calls our attention more to grace of design than to beauty of color. The utmost refinement of taste is the object aimed at; whereas anything like display is banished with religious horror. The very fact that it was invented by a contemplative recluse, in a time when wars and the rumors of wars were incessant, is well calculated to show that this institution was more than a pastime. Before entering the quiet precincts of the tea-room, the company assembling to partake of the ceremony laid aside, together with their swords, the ferocity of the battle-field or the cares of government, there to find peace and friendship.

Cha-no-yu is more than a ceremony—it is a fine art; it is poetry, with articulate gestures for rhythm: it is a *modus operandi* of soul discipline. Its greatest value lies in this last phase. Not infrequently the other phases preponderated in the mind of its votaries, but that does not prove that its essence was not of a spiritual nature.

Politeness will be a great acquisition, if it does no more than impart grace to manners; but its function does not stop here. For propriety, springing as it does from motives of benevolence and modesty, and actuated by tender feelings toward the sensibilities of others, is ever a graceful expression of sympathy. Its requirement is that we should weep with those that weep and rejoice with those that rejoice. Such didactic requirement, when reduced into small every-day details of life, expresses itself in little acts scarcely noticeable, or, if noticed, is, as one missionary lady of twenty years' residence once said to me, "awfully funny." You are out in the hot glaring sun with no shade over you; a Japanese acquaintance passes by; you accost him, and instantly his hat is off—well, that is perfectly natural, but the "awfully funny" performance is, that all the while he talks with you his parasol is down and he stands in the glaring sun also. How foolish!—Yes, exactly so, provided the motive were less than this: "You are in the sun; I sympathize with you; I would willingly take you under my parasol if it were large enough, or if we were familiarly acquainted; as I cannot shade you, I will share your discomforts." Little acts of this kind, equally or more amusing, are not mere gestures or conventionalities. They are the "bodying forth" of thoughtful feelings for the comfort of others.

Another "awfully funny" custom is dictated by our canons of Politeness; but many superficial writers on Japan, have dismissed it by simply attributing it to the general topsy-turvyness of the nation. Every foreigner who has observed it will confess the awkwardness he felt in making proper reply upon the occasion. In America, when you make a gift, you sing its praises to the recipient; in Japan we depreciate or slander it. The underlying idea with you is, "This is a nice gift: if it were not nice I would not dare give it to you; for it will be an insult to give you anything but what is nice." In contrast to this, our logic runs: "You are a nice person, and no gift is nice enough for you. You will not accept anything I can lay at your feet except as a token of my good will; so accept this, not for its intrinsic value, but as a token. It will be an insult to your worth to call the best gift good enough for you." Place the two ideas side by side; and we see that the ultimate idea is one and the same. Neither is "awfully funny." The American speaks of the material which makes the gift; the Japanese speaks of the spirit which prompts the gift.

Bushido - The Soul of Japan

Veracity or Truthfulness

It is perverse reasoning to conclude, because our sense of propriety shows itself in all the smallest ramifications of our deportment, to take the least important of them and uphold it as the type, and pass judgment upon the principle itself. Which is more important, to eat or to observe rules of propriety about eating? A Chinese sage answers, "If you take a case where the eating is all-important, and the observing the rules of propriety is of little importance, and compare them together, why merely say that the eating is of the more importance?" "Metal is heavier than feathers," but does that saying have reference to a single clasp of metal and a wagon-load of feathers? Take a piece of wood a foot thick and raise it above the pinnacle of a temple, none would call it taller than the temple.

To the question, "Which is the more important, to tell the truth or to be polite?" the Japanese are said to give an answer diametrically opposite to what the American will say,—but I forbear any comment until I come to speak of veracity or truthfulness without which Politeness is a farce and a show. "Propriety carried beyond right bounds," says Masamuné, "becomes a lie." An ancient poet has outdone Polonius in the advice he gives: "To thyself be faithful: if in thy heart thou strayest not from truth, without prayer of thine the Gods will keep thee whole." The apotheosis of Sincerity to which Tsu-tsu gives expression in the *Doctrine of the Mean*, attributes to it transcendental powers, almost identifying them with the Divine. "Sincerity is the end and the beginning of all things; without Sincerity there would be nothing." He then dwells with eloquence on its far-reaching and long enduring nature, its power to produce changes without movement and by its mere presence to accomplish its purpose without effort. From the Chinese ideogram for Sincerity, which is a combination of "Word" and "Perfect," one is tempted to draw a parallel between it and the Neo-Platonic doctrine of *Logos*—to such height does the sage soar in his unwonted mystic flight.

Lying or equivocation were deemed equally cowardly. The bushi held that his high social position demanded a loftier standard of veracity than that of the tradesman and peasant. *Bushi no ichi-gon*—the word of a samurai or in exact German equivalent *ein Ritterwort*—was sufficient guaranty of the truthfulness of an assertion. His word carried such weight with it that promises were generally made and fulfilled without a written pledge, which would have been deemed quite beneath his dignity. Many thrilling anecdotes were told of those who atoned by death for *ni-gon*, a double tongue.

The regard for veracity was so high that, unlike the generality of Christians who persistently violate the plain commands of the Teacher not to swear, the best of samurai looked upon an oath as derogatory to their honor. I am well aware that they did swear by different deities or upon their swords; but never has swearing degenerated into wanton form and irreverent interjection. To emphasize our words a practice of literally sealing with blood was sometimes resorted to. For the explanation of such a practice, I need only refer my readers to Goethe's Faust.

A recent American writer is responsible for this statement, that if you ask an ordinary Japanese which is better, to tell a falsehood or be impolite, he will not hesitate to answer "to tell a falsehood!" Dr. Peery [Peery, *The Gist of Japan*, p. 86.] is partly right and partly wrong; right in that an ordinary Japanese, even a samurai, may answer in the way ascribed to him, but wrong in attributing too much weight to the term he translates "falsehood." This word (in Japanese *uso*) is employed to denote anything which is not a truth (*makoto*) or fact (*honto*). Lowell tells us that Wordsworth could not distinguish between truth and fact, and an ordinary Japanese is in this respect as good as Wordsworth. Ask a Japanese, or even an American of any refinement, to tell you whether he dislikes you or whether he is sick at his stomach, and he will not hesitate long to tell falsehoods and answer, "I like you much," or, "I am quite well, thank you." To sacrifice truth merely for the sake of politeness was regarded as an "empty form" (*kyo-rei*) and "deception by sweet words," and was never justified.

I own I am speaking now of the Bushido idea of veracity; but it may not be amiss to devote a few words to our commercial integrity, of which I have heard much complaint in foreign books and journals. A loose business morality has indeed been the worst blot on our national reputation; but before abusing it or hastily condemning the whole race for it, let us calmly study it and we shall be rewarded with consolation for the future.

Of all the great occupations of life, none was farther removed from the profession of arms than commerce. The merchant was placed lowest in the category of vocations,—the knight, the tiller of the soil, the mechanic, the merchant. The samurai derived his income from land and could even indulge, if he had a mind to, in amateur farming; but the counter and abacus were abhorred. We knew the wisdom of this social arrangement. Montesquieu has made it clear that the debarring of the nobility from mercantile pursuits was an admirable social policy, in that it prevented wealth from accumulating in the hands of the powerful. The separation of power and riches kept the distribution of the latter more nearly equable. Professor Dill, the author of "Roman Society in the Last Century of the Western Empire," has brought afresh to our mind that one cause of the decadence of the Roman Empire, was the permission given to the nobility to engage in trade, and the consequent monopoly of wealth and power by a minority of the senatorial families.

Commerce, therefore, in feudal Japan did not reach that degree of development which it would have attained under freer conditions. The obloquy attached to the calling naturally brought within its pale such as cared little for social repute. "Call one a thief and he will steal:" put a stigma on a calling and its followers adjust their morals to it, for it is natural that "the normal conscience," as Hugh Black says, "rises to the demands made on it, and easily falls to the limit of the standard expected from it." It is unnecessary to add that no business, commercial or otherwise, can be transacted without a code of morals. Our merchants of the feudal period had one among themselves, without which they could never have developed, as they did, such fundamental mercantile institutions as the guild, the bank, the bourse, insurance, checks, bills of exchange, etc.; but in their relations with people outside their vocation, the tradesmen lived too true to the reputation of their order.

This being the case, when the country was opened to foreign trade, only the most adventurous and unscrupulous rushed to the ports, while the respectable business houses declined for some time the repeated requests of the authorities to establish branch houses. Was Bushido powerless to stay the current of commercial dishonor? Let us see.

Those who are well acquainted with our history will remember that only a few years after our treaty ports were opened to foreign trade, feudalism was abolished, and when with it the samurai's fiefs were taken and bonds issued to them in compensation, they were given liberty to invest them in mercantile transactions. Now you may ask, "Why could they not bring their much boasted veracity into their new business relations and so reform the old abuses?" Those who had eyes to see could not weep enough, those who had hearts to feel could not sympathize enough, with the fate of many a noble and honest samurai who signally and irrevocably failed in his new and unfamiliar field of trade and industry, through sheer lack of shrewdness in coping with his artful plebeian rival. When we know that eighty per cent. of the business houses fail in so industrial a country as America, is it any wonder that scarcely one among a hundred samurai who went into trade could succeed in his new vocation? It will be long before it will be recognized how many fortunes were wrecked in the attempt to apply Bushido ethics to business methods; but it was soon patent to every observing mind that the ways of wealth were not the ways of honor. In what respects, then, were they different?

Of the three incentives to Veracity that Lecky enumerates, viz: the industrial, the political, and the philosophical, the first was altogether lacking in Bushido. As to the second, it could develop little in a political community under a feudal system. It is in its philosophical, and as Lecky says, in its highest aspect, that Honesty attained elevated rank in our catalogue of virtues. With all my sincere regard for the high commercial integrity of the Anglo-Saxon race, when I ask for the ultimate ground, I am told that "Honesty is the best policy," that it *pays* to be honest. Is not this virtue, then, its own reward? If it is followed because it brings in more cash than falsehood, I am afraid Bushido would rather indulge in lies!

If Bushido rejects a doctrine of *quid pro quo* rewards, the shrewder tradesman will readily accept it. Lecky has very truly remarked that Veracity owes its growth largely to commerce and manufacture; as Nietzsche puts it, "Honesty is the youngest of virtues"—in other words, it is the foster-child of industry, of modern industry. Without this mother, Veracity was like a blue-blood orphan whom only the most cultivated mind could adopt and nourish. Such minds were general among the samurai, but, for want of a more democratic and utilitarian foster-mother, the tender child failed to thrive. Industries advancing, Veracity will prove an easy, nay, a profitable, virtue to practice. Just think, as late as November 1880, Bismarck sent a circular to the professional consuls of the German Empire, warning them of "a lamentable lack of reliability with regard to German shipments *inter alia*, apparent both as to quality and quantity;" now-a-days we hear comparatively little of German carelessness and dishonesty in trade. In twenty years her merchants learned that in the end honesty pays. Already our merchants are finding that out. For the rest I recommend the reader to two recent writers for well-weighed judgment on this point. [Knapp, *Feudal and Modern Japan*, Vol. I, Ch. IV. Ransome, *Japan in Transition*, Ch. VIII.] It is interesting to remark in this connection that integrity and honor were the surest guaranties which even a merchant debtor could present in the form of promissory notes. It was quite a usual thing to insert such clauses as these: "In default of the repayment of the sum lent to me, I shall say nothing against being ridiculed in public;" or, "In case I fail to pay you back, you may call me a fool," and the like.

Often have I wondered whether the Veracity of Bushido had any motive higher than courage. In the absence of any positive commandment against bearing false witness, lying was not condemned as sin, but simply denounced as weakness, and, as such, highly dishonorable. As a matter of fact, the idea of honesty is so intimately blended, and its Latin and its German etymology so identified with honor that it is high time I should pause a few moments for the consideration of this feature of the Precepts of Knighthood.

Bushido - The Soul of Japan

Honor

The sense of honor, implying a vivid consciousness of personal dignity and worth, could not fail to characterize the samurai, born and bred to value the duties and privileges of their profession. Though the word ordinarily given now-a-days as the translation of Honor was not used freely, yet the idea was conveyed by such terms as *na* (name) *men-moku* (countenance), *guai-bun* (outside hearing), reminding us respectively of the biblical use of "name," of the evolution of the term "personality" from the Greek mask, and of "fame." A good name— one's reputation, the immortal part of one's self, what remains being bestial—assumed as a matter of course, any infringement upon its integrity was felt as shame, and the sense of shame (*Ren-chi-shin*) was one of the earliest to be cherished in juvenile education. "You will be laughed at," "It will disgrace you," "Are you not ashamed?" were the last appeal to correct behavior on the part of a youthful delinquent. Such a recourse to his honor touched the most sensitive spot in the child's heart, as though it had been nursed on honor while it was in its mother's womb; for most truly is honor a prenatal influence, being closely bound up with strong family consciousness. "In losing the solidarity of families," says Balzac, "society has lost the fundamental force which Montesquieu named Honor." Indeed, the sense of shame seems to me to be the earliest indication of the moral consciousness of our race. The first and worst punishment which befell humanity in consequence of tasting "the fruit of that forbidden tree" was, to my mind, not the sorrow of childbirth, nor the thorns and thistles, but the awakening of the sense of shame. Few incidents in history excel in pathos the scene of the first mother plying with heaving breast and tremulous fingers, her crude needle on the few fig leaves which her dejected husband plucked for her. This first fruit of disobedience clings to us with a tenacity that nothing else does. All the sartorial ingenuity of mankind has not yet succeeded in sewing an apron that will efficaciously hide our sense of shame. That samurai was right who refused to compromise his character by a slight humiliation in his youth; "because," he said, "dishonor is like a scar on a tree, which time, instead of effacing, only helps to enlarge."

Mencius had taught centuries before, in almost the identical phrase, what Carlyle has latterly expressed,—namely, that "Shame is the soil of all Virtue, of good manners and good morals."

The fear of disgrace was so great that if our literature lacks such eloquence as Shakespeare puts into the mouth of Norfolk, it nevertheless hung like Damocles' sword over the head of every samurai and often assumed a morbid character. In the name of Honor, deeds were perpetrated which can find no justification in the code of Bushido. At the slightest, nay, imaginary insult, the quick-tempered braggart took offense, resorted to the use of the sword, and many an unnecessary strife was raised and many an innocent life lost. The story of a well-meaning citizen who called the attention of a bushi to a flea jumping on his back, and who was forthwith cut in two, for the simple and questionable reason that inasmuch as fleas are parasites which feed on animals, it was an unpardonable insult to identify a noble warrior with a beast—I say, stories like these are too frivolous to believe. Yet, the circulation of such stories implies three things; (1) that they were invented to overawe common people; (2) that abuses were really made of the samurai's profession of honor; and (3) that a very strong sense of shame was developed among them. It is plainly unfair to take an abnormal case to cast blame upon the Precepts, any more than to judge of the true teaching of Christ from the fruits of religious fanaticism and extravagance—inquisitions and hypocrisy. But, as in religious monomania there is something touchingly noble, as compared with the delirium tremens of a drunkard, so in that extreme sensitiveness of the samurai about their honor do we not recognize the substratum of a genuine virtue?

The morbid excess into which the delicate code of honor was inclined to run was strongly counterbalanced by preaching magnanimity and patience. To take offense at slight provocation was ridiculed as "short-tempered." The popular adage said: "To bear what you think you cannot bear is really to bear." The great Iyéyasu left to posterity a few maxims, among which are the following:—"The life of man is like going a long distance with a heavy load upon the shoulders. Haste not. —Reproach none, but be forever watchful of thine own short-comings.

—Forbearance is the basis of length of days." He proved in his life what he preached. A literary wit put a characteristic epigram into the mouths of three well-known personages in our history: to Nobunaga he attributed, "I will kill her, if the nightingale sings not in time;" to Hidéyoshi, "I will force her to sing for me;" and to Iyéyasu, "I will wait till she opens her lips."

Patience and long suffering were also highly commended by Mencius. In one place he writes to this effect: "Though you denude yourself and insult me, what is that to me? You cannot defile my soul by your outrage." Elsewhere he teaches that anger at a petty offense is unworthy a superior man, but indignation for a great cause is righteous wrath.

To what height of unmartial and unresisting meekness Bushido could reach in some of its votaries, may be seen in their utterances. Take, for instance, this saying of Ogawa: "When others speak all manner of evil things against thee, return not evil for evil, but rather reflect that thou wast not more faithful in the discharge of thy duties." Take another of Kumazawa:—"When others blame thee, blame them not; when others are angry at thee, return not anger. Joy cometh only as Passion and Desire part." Still another instance I may cite from Saigo, upon whose overhanging brows "shame is ashamed to sit;"—"The Way is the way of Heaven and Earth: Man's place is to follow it: therefore make it the object of thy life to reverence Heaven. Heaven loves me and others with equal love; therefore with the love wherewith thou lovest thyself, love others. Make not Man thy partner but Heaven, and making Heaven thy partner do thy best. Never condemn others; but see to it that thou comest not short of thine own mark." Some of those sayings remind us of Christian expostulations and show us how far in practical morality natural religion can approach the revealed. Not only did these sayings remain as utterances, but they were really embodied in acts.

It must be admitted that very few attained this sublime height of magnanimity, patience and forgiveness. It was a great pity that nothing clear and general was expressed as to what constitutes Honor, only a few enlightened minds being aware that it "from no condition rises," but that it lies in each acting well his part: for nothing was easier than for youths to forget in the heat of action what they had learned in Mencius in their calmer moments. Said this sage, "'Tis in every man's mind to love honor: but little doth he dream that what is truly honorable lies within himself and not anywhere else. The honor which men confer is not good honor. Those whom Châo the Great ennobles, he can make mean again."

For the most part, an insult was quickly resented and repaid by death, as we shall see later, while Honor—too often nothing higher than vain glory or worldly approbation—was prized as the *summum bonum* of earthly existence. Fame, and not wealth or knowledge, was the goal toward which youths had to strive. Many a lad swore within himself as he crossed the threshold of his paternal home, that he would not recross it until he had made a name in the world: and many an ambitious mother refused to see her sons again unless they could "return home," as the expression is, "caparisoned in brocade." To shun shame or win a name, samurai boys would submit to any privations and undergo severest ordeals of bodily or mental suffering. They knew that honor won in youth grows with age. In the memorable siege of Osaka, a young son of Iyéyasu, in spite of his earnest entreaties to be put in the vanguard, was placed at the rear of the army. When the castle fell, he was so chagrined and wept so bitterly that an old councillor tried to console him with all the resources at his command. "Take comfort, Sire," said he, "at thought of the long future before you. In the many years that you may live, there will come divers occasions to distinguish yourself." The boy fixed his indignant gaze upon the man and said—"How foolishly you talk! Can ever my fourteenth year come round again?"

Life itself was thought cheap if honor and fame could be attained therewith: hence, whenever a cause presented itself which was considered dearer than life, with utmost serenity and celerity was life laid down.

Bushido - The Soul of Japan

The Duty of Loyalty

Of the causes in comparison with which no life was too dear to sacrifice, was the duty of loyalty which was the key-stone making feudal virtues a symmetrical arch. Other virtues feudal morality shares in common with other systems of ethics, with other classes of people, but this virtue—homage and fealty to a superior—is its distinctive feature. I am aware that personal fidelity is a moral adhesion existing among all sorts and conditions of men,—a gang of pickpockets owe allegiance to a Fagin; but it is only in the code of chivalrous honor that Loyalty assumes paramount importance.

In spite of Hegel's criticism that the fidelity of feudal vassals, being an obligation to an individual and not to a Commonwealth, is a bond established on totally unjust principles, [*Philosophy of History* (Eng. trans. by Sibree), Pt. IV, Sec. II, Ch. I] a great compatriot of his made it his boast that personal loyalty was a German virtue. Bismarck had good reason to do so, not because the *Treue* he boasts of was the monopoly of his Fatherland or of any single nation or race, but because this favored fruit of chivalry lingers latest among the people where feudalism has lasted longest. In America where "everybody is as good as anybody else," and, as the Irishman added, "better too," such exalted ideas of loyalty as we feel for our sovereign may be deemed "excellent within certain bounds," but preposterous as encouraged among us. Montesquieu complained long ago that right on one side of the Pyrenees was wrong on the other, and the recent Dreyfus trial proved the truth of his remark, save that the Pyrenees were not the sole boundary beyond which French justice finds no accord. Similarly, Loyalty as we conceive it may find few admirers elsewhere, not because our conception is wrong, but because it is, I am afraid, forgotten, and also because we carry it to a degree not reached in any other country. Griffis [*Religions of Japan.*] was quite right in stating that whereas in China Confucian ethics made obedience to parents the primary human duty, in Japan precedence was given to Loyalty. At the risk of shocking some of my good readers, I will relate of one "who could endure to follow a fall'n lord" and who thus, as Shakespeare assures, "earned a place i' the story."

The story is of one of the purest characters in our history, Michizané, who, falling a victim to jealousy and calumny, is exiled from the capital. Not content with this, his unrelenting enemies are now bent upon the extinction of his family. Strict search for his son—not yet grown—reveals the fact of his being secreted in a village school kept by one Genzo, a former vassal of Michizané. When orders are dispatched to the schoolmaster to deliver the head of the juvenile offender on a certain day, his first idea is to find a suitable substitute for it. He ponders over his school-list, scrutinizes with careful eyes all the boys, as they stroll into the class-room, but none among the children born of the soil bears the least resemblance to his protégé. His despair, however, is but for a moment; for, behold, a new scholar is announced—a comely boy of the same age as his master's son, escorted by a mother of noble mien. No less conscious of the resemblance between infant lord and infant retainer, were the mother and the boy himself. In the privacy of home both had laid themselves upon the altar; the one his life,—the other her heart, yet without sign to the outer world. Unwitting of what had passed between them, it is the teacher from whom comes the suggestion.

Here, then, is the scape-goat!—The rest of the narrative may be briefly told.—On the day appointed, arrives the officer commissioned to identify and receive the head of the youth. Will he be deceived by the false head? The poor Genzo's hand is on the hilt of the sword, ready to strike a blow either at the man or at himself, should the examination defeat his scheme. The officer takes up the gruesome object before him, goes calmly over each feature, and in a deliberate, business-like tone, pronounces it genuine.—That evening in a lonely home awaits the mother we saw in the school. Does she know the fate of her child? It is not for his return that she watches with eagerness for the opening of the wicket. Her father-in-law has been for a long time a recipient of Michizané's bounties, but since his banishment circumstances have forced her husband to follow the service of the enemy of his family's benefactor. He himself could not be untrue to his own cruel master; but his son could serve the cause of the grandsire's lord. As one acquainted with the exile's family, it was he who had been entrusted with the task of identifying the boy's head. Now the day's—yea, the life's—hard work is done, he returns home and as he crosses its threshold, he accosts his wife, saying: "Rejoice, my wife, our darling son has proved of service to his lord!"

"What an atrocious story!" I hear my readers exclaim,—"Parents deliberately sacrificing their own innocent child to save the life of another man's." But this child was a conscious and willing victim: it is a story of vicarious death—as significant as, and not more revolting than, the story of Abraham's intended sacrifice of Isaac. In both cases it was obedience to the call of duty, utter submission to the command of a higher voice, whether given by a visible or an invisible angel, or heard by an outward or an inward ear;—but I abstain from preaching.

The individualism of the West, which recognizes separate interests for father and son, husband and wife, necessarily brings into strong relief the duties owed by one to the other; but Bushido held that the interest of the family and of the members thereof is intact,—one and inseparable. This interest it bound up with affection—natural, instinctive, irresistible; hence, if we die for one we love with natural love (which animals themselves possess), what is that? "For if ye love them that love you, what reward have ye? Do not even the publicans the same?"

In his great history, Sanyo relates in touching language the heart struggle of Shigemori concerning his father's rebellious conduct. "If I be loyal, my father must be undone; if I obey my father, my duty to my sovereign must go amiss." Poor Shigemori! We see him afterward praying with all his soul that kind Heaven may visit him with death, that he may be released from this world where it is hard for purity and righteousness to dwell.

Many a Shigemori has his heart torn by the conflict between duty and affection. Indeed neither Shakespeare nor the Old Testament itself contains an adequate rendering of *ko*, our conception of filial piety, and yet in such conflicts Bushido never wavered in its choice of Loyalty. Women, too, encouraged their offspring to sacrifice all for the king. Ever as resolute as Widow Windham and her illustrious consort, the samurai matron stood ready to give up her boys for the cause of Loyalty.

Since Bushido, like Aristotle and some modern sociologists, conceived the state as antedating the individual—the latter being born into the former as part and parcel thereof—he must live and die for it or for the incumbent of its legitimate authority. Readers of Crito will remember the argument with which Socrates represents the laws of the city as pleading with him on the subject of his escape. Among others he makes them (the laws, or the state) say:—"Since you were begotten and nurtured and educated under us, dare you once to say you are not our offspring and servant, you and your fathers before you!" These are words which do not impress us as any thing extraordinary; for the same thing has long been on the lips of Bushido, with this modification, that the laws and the state were represented with us by a personal being. Loyalty is an ethical outcome of this political theory.

I am not entirely ignorant of Mr. Spencer's view according to which political obedience—Loyalty—is accredited with only a transitional function. [*Principles of Ethics*, Vol. I, Pt. II, Ch. X.] It may be so. Sufficient unto the day is the virtue thereof. We may complacently repeat it, especially as we believe *that* day to be a long space of time, during which, so our national anthem says, "tiny pebbles grow into mighty rocks draped with moss." We may remember at this juncture that even among so democratic a people as the English, "the sentiment of personal fidelity to a man and his posterity which their Germanic ancestors felt for their chiefs, has," as Monsieur Boutmy recently said, "only passed more or less into their profound loyalty to the race and blood of their princes, as evidenced in their extraordinary attachment to the dynasty."

Political subordination, Mr. Spencer predicts, will give place to loyalty to the dictates of conscience. Suppose his induction is realized—will loyalty and its concomitant instinct of reverence disappear forever? We transfer our allegiance from one master to another, without being unfaithful to either; from being subjects of a ruler that wields the temporal sceptre we become servants of the monarch who sits enthroned in the penetralia of our heart. A few years ago a very stupid controversy, started by the misguided disciples of Spencer, made havoc among the reading class of Japan. In their zeal to uphold the claim of the throne to undivided loyalty, they charged Christians with treasonable propensities in that they avow fidelity to their Lord and Master. They arrayed forth sophistical arguments without the wit of Sophists, and scholastic tortuosities minus the niceties of the Schoolmen. Little did they know that we can, in a sense, "serve two masters without holding to the one or despising the other," "rendering unto Caesar the things that are Caesar's and unto God the things that are God's." Did not Socrates, all the while he unflinchingly refused to concede one iota of loyalty to his *daemon*, obey with equal fidelity and equanimity the command of his earthly master, the State? His conscience he followed, alive; his country he served, dying. Alack the day when a state grows so powerful as to demand of its citizens the dictates of their conscience!

Bushido did not require us to make our conscience the slave of any lord or king. Thomas Mowbray was a veritable spokesman for us when he said:

"Myself I throw, dread sovereign, at thy foot.
My life thou shalt command, but not my shame.
The one my duty owes; but my fair name,
Despite of death, that lives upon my grave,
To dark dishonor's use, thou shalt not have."

A man who sacrificed his own conscience to the capricious will or freak or fancy of a sovereign was accorded a low place in the estimate of the Precepts. Such an one was despised as *nei-shin*, a cringeling, who makes court by unscrupulous fawning or as *chô-shin*, a favorite who steals his master's affections by means of servile compliance; these two species of subjects corresponding exactly to those which Iago describes,—the one, a duteous and knee-crooking knave, doting on his own obsequious bondage, wearing out his time much like his master's ass; the other trimm'd in forms and visages of duty, keeping yet his heart attending on himself. When a subject differed from his master, the loyal path for him to pursue was to use every available means to persuade him of his error, as Kent did to King Lear. Failing in this, let the master deal with him as he wills. In cases of this kind, it was quite a usual course for the samurai to make the last appeal to the intelligence and conscience of his lord by demonstrating the sincerity of his words with the shedding of his own blood.

Bushido - The Soul of Japan

Education and Training of a Samurai

Life being regarded as the means whereby to serve his master, and its ideal being set upon honor, the whole education and training of a Samurai were conducted accordingly.

The first point to observe in knightly pedagogics was to build up character, leaving in the shade the subtler faculties of prudence, intelligence and dialectics. We have seen the important part aesthetic accomplishments played in his education. Indispensable as they were to a man of culture, they were accessories rather than essentials of samurai training. Intellectual superiority was, of course, esteemed; but the word *Chi*, which was employed to denote intellectuality, meant wisdom in the first instance and placed knowledge only in a very subordinate place. The tripod that supported the framework of Bushido was said to be *Chi, Jin, Yu*, respectively Wisdom, Benevolence, and Courage. A samurai was essentially a man of action. Science was without the pale of his activity. He took advantage of it in so far as it concerned his profession of arms. Religion and theology were relegated to the priests; he concerned himself with them in so far as they helped to nourish courage. Like an English poet the samurai believed "'tis not the creed that saves the man; but it is the man that justifies the creed." Philosophy and literature formed the chief part of his intellectual training; but even in the pursuit of these, it was not objective truth that he strove after,—literature was pursued mainly as a pastime, and philosophy as a practical aid in the formation of character, if not for the exposition of some military or political problem.

From what has been said, it will not be surprising to note that the curriculum of studies, according to the pedagogics of Bushido, consisted mainly of the following,—fencing, archery, *jiujutsu* or *yawara*, horsemanship, the use of the spear, tactics, caligraphy, ethics, literature and history. Of these, *jiujutsu* and caligraphy may require a few words of explanation. Great stress was laid on good writing, probably because our logograms, partaking as they do of the nature of pictures, possess artistic value, and also because chirography was accepted as indicative of one's personal character. *Jiujutsu* may be briefly defined as an application of anatomical knowledge to the purpose of offense or defense. It differs from wrestling, in that it does not depend upon muscular strength. It differs from other forms of attack in that it uses no weapon. Its feat consists in clutching or striking such part of the enemy's body as will make him numb and incapable of resistance. Its object is not to kill, but to incapacitate one for action for the time being.

A subject of study which one would expect to find in military education and which is rather conspicuous by its absence in the Bushido course of instruction, is mathematics. This, however, can be readily explained in part by the fact that feudal warfare was not carried on with scientific precision. Not only that, but the whole training of the samurai was unfavorable to fostering numerical notions.

Chivalry is uneconomical; it boasts of penury. It says with Ventidius that "ambition, the soldier's virtue, rather makes choice of loss, than gain which darkens him." Don Quixote takes more pride in his rusty spear and skin-and-bone horse than in gold and lands, and a samurai is in hearty sympathy with his exaggerated confrère of La Mancha. He disdains money itself,—the art of making or hoarding it. It is to him veritably filthy lucre. The hackneyed expression to describe the decadence of an age is "that the civilians loved money and the soldiers feared death." Niggardliness of gold and of life excites as much disapprobation as their lavish use is panegyrized. "Less than all things," says a current precept, "men must grudge money: it is by riches that wisdom is hindered." Hence children were brought up with utter disregard of economy. It was considered bad taste to speak of it, and ignorance of the value of different coins was a token of good breeding. Knowledge of numbers was indispensable in the mustering of forces as well, as in the distribution of benefices and fiefs; but the counting of money was left to meaner hands. In many feudatories, public finance was administered by a lower kind of samurai or by priests. Every thinking bushi knew well enough that money formed the sinews of war; but he did not think of raising the appreciation of money to a virtue. It is true that thrift was enjoined by Bushido, but not for economical reasons so much as for the exercise of abstinence. Luxury was thought the greatest menace to manhood, and severest simplicity was required of the warrior class, sumptuary laws being enforced in many of the clans.

We read that in ancient Rome the farmers of revenue and other financial agents were gradually raised to the rank of knights, the State thereby showing its appreciation of their service and of the importance of money itself. How closely this was connected with the luxury and avarice of the Romans may be imagined. Not so with the Precepts of Knighthood. These persisted in systematically regarding finance as something low—low as compared with moral and intellectual vocations.

Money and the love of it being thus diligently ignored, Bushido itself could long remain free from a thousand and one evils of which money is the root. This is sufficient reason for the fact that our public men have long been free from corruption; but, alas, how fast plutocracy is making its way in our time and generation!

The mental discipline which would now-a-days be chiefly aided by the study of mathematics, was supplied by literary exegesis and deontological discussions. Very few abstract subjects troubled the mind of the young, the chief aim of their education being, as I have said, decision of character. People whose minds were simply stored with information found no great admirers. Of the three services of studies that Bacon gives,—for delight, ornament, and ability,—Bushido had decided preference for the last, where their use was "in judgment and the disposition of business." Whether it was for the disposition of public business or for the exercise of self-control, it was with a practical end in view that education was conducted. "Learning without thought," said Confucius, "is labor lost: thought without learning is perilous."

When character and not intelligence, when the soul and not the head, is chosen by a teacher for the material to work upon and to develop, his vocation partakes of a sacred character. "It is the parent who has borne me: it is the teacher who makes me man." With this idea, therefore, the esteem in which one's preceptor was held was very high. A man to evoke such confidence and respect from the young, must necessarily be endowed with superior personality without lacking erudition. He was a father to the fatherless, and an adviser to the erring. "Thy father and thy mother"—so runs our maxim—"are like heaven and earth; thy teacher and thy lord are like the sun and moon."

The present system of paying for every sort of service was not in vogue among the adherents of Bushido. It believed in a service which can be rendered only without money and without price. Spiritual service, be it of priest or teacher, was not to be repaid in gold or silver, not because it was valueless but because it was invaluable. Here the non-arithmetical honor-instinct of Bushido taught a truer lesson than modern Political Economy; for wages and salaries can be paid only for services whose results are definite, tangible, and measurable, whereas the best service done in education,—namely, in soul development (and this includes the services of a pastor), is not definite, tangible or measurable. Being immeasurable, money, the ostensible measure of value, is of inadequate use. Usage sanctioned that pupils brought to their teachers money or goods at different seasons of the year; but these were not payments but offerings, which indeed were welcome to the recipients as they were usually men of stern calibre, boasting of honorable penury, too dignified to work with their hands and too proud to beg. They were grave personifications of high spirits undaunted by adversity. They were an embodiment of what was considered as an end of all learning, and were thus a living example of that discipline of disciplines, self control, which was universally required of samurai.

Self-Control

The discipline of fortitude on the one hand, inculcating endurance without a groan, and the teaching of politeness on the other, requiring us not to mar the pleasure or serenity of another by manifestations of our own sorrow or pain, combined to engender a stoical turn of mind, and eventually to confirm it into a national trait of apparent stoicism. I say apparent stoicism, because I do not believe that true stoicism can ever become the characteristic of a whole nation, and also because some of our national manners and customs may seem to a foreign observer hard-hearted. Yet we are really as susceptible to tender emotion as any race under the sky.

I am inclined to think that in one sense we have to feel more than others—yes, doubly more—since the very attempt to, restrain natural promptings entails suffering. Imagine boys—and girls too—brought up not to resort to the shedding of a tear or the uttering of a groan for the relief of their feelings,—and there is a physiological problem whether such effort steels their nerves or makes them more sensitive.

It was considered unmanly for a samurai to betray his emotions on his face. "He shows no sign of joy or anger," was a phrase used in describing a strong character. The most natural affections were kept under control. A father could embrace his son only at the expense of his dignity; a husband would not kiss his wife,—no, not in the presence of other people, whatever he might do in private! There may be some truth in the remark of a witty youth when he said, "American husbands kiss their wives in public and beat them in private; Japanese husbands beat theirs in public and kiss them in private."

Calmness of behavior, composure of mind, should not be disturbed by passion of any kind. I remember when, during the late war with China, a regiment left a certain town, a large concourse of people flocked to the station to bid farewell to the general and his army. On this occasion an American resident resorted to the place, expecting to witness loud demonstrations, as the nation itself was highly excited and there were fathers, mothers, and sweethearts of the soldiers in the crowd. The

American was strangely disappointed; for as the whistle blew and the train began to move, the hats of thousands of people were silently taken off and their heads bowed in reverential farewell; no waving of handkerchiefs, no word uttered, but deep silence in which only an attentive ear could catch a few broken sobs. In domestic life, too, I know of a father who spent whole nights listening to the breathing of a sick child, standing behind the door that he might not be caught in such an act of parental weakness! I know of a mother who, in her last moments, refrained from sending for her son, that he might not be disturbed in his studies. Our history and everyday life are replete with examples of heroic matrons who can well bear comparison with some of the most touching pages of Plutarch. Among our peasantry an Ian Maclaren would be sure to find many a Marget Howe.

It is the same discipline of self-restraint which is accountable for the absence of more frequent revivals in the Christian churches of Japan. When a man or woman feels his or her soul stirred, the first instinct is to quietly suppress any indication of it. In rare instances is the tongue set free by an irresistible spirit, when we have eloquence of sincerity and fervor. It is putting a premium upon a breach of the third commandment to encourage speaking lightly of spiritual experience. It is truly jarring to Japanese ears to hear the most sacred words, the most secret heart experiences, thrown out in promiscuous audiences. "Dost thou feel the soil of thy soul stirred with tender thoughts? It is time for seeds to sprout. Disturb it not with speech; but let it work alone in quietness and secrecy,"—writes a young samurai in his diary.

To give in so many articulate words one's inmost thoughts and feelings—notably the religious—is taken among us as an unmistakable sign that they are neither very profound nor very sincere. "Only a pomegranate is he"—so runs a popular saying—"who, when he gapes his mouth, displays the contents of his heart."

It is not altogether perverseness of oriental minds that the instant our emotions are moved we try to guard our lips in order to hide them. Speech is very often with us, as the Frenchman defined it, "the art of concealing thought."

Call upon a Japanese friend in time of deepest affliction and he will invariably receive you laughing, with red eyes or moist cheeks. At first you may think him hysterical. Press him for explanation and you will get a few broken commonplaces—"Human life has sorrow;" "They who meet must part;" "He that is born must die;" "It is foolish to count the years of a child that is gone, but a woman's heart will indulge in follies;" and the like. So the noble words of a noble Hohenzollern—"Lerne zu leiden ohne Klagen"—had found many responsive minds among us, long before they were uttered.

Indeed, the Japanese have recourse to risibility whenever the frailties of human nature are put to severest test. I think we possess a better reason than Democritus himself for our Abderian tendency; for laughter with us oftenest veils an effort to regain balance of temper, when disturbed by any untoward circumstance. It is a counterpoise of sorrow or rage.

The suppression of feelings being thus steadily insisted upon, they find their safety-valve in poetical aphorism. A poet of the tenth century writes, "In Japan and China as well, humanity, when moved by sorrow, tells its bitter grief in verse." A mother who tries to console her broken heart by fancying her departed child absent on his wonted chase after the dragon-fly, hums,

"How far to-day in chase, I wonder,
Has gone my hunter of the dragon-fly!"

I refrain from quoting other examples, for I know I could do only scant justice to the pearly gems of our literature, were I to render into a foreign tongue the thoughts which were wrung drop by drop from bleeding hearts and threaded into beads of rarest value. I hope I have in a measure shown that inner working of our minds which often presents an appearance of callousness or of a hysterical mixture of laughter and dejection, and whose sanity is sometimes called in question.

It has also been suggested that our endurance of pain and indifference to death are due to less sensitive nerves. This is plausible as far as it goes. The next question is,—Why are our nerves less tightly strung? It may be our climate is not so stimulating as the American. It may be our monarchical form of government does not excite us as much as the Republic does the Frenchman. It may be that we do not read *Sartor Resartus* as zealously as the Englishman. Personally, I believe it was our very excitability and sensitiveness which made it a necessity to recognize and enforce constant self-repression; but whatever may be the explanation, without taking into account long years of discipline in self-control, none can be correct.

Discipline in self-control can easily go too far. It can well repress the genial current of the soul. It can force pliant natures into distortions and monstrosities. It can beget bigotry, breed hypocrisy or hebetate affections. Be a virtue never so noble, it has its counterpart and counterfeit. We must recognize in each virtue its own positive excellence and follow its positive ideal, and the ideal of self-restraint is to keep our mind *level*—as our expression is—or, to borrow a Greek term, attain the state of *euthymia*, which Democritus called the highest good.

Bushido - The Soul of Japan

The Institutions of Suicide and Redress

The acme of self-control is reached and best illustrated in the first of the two institutions which we shall now bring to view; namely, the institutions of Suicide and Redress of which (the former known as *hara-kiri* and the latter as *kataki-uchi*) many foreign writers have treated more or less fully.

To begin with suicide, let me state that I confine my observations only to *seppuku* or *kappuku*, popularly known as *hara-kiri*—which means self-immolation by disembowelment. "Ripping the abdomen? How absurd!"—so cry those to whom the name is new. Absurdly odd as it may sound at first to foreign ears, it can not be so very foreign to students of Shakespeare, who puts these words in Brutus' mouth— "Thy (Caesar's) spirit walks abroad and turns our swords into our proper entrails." Listen to a modern English poet, who in his *Light of Asia*, speaks of a sword piercing the bowels of a queen:—none blames him for bad English or breach of modesty. Or, to take still another example, look at Guercino's painting of Cato's death, in the Palazzo Rossa in Genoa. Whoever has read the swan-song which Addison makes Cato sing, will not jeer at the sword half-buried in his abdomen. In our minds this mode of death is associated with instances of noblest deeds and of most touching pathos, so that nothing repugnant, much less ludicrous, mars our conception of it. So wonderful is the transforming power of virtue, of greatness, of tenderness, that the vilest form of death assumes a sublimity and becomes a symbol of new life, or else—the sign which Constantine beheld would not conquer the world!

Not for extraneous associations only does *seppuku* lose in our mind any taint of absurdity; for the choice of this particular part of the body to operate upon, was based on an old anatomical belief as to the seat of the soul and of the affections. When Moses wrote of Joseph's "bowels yearning upon his brother," or David prayed the Lord not to forget his bowels, or when Isaiah, Jeremiah and other inspired men of old spoke of the "sounding" or the "troubling" of bowels, they all and each endorsed the belief prevalent among the Japanese that in the abdomen was enshrined the soul. The Semites habitually spoke of the liver and kidneys and surrounding fat as the seat of emotion and of life. The term *hara* was more comprehensive than the Greek *phren* or *thumos>* and the Japanese and Hellenese alike thought the spirit of man to dwell somewhere in that region. Such a notion is by no means confined to the peoples of antiquity. The French, in spite of the theory propounded by one of their most distinguished philosophers, Descartes, that the soul is located in the pineal gland, still insist in using the term *ventre* in a sense, which, if anatomically too vague, is nevertheless physiologically significant. Similarly *entrailles* stands in their language for affection and compassion. Nor is such belief mere superstition, being more scientific than the general idea of making the heart the centre of the feelings. Without asking a friar, the Japanese knew better than Romeo "in what vile part of this anatomy one's name did lodge." Modern neurologists speak of the abdominal and pelvic brains, denoting thereby sympathetic nerve-centres in those parts which are strongly affected by any psychical action. This view of mental physiology once admitted, the syllogism of *seppuku* is easy to construct. "I will open the seat of my soul and show you how it fares with it. See for yourself whether it is polluted or clean."

I do not wish to be understood as asserting religious or even moral justification of suicide, but the high estimate placed upon honor was ample excuse with many for taking one's own life. How many acquiesced in the sentiment expressed by Garth,

> "When honor's lost, 'tis a relief to die;
> Death's but a sure retreat from infamy,"

and have smilingly surrendered their souls to oblivion! Death when honor was involved, was accepted in Bushido as a key to the solution of many complex problems, so that to an ambitious samurai a natural departure from life seemed a rather tame affair and a consummation not devoutly to be wished for. I dare say that many good Christians, if only they are honest enough, will confess the fascination of, if not positive admiration for, the sublime composure with which Cato, Brutus, Petronius and a host of other ancient worthies, terminated their own earthly existence. Is it too bold to hint that the death of the first of the philosophers was partly suicidal? When we are told so minutely by his pupils how their master willingly submitted to the mandate of the state—which he knew was morally mistaken—in spite of the possibilities of escape, and how he took up the cup of hemlock in his own hand, even offering libation from its deadly contents, do we not discern in his whole proceeding and demeanor, an act of self-immolation? No physical compulsion here, as in ordinary cases of execution. True the verdict of the judges was compulsory: it said, "Thou shalt die,—and that by thy own hand." If suicide meant no more than dying by one's own hand, Socrates was a clear case of suicide. But nobody would charge him with the crime; Plato, who was averse to it, would not call his master a suicide.

Now my readers will understand that *seppuku* was not a mere suicidal process. It was an institution, legal and ceremonial. An invention of the middle ages, it was a process by which warriors could expiate their crimes, apologize for errors, escape from disgrace, redeem their friends, or prove their sincerity. When enforced as a legal punishment, it was practiced with due ceremony. It was a refinement of self-destruction, and none could perform it without the utmost coolness of temper and composure of demeanor, and for these reasons it was particularly befitting the profession of bushi.

Antiquarian curiosity, if nothing else, would tempt me to give here a description of this obsolete ceremonial; but seeing that such a description was made by a far abler writer, whose book is not much read now-a-days, I am tempted to make a somewhat lengthy quotation. Mitford, in his "Tales of Old Japan," after giving a translation of a treatise on *seppuku* from a rare Japanese manuscript, goes on to describe an instance of such an execution of which he was an eye-witness:—

"We (seven foreign representatives) were invited to follow the Japanese witness into the *hondo* or main hall of the temple, where the ceremony was to be performed. It was an imposing scene. A large hall with a high roof supported by dark pillars of wood. From the ceiling hung a profusion of those huge gilt lamps and ornaments peculiar to Buddhist temples. In front of the high altar, where the floor, covered with beautiful white mats, is raised some three or four inches from the ground, was laid a rug of scarlet felt. Tall candles placed at regular intervals gave out a dim mysterious light, just sufficient to let all the proceedings be seen. The seven Japanese took their places on the left of the raised floor, the seven foreigners on the right. No other person was present.

"After the interval of a few minutes of anxious suspense, Taki Zenzaburo, a stalwart man thirty-two years of age, with a noble air, walked into the hall attired in his dress of ceremony, with the peculiar hempen-cloth wings which are worn on great occasions. He was accompanied by a *kaishaku* and three officers, who wore the *jimbaori* or war surcoat with gold tissue facings. The word *kaishaku* it should be observed, is one to which our word executioner is no equivalent term. The office is that of a gentleman: in many cases it is performed by a kinsman or friend of the condemned, and the relation between them is rather that of principal and second than that of victim and executioner. In this instance the *kaishaku* was a pupil of Taki Zenzaburo, and was selected by friends of the latter from among their own number for his skill in swordsmanship.

"With the *kaishaku* on his left hand, Taki Zenzaburo advanced slowly towards the Japanese witnesses, and the two bowed before them, then drawing near to the foreigners they saluted us in the same way, perhaps even with more deference; in each case the salutation was ceremoniously returned. Slowly and with great dignity the condemned man mounted on to the raised floor, prostrated himself before the high altar twice, and seated [*Seated himself—that is, in the Japanese fashion, his knees and toes touching the ground and his body resting on his heels. In this position, which is one of respect, he remained until his death.*] himself on the felt carpet with his back to the high altar, the *kaishaku* crouching on his left hand side. One of the three attendant officers then came forward, bearing a stand of the kind used in the temple for offerings, on which, wrapped in paper, lay the *wakizashi*, the short sword or dirk of the Japanese, nine inches and a half in length, with a point and an edge as sharp as a razor's. This he handed, prostrating himself, to the condemned man, who received it reverently, raising it to his head with both hands, and placed it in front of himself.

"After another profound obeisance, Taki Zenzaburo, in a voice which betrayed just so much emotion and hesitation as might be expected from a man who is making a painful confession, but with no sign of either in his face or manner, spoke as follows:—

'I, and I alone, unwarrantably gave the order to fire on the foreigners at Kobe, and again as they tried to escape. For this crime I disembowel myself, and I beg you who are present to do me the honor of witnessing the act.'

"Bowing once more, the speaker allowed his upper garments to slip down to his girdle, and remained naked to the waist. Carefully, according to custom, he tucked his sleeves under his knees to prevent himself from falling backward; for a noble Japanese gentleman should die falling forwards. Deliberately, with a steady hand he took the dirk that lay before him; he looked at it wistfully, almost affectionately; for a moment he seemed to collect his thoughts for the last time, and then stabbing himself deeply below the waist in the left-hand side, he drew the dirk slowly across to his right side, and turning it in the wound, gave a slight cut upwards. During this sickeningly painful operation he never moved a muscle of his face. When he drew out the dirk, he leaned forward and stretched out his neck; an expression of pain for the first time crossed his face, but he uttered no sound. At that moment the *kaishaku*, who, still crouching by his side, had been keenly watching his every movement, sprang to his feet, poised his sword for a second in the air; there was a flash, a heavy, ugly thud, a crashing fall; with one blow the head had been severed from the body.

"A dead silence followed, broken only by the hideous noise of the blood throbbing out of the inert head before us, which but a moment before had been a brave and chivalrous man. It was horrible.

"The *kaishaku* made a low bow, wiped his sword with a piece of paper which he had ready for the purpose, and retired from the raised floor; and the stained dirk was solemnly borne away, a bloody proof of the execution.

"The two representatives of the Mikado then left their places, and crossing over to where the foreign witnesses sat, called to us to witness that the sentence of death upon Taki Zenzaburo had been faithfully carried out. The ceremony being at an end, we left the temple."

I might multiply any number of descriptions of *seppuku* from literature or from the relation of eye-witnesses; but one more instance will suffice.

Two brothers, Sakon and Naiki, respectively twenty-four and seventeen years of age, made an effort to kill Iyéyasu in order to avenge their father's wrongs; but before they could enter the camp they were made prisoners. The old general admired the pluck of the youths who dared an attempt on his life and ordered that they should be allowed to die an honorable death. Their little brother Hachimaro, a mere infant of eight summers, was condemned to a similar fate, as the sentence was pronounced on all the male members of the family, and the three were taken to a monastery where it was to be executed. A physician who was present on the occasion has left us a diary from which the following scene is translated. "When they were all seated in a row for final despatch, Sakon turned to the youngest and said—'Go thou first, for I wish to be sure that thou doest it aright.' Upon the little one's replying that, as he had never seen *seppuku* performed, he would like to see his brothers do it and then he could follow them, the older brothers smiled between their tears:—'Well said, little fellow! So canst thou well boast of being our father's child.' When they had placed him between them, Sakon thrust the dagger into the left side of his own abdomen and asked—'Look, brother! Dost understand now? Only, don't push the dagger too far, lest thou fall back. Lean forward, rather, and keep thy knees well composed.' Naiki did likewise and said to the boy—'Keep thy eyes open or else thou mayst look like a dying woman. If thy dagger feels anything within and thy strength fails, take courage and double thy effort to cut across.' The child looked from one to the other, and when both had expired, he calmly half denuded himself and followed the example set him on either hand."

The glorification of *seppuku* offered, naturally enough, no small temptation to its unwarranted committal. For causes entirely incompatible with reason, or for reasons entirely undeserving of death, hot headed youths rushed into it as insects fly into fire; mixed and dubious motives drove more samurai to this deed than nuns into convent gates. Life was cheap—cheap as reckoned by the popular standard of honor. The saddest feature was that honor, which was always in the *agio*, so to speak, was not always solid gold, but alloyed with baser metals. No one circle in the Inferno will boast of greater density of Japanese population than the seventh, to which Dante consigns all victims of self-destruction!

And yet, for a true samurai to hasten death or to court it, was alike cowardice. A typical fighter, when he lost battle after battle and was pursued from plain to hill and from bush to cavern, found himself hungry and alone in the dark hollow of a tree, his sword blunt with use, his bow broken and arrows exhausted—did not the noblest of the Romans fall upon his own sword in Phillippi under like circumstances?—deemed it cowardly to die, but with a fortitude approaching a Christian martyr's, cheered himself with an impromptu verse:

> "Come! evermore come,
> Ye dread sorrows and pains!
> And heap on my burden'd back;
> That I not one test may lack
> Of what strength in me remains!"

This, then, was the Bushido teaching—Bear and face all calamities and adversities with patience and a pure conscience; for as Mencius taught [*I use Dr. Legge's translation verbatim.*], "When Heaven is about to confer a great office on anyone, it first exercises his mind with suffering and his sinews and bones with toil; it exposes his body to hunger and subjects him to extreme poverty; and it confounds his undertakings. In all these ways it stimulates his mind, hardens his nature, and supplies his incompetencies." True honor lies in fulfilling Heaven's decree and no death incurred in so doing is ignominious, whereas death to avoid what Heaven has in store is cowardly indeed! In that quaint book of Sir Thomas Browne's, *Religio Medici* there is an exact English equivalent for what is repeatedly taught in our Precepts. Let me quote it: "It is a brave act of valor to contemn death, but where life is more terrible than death, it is then the truest valor to dare to live." A renowned priest of the seventeenth century satirically observed—"Talk as he may, a samurai who ne'er has died is apt in decisive moments to flee or hide." Again—Him who once has died in the bottom of his breast, no spears of Sanada nor all the arrows of Tametomo can pierce. How near we come to the portals of the temple whose Builder taught "he that loseth his life for my sake shall find it!" These are but a few of the numerous examples which tend to confirm the moral identity of the human species, notwithstanding an attempt so assiduously made to render the distinction between Christian and Pagan as great as possible.

We have thus seen that the Bushido institution of suicide was neither so irrational nor barbarous as its abuse strikes us at first sight. We will now see whether its sister institution of Redress—or call it Revenge, if you will—has its mitigating features. I hope I can dispose of this question in a few words, since a similar institution, or call it custom, if that suits you better, has at some time prevailed among all peoples and has not yet become entirely obsolete, as attested by the continuance of duelling and lynching. Why, has not an American captain recently challenged Esterhazy, that the wrongs of Dreyfus be avenged? Among a savage tribe which has no marriage, adultery is not a sin, and only the jealousy of a lover protects a woman from abuse: so in a time which has no criminal court, murder is not a crime, and only the vigilant vengeance of the victim's people preserves social order. "What is the most beautiful thing on earth?" said Osiris to Horus. The reply was, "To avenge a parent's wrongs,"—to which a Japanese would have added "and a master's."

In revenge there is something which satisfies one's sense of justice. The avenger reasons:—"My good father did not deserve death. He who killed him did great evil. My father, if he were alive, would not tolerate a deed like this: Heaven itself hates wrong-doing. It is the will of my father; it is the will of Heaven that the evil-doer cease from his work. He must perish by my hand; because he shed my father's blood, I, who am his flesh and blood, must shed the murderer's. The same Heaven shall not shelter him and me." The ratiocination is simple and childish (though we know Hamlet did not reason much more deeply), nevertheless it shows an innate sense of exact balance and equal justice "An eye for an eye, a tooth for a tooth." Our sense of revenge is as exact as our mathematical faculty, and until both terms of the equation are satisfied we cannot get over the sense of something left undone.

In Judaism, which believed in a jealous God, or in Greek mythology, which provided a Nemesis, vengeance may be left to superhuman agencies; but common sense furnished Bushido with the institution of redress as a kind of ethical court of equity, where people could take cases not to be judged in accordance with ordinary law. The master of the forty-seven Ronins was condemned to death;—he had no court of higher instance to appeal to; his faithful retainers addressed themselves to Vengeance, the only Supreme Court existing; they in their turn were condemned by common law,—but the popular instinct passed a different judgment and hence their memory is still kept as green and fragrant as are their graves at Sengakuji to this day.

Though Lao-tse taught to recompense injury with kindness, the voice of Confucius was very much louder, which counselled that injury must be recompensed with justice;—and yet revenge was justified only when it was undertaken in behalf of our superiors and benefactors. One's own wrongs, including injuries done to wife and children, were to be borne and forgiven. A samurai could therefore fully sympathize with Hannibal's oath to avenge his country's wrongs, but he scorns James Hamilton for wearing in his girdle a handful of earth from his wife's grave, as an eternal incentive to avenge her wrongs on the Regent Murray.

Both of these institutions of suicide and redress lost their *raison d'être* at the promulgation of the criminal code. No more do we hear of romantic adventures of a fair maiden as she tracks in disguise the murderer of her parent. No more can we witness tragedies of family vendetta enacted. The knight errantry of Miyamoto Musashi is now a tale of the past. The well-ordered police spies out the criminal for the injured party and the law metes out justice. The whole state and society will see that wrong is righted. The sense of justice satisfied, there is no need of *kataki-uchi*. If this had meant that "hunger of the heart which feeds upon the hope of glutting that hunger with the life-blood of the victim," as a New England divine has described it, a few paragraphs in the Criminal Code would not so entirely have made an end of it.

As to *seppuku*, though it too has no existence *de jure*, we still hear of it from time to time, and shall continue to hear, I am afraid, as long as the past is remembered. Many painless and time-saving methods of self-immolation will come in vogue, as its votaries are increasing with fearful rapidity throughout the world; but Professor Morselli will have to concede to *seppuku* an aristocratic position among them. He maintains that "when suicide is accomplished by very painful means or at the cost of prolonged agony, in ninety-nine cases out of a hundred, it may be assigned as the act of a mind disordered by fanaticism, by madness, or by morbid excitement." [Morselli, *Suicide*, p. 314.] But a normal *seppuku* does not savor of fanaticism, or madness or excitement, utmost *sang froid* being necessary to its successful accomplishment. Of the two kinds into which Dr. Strahan [*Suicide and Insanity*.] divides suicide, the Rational or Quasi, and the Irrational or True, *seppuku* is the best example of the former type.

Bushido - The Soul of Japan

The Sword, the Soul of the Samurai

From these bloody institutions, as well as from the general tenor of Bushido, it is easy to infer that the sword played an important part in social discipline and life. The saying passed as an axiom which called the sword the soul of the Samurai and made it the emblem of power and prowess. When Mahomet proclaimed that "The sword is the key of Heaven and of Hell," he only echoed a Japanese sentiment. Very early the samurai boy learned to wield it. It was a momentous occasion for him when at the age of five he was appareled in the paraphernalia of samurai costume, placed upon a *go*-board and initiated into the rights of the military profession by having thrust into his girdle a real sword, instead of the toy dirk with which he had been playing. [*The game of go is sometimes called Japanese checkers, but is much more intricate than the English game. The go-board contains 361 squares and is supposed to represent a battle-field—the object of the game being to occupy as much space as possible.*]

After this first ceremony of *adoptio per arma*, he was no more to be seen outside his father's gates without this badge of his status, even if it was usually substituted for every-day wear by a gilded wooden dirk. Not many years pass before he wears constantly the genuine steel, though blunt, and then the sham arms are thrown aside and with enjoyment keener than his newly acquired blades, he marches out to try their edge on wood and stone.

When be reaches man's estate at the age of fifteen, being given independence of action, he can now pride himself upon the possession of arms sharp enough for any work. The very possession of the dangerous instrument imparts to him a feeling and an air of self-respect and responsibility. "He beareth not his sword in vain." What he carries in his belt is a symbol of what he carries in his mind and heart—Loyalty and Honor. The two swords, the longer and the shorter—called respectively *daito* and *shoto* or *katana* and *wakizashi*—never leave his side. When at home, they grace the most conspicuous place in study or parlor; by night they guard his pillow within easy reach of his hand. Constant companions, they are beloved, and proper names of endearment given them. Being venerated, they are well-nigh worshiped. The Father of History has recorded as a curious piece of information that the Scythians sacrificed to an iron scimitar. Many a temple and many a family in Japan hoards a sword as an object of adoration. Even the commonest dirk has due respect paid to it. Any insult to it is tantamount to personal affront. Woe to him who carelessly steps over a weapon lying on the floor!

So precious an object cannot long escape the notice and the skill of artists nor the vanity of its owner, especially in times of peace, when it is worn with no more use than a crosier by a bishop or a sceptre by a king. Shark-skin and finest silk for hilt, silver and gold for guard, lacquer of varied hues for scabbard, robbed the deadliest weapon of half its terror; but these appurtenances are playthings compared with the blade itself.

The swordsmith was not a mere artisan but an inspired artist and his workshop a sanctuary. Daily he commenced his craft with prayer and purification, or, as the phrase was, "he committed his soul and spirit into the forging and tempering of the steel." Every swing of the sledge, every plunge into water, every friction on the grindstone, was a religious act of no slight import. Was it the spirit of the master or of his tutelary god that cast a formidable spell over our sword? Perfect as a work of art, setting at defiance its Toledo and Damascus rivals, there is more than art could impart. Its cold blade, collecting on its surface the moment it is drawn the vapors of the atmosphere; its immaculate texture, flashing light of bluish hue; its matchless edge, upon which histories and possibilities hang; the curve of its back, uniting exquisite grace with utmost strength;—all these thrill us with mixed feelings of power and beauty, of awe and terror. Harmless were its mission, if it only remained a thing of beauty and joy! But, ever within reach of the hand, it presented no small temptation for abuse. Too often did the blade flash forth from its peaceful sheath. The abuse sometimes went so far as to try the acquired steel on some harmless creature's neck.

The question that concerns us most is, however,—Did Bushido justify the promiscuous use of the weapon? The answer is unequivocally, no!

As it laid great stress on its proper use, so did it denounce and abhor its misuse. A dastard or a braggart was he who brandished his weapon on undeserved occasions. A self-possessed man knows the right time to use it, and such times come but rarely. Let us listen to the late Count Katsu, who passed through one of the most turbulent times of our history, when assassinations, suicides, and other sanguinary practices were the order of the day. Endowed as he once was with almost dictatorial powers, repeatedly marked out as an object for assassination, he never tarnished his sword with blood. In relating some of his reminiscences to a friend he says, in a quaint, plebeian way peculiar to him:—"I have a great dislike for killing people and so I haven't killed one single man. I have released those whose heads should have been chopped off. A friend said to me one day, 'You don't kill enough. Don't you eat pepper and egg-plants?' Well, some people are no better! But you see that fellow was slain himself. My escape may be due to my dislike of killing. I had the hilt of my sword so tightly fastened to the scabbard that it was hard to draw the blade. I made up my mind that though they cut me, I will not cut. Yes, yes! some people are truly like fleas and mosquitoes and they bite—but what does their biting amount to? It itches a little, that's all; it won't endanger life." These are the words of one whose Bushido training was tried in the fiery furnace of adversity and triumph. The popular apothegm—"To be beaten is to conquer," meaning true conquest consists in not opposing a riotous foe; and "The best won victory is that obtained without shedding of blood," and others of similar import—will show that after all the ultimate ideal of knighthood was Peace.

The Training and Position of Woman

It was a great pity that this high ideal knighthood was left exclusively to priests and moralists to preach, while the samurai went on practicing and extolling martial traits. In this they went so far as to tinge the ideals of womanhood with Amazonian character. Here we may profitably devote a few paragraphs to the subject of The Training and Position of Woman.

The female half of our species has sometimes been called the paragon of paradoxes, because the intuitive working of its mind is beyond the comprehension of men's "arithmetical understanding." The Chinese ideogram denoting "the mysterious," "the unknowable," consists of two parts, one meaning "young" and the other "woman," because the physical charms and delicate thoughts of the fair sex are above the coarse mental calibre of our sex to explain.

In the Bushido ideal of woman, however, there is little mystery and only a seeming paradox. I have said that it was Amazonian, but that is only half the truth. Ideographically the Chinese represent wife by a woman holding a broom—certainly not to brandish it offensively or defensively against her conjugal ally, neither for witchcraft, but for the more harmless uses for which the besom was first invented—the idea involved being thus not less homely than the etymological derivation of the English wife (weaver) and daughter (*duhitar*, milkmaid). Without confining the sphere of woman's activity to *Küche, Kirche, Kinder*, as the present German Kaiser is said to do, the Bushido ideal of womanhood was preeminently domestic. These seeming contradictions—Domesticity and Amazonian traits—are not inconsistent with the Precepts of Knighthood, as we shall see.

Bushido being a teaching primarily intended for the masculine sex, the virtues it prized in woman were naturally far from being distinctly feminine. Winckelmann remarks that "the supreme beauty of Greek art is rather male than female," and Lecky adds that it was true in the moral conception of the Greeks as in their art. Bushido similarly praised those women most "who emancipated themselves from the frailty of their sex and displayed an heroic fortitude worthy of the strongest and the bravest of men." [Lecky, *History of European Morals* II, p. 383.]

Young girls therefore, were trained to repress their feelings, to indurate their nerves, to manipulate weapons,—especially the long-handled sword called *nagi-nata*, so as to be able to hold their own against unexpected odds. Yet the primary motive for exercises of this martial character was not for use in the field; it was twofold—personal and domestic. Woman owning no suzerain of her own, formed her own bodyguard. With her weapon she guarded her personal sanctity with as much zeal as her husband did his master's. The domestic utility of her warlike training was in the education of her sons, as we shall see later.

Fencing and similar exercises, if rarely of practical use, were a wholesome counterbalance to the otherwise sedentary habits of woman. But these exercises were not followed only for hygienic purposes. They could be turned into use in times of need. Girls, when they reached womanhood, were presented with dirks (*kai-ken*, pocket poniards), which might be directed to the bosom of their assailants, or, if advisable, to their own. The latter was very often the case: and yet I will not judge them severely. Even the Christian conscience with its horror of self-immolation, will not be harsh with them, seeing Pelagia and Domnina, two suicides, were canonized for their purity and piety. When a Japanese Virginia saw her chastity menaced, she did not wait for her father's dagger. Her own weapon lay always in her bosom. It was a disgrace to her not to know the proper way in which she had to perpetrate self-destruction. For example, little as she was taught in anatomy, she must know the exact spot to cut in her throat: she must know how to tie her lower limbs together with a belt so that, whatever the agonies of death might be, her corpse be found in utmost modesty with the limbs properly composed.

Is not a caution like this worthy of the Christian Perpetua or the Vestal Cornelia? I would not put such an abrupt interrogation, were it not for a misconception, based on our bathing customs and other trifles, that chastity is unknown among us. [For a very sensible explanation of nudity and bathing see Finck's *Lotos Time in Japan*, pp. 286-297.] On the contrary, chastity was a pre-eminent virtue of the samurai woman, held above life itself. A young woman, taken prisoner, seeing herself in danger of violence at the hands of the rough soldiery, says she will obey their pleasure, provided she be first allowed to write a line to her sisters, whom war has dispersed in every direction. When the epistle is finished, off she runs to the nearest well and saves her honor by drowning. The letter she leaves behind ends with these verses;—

> "For fear lest clouds may dim her light,
> Should she but graze this nether sphere,
> The young moon poised above the height
> Doth hastily betake to flight."

It would be unfair to give my readers an idea that masculinity alone was our highest ideal for woman. Far from it! Accomplishments and the gentler graces of life were required of them. Music, dancing and literature were not neglected. Some of the finest verses in our literature were expressions of feminine sentiments; in fact, women played an important role in the history of Japanese *belles lettres*. Dancing was taught (I am speaking of samurai girls and not of *geisha*) only to smooth the angularity of their movements. Music was to regale the weary hours of their fathers and husbands; hence it was not for the technique, the art as such, that music was learned; for the ultimate object was purification of heart, since it was said that no harmony of sound is attainable without the player's heart being in harmony with herself. Here again we see the same idea prevailing which we notice in the training of youths—that accomplishments were ever kept subservient to moral worth. Just enough of music and dancing to add grace and brightness to life, but never to foster vanity and extravagance. I sympathize with the Persian prince, who, when taken into a ball-room in London and asked to take part in the merriment, bluntly remarked that in his country they provided a particular set of girls to do that kind of business for them.

The accomplishments of our women were not acquired for show or social ascendency. They were a home diversion; and if they shone in social parties, it was as the attributes of a hostess,—in other words, as a part of the household contrivance for hospitality. Domesticity guided their education. It may be said that the accomplishments of the women of Old Japan, be they martial or pacific in character, were mainly intended for the home; and, however far they might roam, they never lost sight of the hearth as the center. It was to maintain its honor and integrity that they slaved, drudged and gave up their lives. Night and day, in tones at once firm and tender, brave and plaintive, they sang to their little nests. As daughter, woman sacrificed herself for her father, as wife for her husband, and as mother for her son. Thus from earliest youth she was taught to deny herself. Her life was not one of independence, but of dependent service. Man's helpmeet, if her presence is helpful she stays on the stage with him: if it hinders his work, she retires behind the curtain. Not infrequently does it happen that a youth becomes enamored of a maiden who returns his love with equal ardor, but, when she realizes his interest in her makes him forgetful of his duties, disfigures her person that her attractions may cease. Adzuma, the ideal wife in the minds of samurai girls, finds herself loved by a man who, in order to win her affection, conspires against her husband. Upon pretence of joining in the guilty plot, she manages in the dark to take her husband's place, and the sword of the lover assassin descends upon her own devoted head.

The following epistle written by the wife of a young daimio, before taking her own life, needs no comment:—"Oft have I heard that no accident or chance ever mars the march of events here below, and that all moves in accordance with a plan. To take shelter under a common bough or a drink of the same river, is alike ordained from ages prior to our birth. Since we were joined in ties of eternal wedlock, now two short years ago, my heart hath followed thee, even as its shadow followeth an object, inseparably bound heart to heart, loving and being loved. Learning but recently, however, that the coming battle is to be the last of thy labor and life, take the farewell greeting of thy loving partner. I have heard that Kō-u, the mighty warrior of ancient China, lost a battle, loth to part with his favorite Gu. Yoshinaka, too, brave as he was, brought disaster to his cause, too weak to bid prompt farewell to his wife. Why should I, to whom earth no longer offers hope or joy—why should I detain thee or thy thoughts by living? Why should I not, rather, await thee on the road which all mortal kind must sometime tread? Never, prithee, never forget the many benefits which our good master Hideyori hath heaped upon thee. The gratitude we owe him is as deep as the sea and as high as the hills."

Woman's surrender of herself to the good of her husband, home and family, was as willing and honorable as the man's self-surrender to the good of his lord and country. Self-renunciation, without which no life-enigma can be solved, was the keynote of the Loyalty of man as well as of the Domesticity of woman. She was no more the slave of man than was her husband of his liege-lord, and the part she played was recognized as *Naijo*, "the inner help." In the ascending scale of service stood woman, who annihilated herself for man, that he might annihilate himself for the master, that he in turn might obey heaven. I know the weakness of this teaching and that the superiority of Christianity is nowhere more manifest than here, in that it requires of each and every living soul direct responsibility to its Creator. Nevertheless, as far as the doctrine of service—the serving of a cause higher than one's own self, even at the sacrifice of one's individuality; I say the doctrine of service, which is the greatest that Christ preached and is the sacred keynote of his mission—as far as that is concerned, Bushido is based on eternal truth.

My readers will not accuse me of undue prejudice in favor of slavish surrender of volition. I accept in a large measure the view advanced with breadth of learning and defended with profundity of thought by Hegel, that history is the unfolding and realization of freedom. The point I wish to make is that the whole teaching of Bushido was so thoroughly imbued with the spirit of self-sacrifice, that it was required not only of woman but of man. Hence, until the influence of its Precepts is entirely done away with, our society will not realize the view rashly expressed by an American exponent of woman's rights, who exclaimed, "May all the daughters of Japan rise in revolt against ancient customs!" Can such a revolt succeed? Will it improve the female status? Will the rights they gain by such a summary process repay the loss of that sweetness of disposition, that gentleness of manner, which are their present heritage? Was not the loss of domesticity on the part of Roman matrons followed by moral corruption too gross to mention? Can the American reformer assure us that a revolt of our daughters is the true course for their historical development to take? These are grave questions. Changes must and will come without revolts! In the meantime let us see whether the status of the fair sex under the Bushido regimen was really so bad as to justify a revolt.

We hear much of the outward respect European knights paid to "God and the ladies,"—the incongruity of the two terms making Gibbon blush; we are also told by Hallam that the morality of Chivalry was coarse, that gallantry implied illicit love. The effect of Chivalry on the weaker vessel was food for reflection on the part of philosophers, M. Guizot contending that Feudalism and Chivalry wrought wholesome influences, while Mr. Spencer tells us that in a militant society (and what is feudal society if not militant?) the position of woman is necessarily low, improving only as society becomes more industrial. Now is M. Guizot's theory true of Japan, or is Mr. Spencer's? In reply I might aver that both are right. The military class in Japan was restricted to the samurai, comprising nearly 2,000,000 souls. Above them were the military nobles, the *daimio*, and the court nobles, the *kugé*—these higher, sybaritical nobles being fighters only in name. Below them were masses of the common people—mechanics, tradesmen, and peasants—whose life was devoted to arts of peace. Thus what Herbert Spencer gives as the characteristics of a militant type of society may be said to have been exclusively confined to the samurai class, while those of the industrial type were applicable to the classes above and below it. This is well illustrated by the position of woman; for in no class did she experience less freedom than among the samurai. Strange to say, the lower the social class—as, for instance, among small artisans—the more equal was the position of husband and wife. Among the higher nobility, too, the difference in the relations of the sexes was less marked, chiefly because there were few occasions to bring the differences of sex into prominence, the leisurely nobleman having become literally effeminate. Thus Spencer's dictum was fully exemplified in Old Japan. As to Guizot's, those who read his presentation of a feudal community will remember that he had the higher nobility especially under consideration, so that his generalization applies to the *daimio* and the *kugé*.

I shall be guilty of gross injustice to historical truth if my words give one a very low opinion of the status of woman under Bushido. I do not hesitate to state that she was not treated as man's equal; but until we learn to discriminate between difference and inequalities, there will always be misunderstandings upon this subject.

When we think in how few respects men are equal among themselves, *e.g.*, before law courts or voting polls, it seems idle to trouble ourselves with a discussion on the equality of sexes. When, the American Declaration of Independence said that all men were created equal, it had no reference to their mental or physical gifts: it simply repeated what Ulpian long ago announced, that before the law all men are equal. Legal rights were in this case the measure of their equality. Were the law the only scale by which to measure the position of woman in a community, it would be as easy to tell where she stands as to give her avoirdupois in pounds and ounces. But the question is: Is there a correct standard in comparing the relative social position of the sexes? Is it right, is it enough, to compare woman's status to man's as the value of silver is compared with that of gold, and give the ratio numerically? Such a method of calculation excludes from consideration the most important kind of value which a human being possesses; namely, the intrinsic. In view of the manifold variety of requisites for making each sex fulfil its earthly mission, the standard to be adopted in measuring its relative position must be of a composite character; or, to borrow from economic language, it must be a multiple standard. Bushido had a standard of its own and it was binomial. It tried to guage the value of woman on the battle-field and by the hearth. There she counted for very little; here for all. The treatment accorded her corresponded to this double measurement;—as a social-political unit not much, while as wife and mother she received highest respect and deepest affection. Why among so military a nation as the Romans, were their matrons so highly venerated? Was it not because they were *matrona*, mothers? Not as fighters or law-givers, but as their mothers did men bow before them. So with us. While fathers and husbands were absent in field or camp, the government of the household was left entirely in the hands of mothers and wives. The education of the young, even their defence, was entrusted to them. The warlike exercises of women, of which I have spoken, were primarily to enable them intelligently to direct and follow the education of their children.

I have noticed a rather superficial notion prevailing among half-informed foreigners, that because the common Japanese expression for one's wife is "my rustic wife" and the like, she is despised and held in little esteem. When it is told that such phrases as "my foolish father," "my swinish son," "my awkward self," etc., are in current use, is not the answer clear enough?

To me it seems that our idea of marital union goes in some ways further than the so-called Christian. "Man and woman shall be one flesh." The individualism of the Anglo-Saxon cannot let go of the idea that husband and wife are two persons;—hence when they disagree, their separate *rights* are recognized, and when they agree, they exhaust their vocabulary in all sorts of silly pet-names and—nonsensical blandishments. It sounds highly irrational to our ears, when a husband or wife speaks to a third party of his other half—better or worse—as being lovely, bright, kind, and what not. Is it good taste to speak of one's self as "my bright self," "my lovely disposition," and so forth? We think praising one's own wife or one's own husband is praising a part of one's own self, and self-praise is regarded, to say the least, as bad taste among us,—and I hope, among Christian nations too! I have diverged at some length because the polite debasement of one's consort was a usage most in vogue among the samurai.

The Teutonic races beginning their tribal life with a superstitious awe of the fair sex (though this is really wearing off in Germany!), and the Americans beginning their social life under the painful consciousness of the numerical insufficiency of women [*I refer to those days when girls were imported from England and given in marriage for so many pounds of tobacco, etc.*] (who, now increasing, are, I am afraid, fast losing the prestige their colonial mothers enjoyed), the respect man pays to woman has in Western civilization become the chief standard of morality. But in the martial ethics of Bushido, the main water-shed dividing the good and the bad was sought elsewhere. It was located along the line of duty which bound man to his own divine soul and then to other souls, in the five relations I have mentioned in the early part of this paper. Of these we have brought to our reader's notice, Loyalty, the relation between one man as vassal and another as lord. Upon the rest, I have only dwelt incidentally as occasion presented itself; because they were not peculiar to Bushido. Being founded on natural affections, they could but be common to all mankind, though in some particulars they may have been accentuated by conditions which its teachings induced.

In this connection, there comes before me the peculiar strength and tenderness of friendship between man and man, which often added to the bond of brotherhood a romantic attachment doubtless intensified by the separation of the sexes in youth,—a separation which denied to affection the natural channel open to it in Western chivalry or in the free intercourse of Anglo-Saxon lands. I might fill pages with Japanese versions of the story of Damon and Pythias or Achilles and Patroclos, or tell in Bushido parlance of ties as sympathetic as those which bound David and Jonathan.

Bushido - The Soul of Japan

The Influence of Bushido

It is not surprising, however, that the virtues and teachings unique in the Precepts of Knighthood did not remain circumscribed to the military class. This makes us hasten to the consideration of the influence of Bushido on the nation at large.

We have brought into view only a few of the more prominent peaks which rise above the range of knightly virtues, in themselves so much more elevated than the general level of our national life. As the sun in its rising first tips the highest peaks with russet hue, and then gradually casts its rays on the valley below, so the ethical system which first enlightened the military order drew in course of time followers from amongst the masses. Democracy raises up a natural prince for its leader, and aristocracy infuses a princely spirit among the people. Virtues are no less contagious than vices. "There needs but one wise man in a company, and all are wise, so rapid is the contagion," says Emerson. No social class or caste can resist the diffusive power of moral influence.

Prate as we may of the triumphant march of Anglo-Saxon liberty, rarely has it received impetus from the masses. Was it not rather the work of the squires and *gentlemen*? Very truly does M. Taine say, "These three syllables, as used across the channel, summarize the history of English society." Democracy may make self-confident retorts to such a statement and fling back the question—"When Adam delved and Eve span, where then was the gentleman?" All the more pity that a gentleman was not present in Eden! The first parents missed him sorely and paid a high price for his absence. Had he been there, not only would the garden have been more tastefully dressed, but they would have learned without painful experience that disobedience to Jehovah was disloyalty and dishonor, treason and rebellion.

What Japan was she owed to the samurai. They were not only the flower of the nation but its root as well. All the gracious gifts of Heaven flowed through them. Though they kept themselves socially aloof from the populace, they set a moral standard for them and guided them by their example. I admit Bushido had its esoteric and exoteric teachings; these were eudemonistic, looking after the welfare and happiness of the commonalty, while those were aretaic, emphasizing the practice of virtues for their own sake.

In the most chivalrous days of Europe, Knights formed numerically but a small fraction of the population, but, as Emerson says—"In English Literature half the drama and all the novels, from Sir Philip Sidney to Sir Walter Scott, paint this figure (gentleman)." Write in place of Sidney and Scott, Chikamatsu and Bakin, and you have in a nutshell the main features of the literary history of Japan.

The innumerable avenues of popular amusement and instruction—the theatres, the story-teller's booths, the preacher's dais, the musical recitations, the novels—have taken for their chief theme the stories of the samurai. The peasants round the open fire in their huts never tire of repeating the achievements of Yoshitsuné and his faithful retainer Benkei, or of the two brave Soga brothers; the dusky urchins listen with gaping mouths until the last stick burns out and the fire dies in its embers, still leaving their hearts aglow with the tale that is told. The clerks and the shop-boys, after their day's work is over and the *amado* [*Outside shutters.*] of the store are closed, gather together to relate the story of Nobunaga and Hidéyoshi far into the night, until slumber overtakes their weary eyes and transports them from the drudgery of the counter to the exploits of the field. The very babe just beginning to toddle is taught to lisp the adventures of Momotaro, the daring conqueror of ogre-land. Even girls are so imbued with the love of knightly deeds and virtues that, like Desdemona, they would seriously incline to devour with greedy ear the romance of the samurai.

The samurai grew to be the *beau ideal* of the whole race. "As among flowers the cherry is queen, so among men the samurai is lord," so sang the populace. Debarred from commercial pursuits, the military class itself did not aid commerce; but there was no channel of human activity, no avenue of thought, which did not receive in some measure an impetus from Bushido. Intellectual and moral Japan was directly or indirectly the work of Knighthood.

Mr. Mallock, in his exceedingly suggestive book, "Aristocracy and Evolution," has eloquently told us that "social evolution, in so far as it is other than biological, may be defined as the unintended result of the intentions of great men;" further, that historical progress is produced by a struggle "not among the community generally, to live, but a struggle amongst a small section of the community to lead, to direct, to employ, the majority in the best way." Whatever may be said about the soundness of his argument, these statements are amply verified in the part played by bushi in the social progress, as far as it went, of our Empire.

How the spirit of Bushido permeated all social classes is also shown in the development of a certain order of men, known as *otoko-daté*, the natural leaders of democracy. Staunch fellows were they, every inch of them strong with the strength of massive manhood. At once the spokesmen and the guardians of popular rights, they had each a following of hundreds and thousands of souls who proffered in the same fashion that samurai did to daimio, the willing service of "limb and life, of body, chattels and earthly honor." Backed by a vast multitude of rash and impetuous working-men, those born "bosses" formed a formidable check to the rampancy of the two-sworded order.

In manifold ways has Bushido filtered down from the social class where it originated, and acted as leaven among the masses, furnishing a moral standard for the whole people. The Precepts of Knighthood, begun at first as the glory of the elite, became in time an aspiration and inspiration to the nation at large; and though the populace could not attain the moral height of those loftier souls, yet *Yamato Damashii*, the Soul of Japan, ultimately came to express the *Volksgeist* of the Island Realm. If religion is no more than "Morality touched by emotion," as Matthew Arnold defines it, few ethical systems are better entitled to the rank of religion than Bushido. Motoori has put the mute utterance of the nation into words when he sings:—

"Isles of blest Japan!
Should your Yamato spirit

Strangers seek to scan,
Say—scenting morn's sun-lit air,
Blows the cherry wild and fair!"

Yes, the *sakura* [*Cerasus pseudo-cerasus*, Lindley.] has for ages been the favorite of our people and the emblem of our character. Mark particularly the terms of definition which the poet uses, the words the *wild cherry flower scenting the morning sun.*

The Yamato spirit is not a tame, tender plant, but a wild—in the sense of natural—growth; it is indigenous to the soil; its accidental qualities it may share with the flowers of other lands, but in its essence it remains the original, spontaneous outgrowth of our clime. But its nativity is not its sole claim to our affection. The refinement and grace of its beauty appeal to *our* aesthetic sense as no other flower can. We cannot share the admiration of the Europeans for their roses, which lack the simplicity of our flower. Then, too, the thorns that are hidden beneath the sweetness of the rose, the tenacity with which she clings to life, as though loth or afraid to die rather than drop untimely, preferring to rot on her stem; her showy colors and heavy odors—all these are traits so unlike our flower, which carries no dagger or poison under its beauty, which is ever ready to depart life at the call of nature, whose colors are never gorgeous, and whose light fragrance never palls. Beauty of color and of form is limited in its showing; it is a fixed quality of existence, whereas fragrance is volatile, ethereal as the breathing of life. So in all religious ceremonies frankincense and myrrh play a prominent part. There is something spirituelle in redolence. When the delicious perfume of the *sakura* quickens the morning air, as the sun in its course rises to illumine first the isles of the Far East, few sensations are more serenely exhilarating than to inhale, as it were, the very breath of beauteous day.

When the Creator himself is pictured as making new resolutions in his heart upon smelling a sweet savor (Gen. VIII, 21), is it any wonder that the sweet-smelling season of the cherry blossom should call forth the whole nation from their little habitations? Blame them not, if for a time their limbs forget their toil and moil and their hearts their pangs and sorrows. Their brief pleasure ended, they return to their daily tasks with new strength and new resolutions. Thus in ways more than one is the sakura the flower of the nation.

Is Bushido Still Alive?

Is, then, this flower, so sweet and evanescent, blown whithersoever the wind listeth, and, shedding a puff of perfume, ready to vanish forever, is this flower the type of the Yamato spirit? Is the Soul of Japan so frailly mortal?

Is Bushido still alive? Or has Western civilization, in its march through the land, already wiped out every trace of its ancient discipline?

It were a sad thing if a nation's soul could die so fast. That were a poor soul that could succumb so easily to extraneous influences. The aggregate of psychological elements which constitute a national character, is as tenacious as the "irreducible elements of species, of the fins of fish, of the beak of the bird, of the tooth of the carnivorous animal." In his recent book, full of shallow asseverations and brilliant generalizations, M. LeBon [*The Psychology of Peoples*, p. 33.] says, "The discoveries due to the intelligence are the common patrimony of humanity; qualities or defects of character constitute the exclusive patrimony of each people: they are the firm rock which the waters must wash day by day for centuries, before they can wear away even its external asperities." These are strong words and would be highly worth pondering over, provided there were qualities and defects of character which *constitute the exclusive patrimony* of each people. Schematizing theories of this sort had been advanced long before LeBon began to write his book, and they were exploded long ago by Theodor Waitz and Hugh Murray. In studying the various virtues instilled by Bushido, we have drawn upon European sources for comparison and illustrations, and we have seen that no one quality of character was its *exclusive* patrimony. It is true the aggregate of moral qualities presents a quite unique aspect. It is this aggregate which Emerson names a "compound result into which every great force enters as an ingredient." But, instead of making it, as LeBon does, an exclusive patrimony of a race or people, the Concord philosopher calls it "an element which unites the most forcible persons of every country; makes them intelligible and agreeable to each other; and is somewhat so precise that it is at once felt if an individual lack the Masonic sign."

The character which Bushido stamped on our nation and on the samurai in particular, cannot be said to form "an irreducible element of species," but nevertheless as to the vitality which it retains there is no doubt. Were Bushido a mere physical force, the momentum it has gained in the last seven hundred years could not stop so abruptly. Were it transmitted only by heredity, its influence must be immensely widespread. Just think, as M. Cheysson, a French economist, has calculated, that supposing there be three generations in a century, "each of us would have in his veins the blood of at least twenty millions of the people living in the year 1000 A.D." The merest peasant that grubs the soil, "bowed by the weight of centuries," has in his veins the blood of ages, and is thus a brother to us as much as "to the ox."

An unconscious and irresistible power, Bushido has been moving the nation and individuals. It was an honest confession of the race when Yoshida Shoin, one of the most brilliant pioneers of Modern Japan, wrote on the eve of his execution the following stanza;—

> "Full well I knew this course must end in death;
> It was Yamato spirit urged me on
> To dare whate'er betide."

Unformulated, Bushido was and still is the animating spirit, the motor force of our country.

Mr. Ransome says that "there are three distinct Japans in existence side by side to-day,—the old, which has not wholly died out; the new, hardly yet born except in spirit; and the transition, passing now through its most critical throes." While this is very true in most respects, and particularly as regards tangible and concrete institutions, the statement, as applied to fundamental ethical notions, requires some modification; for Bushido, the maker and product of Old Japan, is still the guiding principle of the transition and will prove the formative force of the new era.

The great statesmen who steered the ship of our state through the hurricane of the Restoration and the whirlpool of national rejuvenation, were men who knew no other moral teaching than the Precepts of Knighthood. Some writers [Speer; *Missions and Politics in Asia*, Lecture IV, pp. 189-190; Dennis: *Christian Missions and Social Progress*, Vol. I, p. 32, Vol. II, p. 70, etc.] have lately tried to prove that the Christian missionaries contributed an appreciable quota to the making of New Japan. I would fain render honor to whom honor is due: but this honor can hardly be accorded to the good missionaries. More fitting it will be to their profession to stick to the scriptural injunction of preferring one another in honor, than to advance a claim in which they have no proofs to back them. For myself, I believe that Christian missionaries are doing great things for Japan—in the domain of education, and especially of moral education:—only, the mysterious though not the less certain working of the Spirit is still hidden in divine secrecy.

Whatever they do is still of indirect effect. No, as yet Christian missions have effected but little visible in moulding the character of New Japan. No, it was Bushido, pure and simple, that urged us on for weal or woe. Open the biographies of the makers of Modern Japan—of Sakuma, of Saigo, of Okubo, of Kido, not to mention the reminiscences of living men such as Ito, Okuma, Itagaki, etc.:—and you will find that it was under the impetus of samuraihood that they thought and wrought. When Mr. Henry Norman declared, after his study and observation of the Far East, [*The Far East*, p. 375.] that only the respect in which Japan differed from other oriental despotisms lay in "the ruling influence among her people of the strictest, loftiest, and the most punctilious codes of honor that man has ever devised," he touched the main spring which has made new Japan what she is and which will make her what she is destined to be.

The transformation of Japan is a fact patent to the whole world. In a work of such magnitude various motives naturally entered; but if one were to name the principal, one would not hesitate to name Bushido. When we opened the whole country to foreign trade, when we introduced the latest improvements in every department of life, when we began to study Western politics and sciences, our guiding motive was not the development of our physical resources and the increase of wealth; much less was it a blind imitation of Western customs. A close observer of oriental institutions and peoples has written:—"We are told every day how Europe has influenced Japan, and forget that the change in those islands was entirely self-generated, that Europeans did not teach Japan, but that Japan of herself chose to learn from Europe methods of organization, civil and military, which have so far proved successful. She imported European mechanical science, as the Turks years before imported European artillery. That is not exactly influence," continues Mr. Townsend, "unless, indeed, England is influenced by purchasing tea of China. Where is the European apostle," asks our author, "or philosopher or statesman or agitator who has re-made Japan?" [Meredith Townsend, *Asia and Europe*, N.Y., 1900, 28.] Mr. Townsend has well perceived that the spring of action which brought about the changes in Japan lay entirely within our own selves; and if he had only probed into our psychology, his keen powers of observation would easily have convinced him that that spring was no other than Bushido. The sense of honor which cannot bear being looked down upon as an inferior power,—that was the strongest of motives. Pecuniary or industrial considerations were awakened later in the process of transformation.

The influence of Bushido is still so palpable that he who runs may read. A glimpse into Japanese life will make it manifest. Read Hearn, the most eloquent and truthful interpreter of the Japanese mind, and you see the working of that mind to be an example of the working of Bushido. The universal politeness of the people, which is the legacy of knightly ways, is too well known to be repeated anew. The physical endurance, fortitude and bravery that "the little Jap" possesses, were sufficiently proved in the China-Japanese war. [Among other works on the subject, read Eastlake and Yamada on *Heroic Japan*, and Diosy on *The New Far East*.] "Is there any nation more loyal and patriotic?" is a question asked by many; and for the proud answer, "There is not," we must thank the Precepts of Knighthood.

On the other hand, it is fair to recognize that for the very faults and defects of our character, Bushido is largely responsible. Our lack of abstruse philosophy—while some of our young men have already gained international reputation in scientific researches, not one has achieved anything in philosophical lines—is traceable to the neglect of metaphysical training under Bushido's regimen of education. Our sense of honor is responsible for our exaggerated sensitiveness and touchiness; and if there is the conceit in us with which some foreigners charge us, that, too, is a pathological outcome of honor.

Have you seen in your tour of Japan many a young man with unkempt hair, dressed in shabbiest garb, carrying in his hand a large cane or a book, stalking about the streets with an air of utter indifference to mundane things? He is the *shosei* (student), to whom the earth is too small and the Heavens are not high enough. He has his own theories of the universe and of life. He dwells in castles of air and feeds on ethereal words of wisdom. In his eyes beams the fire of ambition; his mind is athirst for knowledge. Penury is only a stimulus to drive him onward; worldly goods are in his sight shackles to his character. He is the repository of Loyalty and Patriotism. He is the self-imposed guardian of national honor. With all his virtues and his faults, he is the last fragment of Bushido.

Deep-rooted and powerful as is still the effect of Bushido, I have said that it is an unconscious and mute influence. The heart of the people responds, without knowing the reason why, to any appeal made to what it has inherited, and hence the same moral idea expressed in a newly translated term and in an old Bushido term, has a vastly different degree of efficacy. A backsliding Christian, whom no pastoral persuasion could help from downward tendency, was reverted from his course by an appeal made to his loyalty, the fidelity he once swore to his Master. The word "Loyalty" revived all the noble sentiments that were permitted to grow lukewarm. A band of unruly youths engaged in a long continued "students' strike" in a college, on account of their dissatisfaction with a certain teacher, disbanded at two simple questions put by the Director,—"Is your professor a blameless character? If so, you ought to respect him and keep him in the school.

Is he weak? If so, it is not manly to push a falling man." The scientific incapacity of the professor, which was the beginning of the trouble, dwindled into insignificance in comparison with the moral issues hinted at. By arousing the sentiments nurtured by Bushido, moral renovation of great magnitude can be accomplished.

One cause of the failure of mission work is that most of the missionaries are grossly ignorant of our history—"What do we care for heathen records?" some say—and consequently estrange their religion from the habits of thought we and our forefathers have been accustomed to for centuries past. Mocking a nation's history!—as though the career of any people—even of the lowest African savages possessing no record—were not a page in the general history of mankind, written by the hand of God Himself. The very lost races are a palimpsest to be deciphered by a seeing eye. To a philosophic and pious mind, the races themselves are marks of Divine chirography clearly traced in black and white as on their skin; and if this simile holds good, the yellow race forms a precious page inscribed in hieroglyphics of gold! Ignoring the past career of a people, missionaries claim that Christianity is a new religion, whereas, to my mind, it is an "old, old story," which, if presented in intelligible words,—that is to say, if expressed in the vocabulary familiar in the moral development of a people—will find easy lodgment in their hearts, irrespective of race or nationality. Christianity in its American or English form—with more of Anglo-Saxon freaks and fancies than grace and purity of its founder—is a poor scion to graft on Bushido stock. Should the propagator of the new faith uproot the entire stock, root and branches, and plant the seeds of the Gospel on the ravaged soil? Such a heroic process may be possible—in Hawaii, where, it is alleged, the church militant had complete success in amassing spoils of wealth itself, and in annihilating the aboriginal race: such a process is most decidedly impossible in Japan—nay, it is a process which Jesus himself would never have employed in founding his kingdom on earth. It behooves us to take more to heart the following words of a saintly man, devout Christian and profound scholar:—"Men have divided the world into heathen and Christian, without considering how much good may have been hidden in the one, or how much evil may have been mingled with the other. They have compared the best part of themselves with the worst of their neighbors, the ideal of Christianity with the corruption of Greece or the East. They have not aimed at impartiality, but have been contented to accumulate all that could be said in praise of their own, and in dispraise of other forms of religion." [Jowett, *Sermons on Faith and Doctrine*, II.]

Bushido - The Soul of Japan

The Future of Bushido

Whatever may be the error committed by individuals, there is little doubt that the fundamental principle of the religion they profess is a power which we must take into account in reckoning the future of Bushido whose days seem to be already numbered. Ominous signs are in the air, that betoken its future. Not only signs, but redoubtable forces are at work to threaten it.

Few historical comparisons can be more judiciously made than between the Chivalry of Europe and the Bushido of Japan, and, if history repeats itself, it certainly will do with the fate of the latter what it did with that of the former. The particular and local causes for the decay of Chivalry which St. Palaye gives, have, of course, little application to Japanese conditions; but the larger and more general causes that helped to undermine Knighthood and Chivalry in and after the Middle Ages are as surely working for the decline of Bushido.

One remarkable difference between the experience of Europe and of Japan is, that, whereas in Europe when Chivalry was weaned from Feudalism and was adopted by the Church, it obtained a fresh lease of life, in Japan no religion was large enough to nourish it; hence, when the mother institution, Feudalism, was gone, Bushido, left an orphan, had to shift for itself. The present elaborate military organization might take it under its patronage, but we know that modern warfare can afford little room for its continuous growth. Shintoism, which fostered it in its infancy, is itself superannuated. The hoary sages of ancient China are being supplanted by the intellectual parvenu of the type of Bentham and Mill. Moral theories of a comfortable kind, flattering to the Chauvinistic tendencies of the time, and therefore thought well-adapted to the need of this day, have been invented and propounded; but as yet we hear only their shrill voices echoing through the columns of yellow journalism.

Principalities and powers are arrayed against the Precepts of Knighthood. Already, as Veblen says, "the decay of the ceremonial code—or, as it is otherwise called, the vulgarization of life—among the industrial classes proper, has become one of the chief enormities of latter-day civilization in the eyes of all persons of delicate sensibilities." The irresistible tide of triumphant democracy, which can tolerate no form or shape of trust—and Bushido was a trust organized by those who monopolized reserve capital of intellect and culture, fixing the grades and value of moral qualities—is alone powerful enough to engulf the remnant of Bushido. The present societary forces are antagonistic to petty class spirit, and Chivalry is, as Freeman severely criticizes, a class spirit. Modern society, if it pretends to any unity, cannot admit "purely personal obligations devised in the interests of an exclusive class." [*Norman Conquest*, Vol. V, p. 482.] Add to this the progress of popular instruction, of industrial arts and habits, of wealth and city-life,—then we can easily see that neither the keenest cuts of samurai's sword nor the sharpest shafts shot from Bushido's boldest bows can aught avail. The state built upon the rock of Honor and fortified by the same—shall we call it the *Ehrenstaat* or, after the manner of Carlyle, the Heroarchy?—is fast falling into the hands of quibbling lawyers and gibbering politicians armed with logic-chopping engines of war. The words which a great thinker used in speaking of Theresa and Antigone may aptly be repeated of the samurai, that "the medium in which their ardent deeds took shape is forever gone."

Alas for knightly virtues! alas for samurai pride! Morality ushered into the world with the sound of bugles and drums, is destined to fade away as "the captains and the kings depart."

If history can teach us anything, the state built on martial virtues—be it a city like Sparta or an Empire like Rome—can never make on earth a "continuing city." Universal and natural as is the fighting instinct in man, fruitful as it has proved to be of noble sentiments and manly virtues, it does not comprehend the whole man. Beneath the instinct to fight there lurks a diviner instinct to love. We have seen that Shintoism, Mencius and Wan Yang Ming, have all clearly taught it; but Bushido and all other militant schools of ethics, engrossed, doubtless, with questions of immediate practical need, too often forgot duly to emphasize this fact. Life has grown larger in these latter times.

Callings nobler and broader than a warrior's claim our attention to-day. With an enlarged view of life, with the growth of democracy, with better knowledge of other peoples and nations, the Confucian idea of Benevolence—dare I also add the Buddhist idea of Pity?—will expand into the Christian conception of Love. Men have become more than subjects, having grown to the estate of citizens: nay, they are more than citizens, being men.

Though war clouds hang heavy upon our horizon, we will believe that the wings of the angel of peace can disperse them. The history of the world confirms the prophecy the "the meek shall inherit the earth." A nation that sells its birthright of peace, and backslides from the front rank of Industrialism into the file of Filibusterism, makes a poor bargain indeed!

When the conditions of society are so changed that they have become not only adverse but hostile to Bushido, it is time for it to prepare for an honorable burial. It is just as difficult to point out when chivalry dies, as to determine the exact time of its inception. Dr. Miller says that Chivalry was formally abolished in the year 1559, when Henry II. of France was slain in a tournament. With us, the edict formally abolishing Feudalism in 1870 was the signal to toll the knell of Bushido. The edict, issued two years later, prohibiting the wearing of swords, rang out the old, "the unbought grace of life, the cheap defence of nations, the nurse of manly sentiment and heroic enterprise," it rang in the new age of "sophisters, economists, and calculators."

It has been said that Japan won her late war with China by means of Murata guns and Krupp cannon; it has been said the victory was the work of a modern school system; but these are less than half-truths. Does ever a piano, be it of the choicest workmanship of Ehrbar or Steinway, burst forth into the Rhapsodies of Liszt or the Sonatas of Beethoven, without a master's hand? Or, if guns win battles, why did not Louis Napoleon beat the Prussians with his *Mitrailleuse*, or the Spaniards with their Mausers the Filipinos, whose arms were no better than the old-fashioned Remingtons? Needless to repeat what has grown a trite saying that it is the spirit that quickeneth, without which the best of implements profiteth but little. The most improved guns and cannon do not shoot of their own accord; the most modern educational system does not make a coward a hero. No! What won the battles on the Yalu, in Corea and Manchuria, was the ghosts of our fathers, guiding our hands and beating in our hearts. They are not dead, those ghosts, the spirits of our warlike ancestors. To those who have eyes to see, they are clearly visible. Scratch a Japanese of the most advanced ideas, and he will show a samurai. The great inheritance of honor, of valor and of all martial virtues is, as Professor Cramb very fitly expresses it, "but ours on trust, the fief inalienable of the dead and of the generation to come," and the summons of the present is to guard this heritage, nor to bate one jot of the ancient spirit; the summons of the future will be so to widen its scope as to apply it in all walks and relations of life.

It has been predicted—and predictions have been corroborated by the events of the last half century—that the moral system of Feudal Japan, like its castles and its armories, will crumble into dust, and new ethics rise phoenix-like to lead New Japan in her path of progress. Desirable and probable as the fulfilment of such a prophecy is, we must not forget that a phoenix rises only from its own ashes, and that it is not a bird of passage, neither does it fly on pinions borrowed from other birds. "The Kingdom of God is within you." It does not come rolling down the mountains, however lofty; it does not come sailing across the seas, however broad. "God has granted," says the Koran, "to every people a prophet in its own tongue." The seeds of the Kingdom, as vouched for and apprehended by the Japanese mind, blossomed in Bushido. Now its days are closing—sad to say, before its full fruition—and we turn in every direction for other sources of sweetness and light, of strength and comfort, but among them there is as yet nothing found to take its place. The profit and loss philosophy of Utilitarians and Materialists finds favor among logic-choppers with half a soul. The only other ethical system which is powerful enough to cope with Utilitarianism and Materialism is Christianity, in comparison with which Bushido, it must be confessed, is like "a dimly burning wick" which the Messiah was proclaimed not to quench but to fan into a flame. Like His Hebrew precursors, the prophets—notably Isaiah, Jeremiah, Amos and Habakkuk—Bushido laid particular stress on the moral conduct of rulers and public men and of nations, whereas the Ethics of Christ, which deal almost solely with individuals and His personal followers, will find more and more practical application as individualism, in its capacity of a moral factor, grows in potency. The domineering, self-assertive, so-called master-morality of Nietzsche, itself akin in some respects to Bushido, is, if I am not greatly mistaken, a passing phase or temporary reaction against what he terms, by morbid distortion, the humble, self-denying slave-morality of the Nazarene.

Christianity and Materialism (including Utilitarianism)—or will the future reduce them to still more archaic forms of Hebraism and Hellenism?—will divide the world between them. Lesser systems of morals will ally themselves on either side for their preservation. On which side will Bushido enlist? Having no set dogma or formula to defend, it can afford to disappear as an entity; like the cherry blossom, it is willing to die at the first gust of the morning breeze. But a total extinction will never be its lot. Who can say that stoicism is dead? It is dead as a system; but it is alive as a virtue: its energy and vitality are still felt through many channels of life—in the philosophy of Western nations, in the jurisprudence of all the civilized world. Nay, wherever man struggles to raise himself above himself, wherever his spirit masters his flesh by his own exertions, there we see the immortal discipline of Zeno at work.

Bushido as an independent code of ethics may vanish, but its power will not perish from the earth; its schools of martial prowess or civic honor may be demolished, but its light and its glory will long survive their ruins. Like its symbolic flower, after it is blown to the four winds, it will still bless mankind with the perfume with which it will enrich life. Ages after, when its customaries shall have been buried and its very name forgotten, its odors will come floating in the air as from a far-off unseen hill, "the wayside gaze beyond;"—then in the beautiful language of the Quaker poet,

"The traveler owns the grateful sense
Of sweetness near he knows not whence,
And, pausing, takes with forehead bare
The benediction of the air."

横川勘平藤原宗則

徒頭　禄　廿五両五人扶持

芝新銭座森屋の
家中の伯父ありしが
この家に同居あり
日ゝ堀部安兵エが
来所の宅にいるや
「万更をとりさうひ
討への切ろ要用の
道具を取あつらさ
支うにらう心を用ひ
なり本意と達して後
死所のさとく
すく去て一死出の
逆法へありしなる
被先生て九えらん

法号

刃常水劔信士

行年
三十七才

Printed in the United States
104321LV00005B/322-351/A

9 781934 255018